Becoming a Spiritual Being in a Physical Body

A Manual For Your Spiritual Journey

Other Books by Art Martin

Psychoneuroimmunology, Mind/Body Medicine Connection
Opening Communication with GOD Source
Your Body is Talking; Are You Listening?
2011: The New Millennium Begins
Recovering Your Lost Self
Journey into the Light
In Search for Meaning

Becoming a
Spiritual Being
in a Physical Body

A Manual For Your Spiritual Journey

Learning to listen to the lessons presented each day,
to recover your soul's flight plan and reclaim
your personal power.

Art Martin, D.D., M.A.

Personal Transformation Press
A Division of the Wellness Institute

Becoming a Spiritual Being in a Physical Body:
A Manual for Your Spiritual Journey
by Art Martin, D.D., M.A.

Published by:
Personal Transformation Press
8300 Rock Springs Road
Penryn, CA 95663
Phone: (916) 663-9178
Fax: (916) 663-0134
Orders only: (800) 655-3846

Copyright © 1992 Personal Transformation Press
First printing: November 1992
Second edition printing: September 2001

ISBN 1-891962-03-5

This book explores the body/mind connection as the actual cause of all mental/emotional dysfunction and physical disease. However, the author in no way makes any diagnosis of medical condition or prescribes any medical treatment whatsoever.

Printed in Canada

Table Of Contents

Let There Be Peace On Earth

Let there be peace on earth
And let it begin with me.
Let there be peace on earth,
The peace that was meant to be.

With God as our one source
United all are we,
Let us walk with each other
In perfect harmony.

Let peace begin with me,
Let this be the moment now
With every step I take,
Let this be my solemn vow:

To take each moment
And live each moment
In peace eternally.

Let there be peace on earth
And let it begin with me.

— Anon

Dedication

This book is dedicated to Paul Solomon, one of my first teachers
who made an indelible imprint on my life.

With his direction, I was able to commit to stepping out
of the illusion and take the path to enlightenment.

When he left the physical plane in 1994,
the world lost a great teacher.

Acknowledgments

No matter how hard I applied myself to the spiritual journey, it wasn't working. However, I stuck to it and, as the old adage says, "When the student is ready the teacher will appear," they did. Some I would never have picked as teachers, but they all gave me just the right nudge in the right direction.

My first teacher was the night manager in my restaurant. He helped me recognize that I was way off the path, and after a year of working with him, I decided to sell the restaurant, find who I was, and get on with the journey. Teachers then began to appear in droves, some taking me down blind roads, with lectures and workshops that offered little except lessons in discernment. That all changed in 1978, however, when I met Paul Solomon and Ronald Beesley.

Paul gave me the tools, guidance and the basic structure of spiritual psychology. Beesley gave me a basic understanding of the theory of hands-on healing and how the body interacts with its environment. Paul's teaching not only turned my life around but also gave me a career goal. I committed to eschew the business world. True, I was in unfamiliar territory, but I was driven to explore it. My teachers helped me bridge the third-dimensional reality and the esoteric realms. Armed with this new knowledge, I shifted from hit-and-miss psychic and faith healing to understandable, predictable processes that anyone could duplicate, to processes that can be explained in both scientific/medical and spiritual terminology.

When I first entered the healing field, I observed that some people would be healed and others would not, with no explanation of why. Once Solomon and Beasley opened my eyes as to why and how of healing, it all became clear. I'm very appreciative and supportive of their work and the understanding I got from them. I thank them for becoming a part of my life and defining the spiritual journey for me so that I could see, follow, and understand the path. They provided me with a priceless foundation of knowledge from which I've since gone on to create my own theories and processes as described in my books.

At the Solomon workshops, I met Joshua Stone, who became a close friend and encouraged me to further my education and get a master's degree in psychology. I appreciate the help and support he provided for me and my family during the early years of my search. Together we opened a counseling center and bookstore in Sacramento, CA. It's now history, but it provided a new avenue for my spiritual journey.

If it hadn't been for my clients who let me practice on them in the early years, Neuro/Cellular Repatterning would never have happened. Life is the best teacher, and I've learned more from my work than I ever learned in a classroom. My best teachers have always been and continue to be my clients. I thank all who trained me and supported my practice, lectures and seminars over the last 15 years.

I also want to thank all the people who supported me in presenting my lectures and workshops. First, in 1987, Chris Issel suggested that I teach my healing process, and her confidence in me pushed me to new heights. Through Chris, I met Jim Ingram. He and Pattie Marshall were pivotal in helping me get the word out to the community. Many others sponsored workshops and I thank you all for your support. For example, in 1989, Mike Hammer and I co-presented workshops, and I appreciated his confidence in my work. He has since gone on to other ventures.

A meeting with Dr. John Craig at the 1991 Whole Life Expo in Los Angeles turned my life upside down by demonstrating to me that we never really clear all the blocks from our reality, and that it's a lifelong experience. He spurred me on to new research that spawned even more theories and started me on a new path—that of being a spiritual being in a physical body.

Last, but not least, I want to thank my sponsors over the years— Pattie Marshall, Helen Phelps, Chris Issel, Lesley Gregory, Joy Johnston, Oshara Miller, Joline Stone, Araya Lawrence, Betts Richter, Nancy Worthington, Ilene Botting, Amy Kinder, Rob Perala, Joyce Techel, Barbara Stone, Nadeen Gotlieb, Ruth Johnston, Joan Noel, Kitty Karteala, Steve Kaplan, Morningstar Black, Dave Winter, Dr. John Hammer and, again, Jim Ingram and many more. I've had many sponsors in the last 20 years and I appreciate all the help I've received from them. For example, Ken Peterson took what I had to offer and ran with it; he continues to be an inspiration to me to this day. And in 1993, Bernard Eckes attended a training workshop I presented on N/CR, and has since become a partner in my ongoing research in the field of personal transformation.

This book has been six years in the writing and revising. Thank you, to my wife, Susie, and Mary Best for your help and support in editing. The final editing and getting to the point of publishing would not have happened without the help of Tony Stubbs. Tony has provided the inspiration to publish my books. His knowledge and expertise have put my books in the professional category, and without his help, this book would not have been published.

Finally, I want to thank my wife, Susie, again and my sons, Ross and Ryan, for their acceptance and cooperation on the rocky road to transformation and their personal and financial sacrifices. The well-trodden path of conventional psychology would have led to financial security, but not believing in that approach, I took the riskier road of carving out my own, and I appreciate my family for sticking by me. I know that we're now entering the period of abundance for all of us.

Preface

Many people feel that they've found the path and are well on the way in their spiritual journey. However, I'm not going to set myself up as the judge as to where people are in their transformation—I let the inner self reveal that to each person, for you cannot fool your Holographic Mind that's in direct contact with your Soul and Higher Self, and knows the lessons you've set yourself up to learn. You can delude yourself, but you can't fool your Soul, Higher Self, or your Holographic Mind. They wrote your flight plan so they know the path you should be on. They are the still small voice within, and when we listen to them without manipulation, control or justification, they will show us the proper path.

This book is about self-empowerment and finding the path to your spiritual journey. It's not about creating a following for me as a teacher. Self-empowerment can be easy if you know and follow universal law and spiritual principles. The challenge is to recognize the Law of Attraction and work effectively with it. The Universal Law of Attraction is one of life's major rules. Since we create all that happens to us, we must realize that whatever we say or think is what we will experience in life.

Our intention creates what we draw to ourselves. If we focus on have-nots, that's what we receive in life. We manifest exactly what we want from our thoughts, feelings and actions. If we go through life wanting or wishing, we will not manifest the objects of those wants and wishes, but just more wanting and wishing. We must become aware that we're entitled to our desires and be willing to receive them. Unless we know that we can have or bring an object or a situation in life, we will continue to want it. The difference is a matter of being a human *doing* and a human *being*. If we think that we must *do* to get what we desire, we'll be faced with a long tough journey. When we realize that we just need to *be*, then we can have it all.

This spiritual journey can be a tough path to follow in the beginning, but sticking to it with discipline brings peace, happiness, harmony, joy, and an abundance of love and support.

To all those who choose to be transformers and enter into world service, today's massive changes make you critically important. Many doomsayers predict global disasters, but we can avert them by spreading the word of love, forgiveness, and by letting go of judgment and control. Our reward will be a peaceful, more beautiful world. The only catch is that we must walk our talk to make the transition into the New Millennium.

In 1992, when I started to write this book, I began to notice the build-up of pressure, the speeding up of time, and the accelerating nature of change. I became aware that the title of this book described my path; I was indeed a spiritual being having a human experience, yet I knew that I had to take the next step, whatever that was. I was trapped in the mire of physical experiences, feeling lost and not knowing how to find the path, but as with any ready and willing student, the teacher appeared—two, in fact, who came at almost the same time. I'd been looking for a teacher for over a year. Many candidates who looked inviting had passed through my life, but I had used my discernment to evaluate them. Some were tempting, but they just didn't ring true. When I met Paul Solomon and Ronald Beesley, I knew I had found the teacher.

Most times, we're not ready for our teachers or even recognize them in the beginning, but if we have the desire, discipline and commitment, are true to ourselves and are willing stay on the path, we'll find the answers we need. I did, and a whole new reality opened up when I trained myself to listen to "the still small voice within." This opened a whole new level of awareness for me.

Many of us yearn to be spiritual beings yet we're mired in the physical. Rather than deal with physical world body/mind experiences, we try to leap on to the spiritual path without really knowing who we are. Unfortunately, it doesn't work that way. We must first build a solid foundation, otherwise any progress is illusory and can come crashing down on top of us, rather than lead to our goal of personal transformation. The reason for the detour may be unclear but we cannot complete the spiritual journey unless we follow all the steps to get to the goal.

In my case, I kept running into denials and walls I'd erected to protect myself from rejection and feeling unaccepted. As we'll see in this book, these denials and walls take the form of programs locked in the Subconscious Mind. Some of these programs were also locked in denial-of-denial, and continue to influence me even today.

The programs are locked into time-lines at the point when they were created, and will come up as you clear other programs around them. Our mind seems to process its programs in a certain way and we cannot jump over some to select the ones *we* want to clear; they have to go in order.

~~~

In my practice, I find that few people have gone through the spiritual "boot camp" necessary to begin the spiritual journey. I find that most people lack the necessary discipline and commitment. Oh, they have the desire but not the discipline to follow through. Many of us delude ourselves into thinking that we've made considerable progress, but deep down, we know the truth. Now these statements are repeated many times throughout this book, and this is not an error, for we're planting a seed so it will germinate and blossom in your psyche. The advertising world knows the value of repeated exposure, and many times in this book, we indulge in "total immersion"—if we read or hear something often enough, it will sink in. So, when you read something more than once, you can be sure that it's one of those critical points in our growth.

The journey to the light can be rigorous, even traumatic. Many of us hold beliefs, emotions and circumstances in denial, and this can force a "dark night of the soul." Getting through the illusions and denials can be tough, but there's no way around them. We carry with us the truth about our past encounters with every person who has crossed our path, including our parents, and we must go back and rewrite that history with love and forgiveness. Only then can we can begin the spiritual journey. (Later, we'll examine the differences between the spiritual journey, a spiritual path and spirituality.)

Throughout this book, we'll stress that we must reclaim our personal power and heal the separation with self. To do so, we must deal with the lessons we came here to work out. We are eternal beings (even though most people cannot see that big of a picture), and the life you're living now is only a tiny fraction of your duration in this universe. When you're in the world of spirit, you set up lessons for your next lifetime, but you cannot clear them until you're in a physical body, for there are certain lessons that simply can't be learned any other way.

If you try to skip these lessons, then you'll be trapped in the cycle of return, reincarnating again and again until you "get it." There's no other way—to get to the other side of the mountain, you must either climb it or tunnel through it. Universal law supersedes our limited belief systems and will not allow us to dodge the lessons. Ignoring them or refusing to face them in this lifetime doesn't let you off the hook.

My intent in this lifetime is to step off the "cycle of return," or the reincarnation loop, and this means clearing all the karmic contracts and agreements from past lives. The progress in this clearing work is a measure of our level of enlightenment.

We can make all the claims we want, but the truth will always come to bear in our final days in this third-dimensional world. At the fork in the road to final transfiguration, you have only two ways to go:

- Death of the body and the cycle of return, which returns you to the spiritual plane to review the lessons, successes and failures of the recent lifetime. This fork takes your freedom away and forces you to take stock of where you are. You then have another chance to review the mistakes and detours before you create a new body. You go before the Lords of Karma, they meet with your inner-plane teacher and help you file another flight plan to release the karmic contracts and agreements. You start all over again at the same place you left the physical plane.

- The path of light and ascension, in which you take your body with you, and have ultimate freedom to move where you wish, unhindered by the physical world. You're able to join other ascended beings in the Great White Brotherhood who have become part of the GOD Source again. You can now take on the role of true teacher if you so chose.

Most readers will be aware of the many doom-laden prophecies made by myself and many others. Until recently, I believed them accurate and expected them to unfold as predicted. However, in light of recent major shifts, this must all be revised. We're playing by new rules now and are headed toward a quantum leap as changes approach critical mass. (See my book *2011: The New Millennium Begins* for more detail.)

Due to a process known as "The Quickening," consciousness is shifting so quickly that a quantum leap is inevitable. Much of what was written only two years ago is outdated. Our lives now change as quickly as the computer industry, in which power, speed, and capacity double every 18 months. What we based our experience and forecasts on just two years ago is now invalid. Of course, the qualities of peace, happiness, harmony, joy, and love remain constant, but how we experience them is undergoing rapid change. The illusions of the past no longer work. We can try to maintain our delusions of stability, but we will find it increasingly difficult to control our lives, and maintain our balance and centeredness.

For proof of this, simply observe the pressure building as we move toward the dimensional shift. Random murders, school shootings, arson fires and other aberrant behavior appear regularly in the news. Note the senseless wars over power and control. Observe how the "X" generation dresses and behaves, and how politicians do whatever they think they can get away with. The list is endless, and the result is that citizens are beginning to fear their government and its top-heavy bureaucracy. Somehow, the politicians think they can control the world with money and rule it with armies. Even Mother Nature is in on the act, with bizarre weather patterns, raging forest fires and ecological disruption at every turn.

The majority of the population lives in fear and survival mode. People work harder for less disposable income. Sure, salaries and wages increase steadily, but stretching them to the end of the month is getting harder. The media deliver such a steady stream of controlled, depressing news stories into our homes that most people simply pull back into their shells.

Another effect of "The Quickening" is that our sense of time speeds up, which causes stress and friction. The friction causes people's bodies to heat up and act uncharacteristically, and triggers anger and fear, resulting in such phenomena as road rage and lately, air rage. Friction also causes the body's frequency to increase beyond the norm that, in turn, drains the endocrine system and taxes the immune system. The adrenal glands must then produce more adrenaline to help you keep up with the stress and, suddenly, and you're in a "Catch 22" situation. If your body frequency is above 60 Hz, adrenaline is pumping all the time, which causes a shut down in interferon, interlukins, serratonin and all the other chemicals that keep you in balance. If this stress continues for an extended period, your adrenal glands become exhausted. Your immune system comes under stress as the neuropeptides and cytokinins that control the immune function are depressed, which robs you of your first line of defense against disease and illness (as the leukocytes and the NPKs are unable to reproduce in effective numbers to fight off invaders). The next phase is depression. Of course, drugs will mask and suppress the symptom but will not relieve the cause of the stress so that you can release it (see Appendix).

However, now that we've reached the year 2000, there's a positive note to all this. We can no longer turn back. For those willing to commit to, and take responsibility for and control of their life, the future is xviii • Becoming a Spiritual Being in a Physical Body

much brighter and clearer. I'm aware of the new life we can have because I've now entered into that place in my own life.

Until 1997, when working on my books, I would literally pass out on the computer keyboard. After some inner probing, I discovered a deep worry that I was not all right and that no one would be interested in what I was writing. The books wouldn't sell, so why bother? Why set myself up for failure? So I struggled along as best I could publishing my books on my photocopier and selling them at lectures and workshops.

In 1997, a shift occurred that moved me from "fear of failure" to "I'm all right." I had many "I wants" that that were not manifesting—actually "don't wants" but I didn't know the difference. (When we say, "I don't want this in my life anymore," our mind cancels out the negative, so that what we say we don't want actually continues to manifest. As long as we're in confusion and indecision, our mind will create sub-personalities to control our life. When we're on "autopilot," our inner Conscious Mind operates from as many as twenty sub-personalities, and until we take full responsibility, it will continue to create these sub-personalities in our life. When we break free by learning how to take full control of life and reclaim our personal power, then our mind begins to work with us instead of trying to protect and control us.)

For 17 years, I knew the rules but was unable to put them into practice in my life until 1997, and then everything shifted. People began to support my work. My life felt as if I was flowing with the river rather than pushing upstream against the current. Money started to come in easily. I felt renewed confidence in my books and began looking for a publisher. But an unexpected block reared up in my face. Publishers simply weren't interested. Of course, the vanity publishers courted me, but more for my bank balance than the wisdom in the books. Things were stalled until I met Tony Stubbs. He was working with Robert Perala on the book *The Divine Blueprint*, which Robert was going to self-publish with Tony's help. I met with Tony, who suggested establishing my own publishing house.

In March 1999, with Tony's help, I published my first book (*2011: The New Millennium Begins*), and was so excited that we published the second book (*Your Body Is Talking; Are You Listening?*) just three months later. A few months after that, we began work on a third (*Opening Communication With GOD Source*), and then on this book, the fourth.

When we don't have the blocks that stop us, success comes naturally and effortlessly. Some people have described my accomplishment as a publishing miracle. Maybe it is; four books in 18 months with no outside financial help, PR firm or distributor. Yet my books are carried by bookstores around the world, with only me as order-taker, shipper and promoter. However, with the desire, self-discipline and willingness to take a risk, you, too, could easily do this.

The programs in our Subconscious Mind will block us from perceived failure and rejection by stopping us from doing anything that threatens our security. If our lives are running on autopilot, our Subconscious Mind will ensure that our control sub-personalities prevent us undertaking any threatening projects. I discovered this when my colleagues and I began our research into why I'd sabotaged myself all my life. For example, if I were buying something, I would somehow choose the only defective item in the batch. Or if two people were offering to collaborate on a project with me, I would invariably choose the person who would take advantage of me and sabotage the project.

In 1995, we discovered the cause—encrypted and encoded programs that were locked into my body before I was born, and the interpretations and beliefs I created from the sensory input I received as a child from my parents. When we released the encrypted programs, I literally watched my life turn around 180 degrees. The sabotaging behavior disappeared, people began treating me more positively and supportively, and good choices replaced poor ones.

In my lectures, people began to tell me they were attracted by the energy coming from the flyer, yet the wording was exactly as before. It became clear to me then that we transmit an image that's projected on to everything we do. When we change who we are, we change the image we project. But because this projection is below the level of the Conscious Mind, we can't fake it; the only way we can change what we transmit is to change who we are, and this means healing the separation from self, and releasing the self-rejection and feeling of not being all right. When we do this, we build self-appreciation and self-love. We then project a new image of self-value out to the world that flows out with everything we touch. Other people unconsciously sense who we are from our projected image, but don't know why they're immediately attracted to us.

After two decades of working with clients, I've gathered enough pragmatic evidence to state that releasing your cellular memory, sub-personalities, and encrypted programs will rewrite your life script completely—and this book shows you how. So welcome to your spiritual journey. Have a wonderful trip!

— Art Martin, Penryn CA August 2000

Introduction

In the very beginning, we were all once sparks of light in a Universe of Love. Motivated by our interest in finding out how the physical universe operated, we entered bodies to experience the dense material world. But over countless such physical forays, we lost direction because we immersed ourselves in competition, control, and physical pleasures, often fighting for our very survival.

Life is not meant to be about work and suffering. We come here to have fun, and understand how to love and forgive each other. *We come here to evolve our consciousness*, not our soul as some writers have contended. Unfortunately that plan has backfired on most of us, as we got caught up in the physical world of desires. Each time we entered a physical body, we lost our flight plan and lesson list, our road map and our directions. Many of us also lost ourselves, along with the knowledge of who and why we're here, so we keep adding to the list of failures and programs that sabotage our lives and evolution.

For millennia, we've been trying to find the way back to our creator consciousness. Many of us have participated in almost destroying the planet itself, thinking that some power outside of us created this universe. In fact, *we* are the co-creators *and* the destroyers. I once asked the GOD Source, "Why, if you created us in your image, did we get so fouled up?"

Their response was, "If we had created you in our image, you would be perfect. You created us in *your* image. When you see the truth of who you are, you will step out of where you are. But, you will have to believe it first before you can see it. Therefore, you created the God concept *in your image*, and not the other way round." (For details of my search for God and what I found, please see my book *Opening Communication with the GOD Source.*)

We are fast approaching the same conditions that led to the destruction of Atlantis, and for the same reasons. This time, however, enough people may be aware of the potential for disaster to avoid repeating it. Many are predicting catastrophes in the next ten years, but most people cannot grasp that *we*, not God, determine our future. Only time will tell if we can change the doom-laden predictions, but to do so, we must first change our consciousness. It's imperative that as many people as possible know that we can choose which future probabilities we will experience, know how to choose, and begin to do just that.

Few people can suspend judgment and control long enough to listen to their inner selves or the world around them or beyond. For many of us, however, there comes a point in life when we recognize that our life is waiting for us to wake up. I've found that, for most people, this point comes around age 40—that's when they wake up and begin the journey into transformation—and the first steps involve letting go of judgment, justification, need to control, authority, and self-righteousness.

The various levels of our mind are in constant dialogue with our body, but we don't listen. Furthermore, few people know that there's a Higher Source of their being that would love to talk to them and offer guidance. If only we can let go of the need to control, and make peace with our Middle Selves and Ego, then we can receive the messages that are coming to us.

Most of the time, we're too busy making a living or impressing other people to see that we've something of value to offer, and to really begin living our life. In the "busyness" of growing up, most of us lose our connection with the GOD Source and our Higher Self. Locked in the struggle to make a living and get validation from the outside world, we separate from and shut ourselves off from the rich inner world. In our neediness, we lose sight of the true goal. In our search for "alrightness," and validation and approval from the outside, we compromise our true identity to the point where we no longer know who we are. We set up our life structure so that threatening traumatic feelings are blocked out, and we lock all the threatening emotions into denial or, even deeper, into denial-of-denial. We set up an elaborate structure so that we can feel safe and secure.

Autopilot programs in either the Conscious Mind or Middle Self run most people's lives, and if those programs become too threatening, we even lock them into denial. The majority of our population lives their lives alone and lost, seldom feeling the peace, happiness, harmony, joy and love that is their birthright. They may think that they're experiencing these qualities, but it's usually an illusion fostered to make them feel better.

Until 1977, the above described my life perfectly, but then that all changed. Driven by a desire to find out who I was and why I was here, I sold my restaurant and went on a crash course to "find myself." I was willing try anything to resume my spiritual journey. What I learned since then works well, and I've "charted a course" for the spiritual journey.

Now, I don't claim to be a guru, shaman, or any authority on the subject, and can only say that I've walked my talk for the last 20 years and have finally reaped the rewards. My experiences of those two decades form the basis for my conclusions about where we are in our life. When I began, I had no idea who I really was or what love was but, over the years, I began to understand how to recover my lost Self. In this book, I share with you what I learned, in the hope that you'll find it useful.

The path to enlightenment can be smooth sailing if you let go and work through the lessons without control, judgment or justification. If you listen and watch for the lessons, you'll find that you're being clearly directed. But if you get angry, fearful, try to justify your authority, and control events or results, you'll fall back into autopilot mode, and one of your sub-personalities will take control. Your Conscious Mind and Middle Self autopilot's sub-personalities like you to lose control of your emotional balance so that they can step in and take over. (One of the main intents of this book is for you to make friends with your Middle Self and Ego,* so they will support and work *with* you rather than *against* you.)

Another main focus of this book is to understand what reality is. Most of us "interpret" reality by placing conditions on it. We then live in illusion overlaid with denial. If that's what we're doing, we're most likely unaware that we're doing it. Our intent is to perceive reality *as it is*, with no judgment, need to control or manipulate, justify or have authority over the outcome of anything in our life. We'll find that this path leads us from the illusion of freedom, to having no freedom, and, as we let go further, back to *true* freedom. The path can seem upsetting, even hazardous, at times, with storms and boulders in the way, but if we take full responsibility for our life, have the commitment and discipline, and are consistent, we will prevail.

We may have to go through a "dark night of the soul" if we refuse to recognize the lessons. I did, and it seemed as if I was in a vast wasteland where nobody was there for me. My connection to Source seemed

---

* As we'll see later, Ego is the "file manager" for your "computer" in Subconscious Mind. Many people believe that Ego is the enemy, but I feel that Ego must come to trust you, and you must make friends with it. If Ego and Middle Self are not working with you, nothing gets past them. As a result, they control your life, affirmations do not work, and your memory seems to lose its acuity. Ego is the "file server" for your memory. If it refuses to work with you, your memory will shut down.

to be blocked, so I had no guidance of any kind. When I woke up to what I was doing, it all turned back on. My teachers were just letting me go blind to see how long it would take me to wake up to the fact that I had full control but didn't know that I did.

This book, then, describes the path back to our true Self, the steps to get there, and the requirements. All we need do is choose to follow the steps. Remember, you have complete freedom to choose any path or direction you wish, and to believe any illusion you want. No one compels you to do anything. You have the right to deny any truth that's presented to you and to create any reality you wish. You're not a victim of anyone or anything. You create it all. You're even free to ignore the universal truth that the universe is based on *love and forgiveness.*

Are you willing to let go of judgment, control, authority, and justification, and accept what is as is? If you can live in integrity, honesty, and in an ethical manner, it will all come to you. But what if a teacher in disguise tells us a truth about reality that conflicts with our *interpretation* of reality? Could we step out of our denial and recognize our own personal beliefs as illusion?

On the other hand, transformational principles are very simple, yet many teachers seem to complicate them. I have worked and studied with many effective, knowledgeable teachers, while others were ungrounded and made their material overly complex in order to appear special. Since I am results-oriented, I evaluate the success of teachers based on their students' success in obtaining the desired results. Most teachers disappointed me in this regard by not walking their talk. Many have grasped valuable concepts, but fail to apply them to their own lives. However, they will adamantly deny this failing.

Most of my fellow students have fallen from the path and are not even applying what they've learned. Life is a hard struggle for many of the people I talk with. Some of them even wish they'd never even stepped on the path. A few, though, are shining examples of intent, commitment, and discipline, and have turned their lives around. Some have made major contributions to serve and help others in their path by becoming teachers themselves.

Paul Solomon warned us that self-proclaimed spiritual teachers would soon appear on every street corner. He was right. He also said, "Many of these teachers will have valuable information, but you will have to separate the pearls from the garbage. They may have only one statement or concept of value, and you must discern what it is." Unfortunately, discernment may be difficult if you're in illusion and denial.

Personally, the past twenty years have been hard for the most part, but I never gave up. Some of my biggest battles have been won just in the last five years. I always kept looking for the light at the end of the tunnel, but it never seemed to appear. In fact, just when I thought the day was dawning, it would get darker, the lessons even more intense. But finally, that light dawned following an initiation that opened my life up to some major miracles. I realized that all I need do is *be who I am* and miracles just happen in my presence. I am now a human *being* rather than a human *doing*. After a long, hard struggle, I've finally overcome the false self, and now my creator self is running the show.

A major stumbling point along my path was clearing self-rejection. Many of us self-reject without knowing that that's what we're doing. Due to societal programming and beliefs, our "committee" of the Middle Self's sub-personalities will react to any input that comes to us and hurry to protect us from any imagined harm. This then creates negative thoughtforms that in turn create programs in our Subconscious Mind, of which we are unaware. If we're not even aware of a program, we cannot rewrite its dialogue. If this program runs without our awareness, it can result in self-rejection, something that happened to me over and over again. I thought I'd cleared a program but self-rejection would pop up again. Now, however, I'm very much aware of my self-talk and monitor it all the time. When my body starts talking, I listen.

If autopilot has control over your mind, it will operate on its own, almost as a separate personality. We must be in control of our mind at all times, and I vigilantly watch for the temptation to give away my power and lose sight of the path.

We all want recognition and approval. If you're on the appropriate path, your teachers and the other students will recognize when you become detached from the need for approval. Personally, in the eighties, I strove for recognition but seldom received it. Then I discovered that when you give up everything, you can have it all, but then you don't *need* it. And when you don't need it, everyone begins to appreciate your value, ability and accomplishments, and you're bathed in recognition and approval. Accepting your self-worth and self-esteem are the key to self-acceptance. I'll repeat this statement many times over in this book, for this simple little irony is one of the main gifts I share with you here.

We must become aware that universal law stipulates that everything we do, say, and think has consequences. To think otherwise is to live in illusion. If we're in illusion and our Middle Self has programs that justify unethical behavior, we won't recognize or feel that our unethical behavior is wrong. But if we know the laws of karma, we won't act in a way that needs to be rebalanced in the future. The major lesson here is that we must learn to live ethically and honestly. Ignorance of the law of karma does not justify karmic behavior in any way, and until we recognize this truth, our transformation will be blocked. So we must walk our talk and live in honesty, ethics, and integrity.

Furthermore, the apparent speeding up of our sense of time results in our karmic lessons coming at us more quickly. At one time, karma incurred in one lifetime wouldn't pop up to be dealt with until a later lifetime. That allowed us to make a mistake and discount it with, "I'll atone for that in my next life." Nowadays, however, karmic effects, both positive and negative, bounce back within the same lifetime, often producing almost immediate results.

Much has been written about the soul and its journey, and many tools allow us access to information on the path. Yet there is considerable controversy as to what the soul is and what it knows about your spiritual journey. Although we may not consciously understand the concept, our soul, operating through the Holographic Mind, already knows the path. Therefore, we must connect to our inner reality, bring it to our external awareness, accept our soul's path, and follow it, thereby removing ourselves from duality.

My experience and the information I have received from GOD Source is that the soul is complete and whole in itself. It has total knowing of where you are on the path as it's connected with and is part of your Higher Self. It can help you traverse the path, but it *per se* doesn't need to learn any lessons as it's your direct connection to the presence of GOD. The Holographic Mind is its connection to your physical self. The soul has no agenda as to how quickly you learn the lessons that are placed before you, and waits patiently for you to wake up and get on with your spiritual journey.

Transformation takes considerable discipline. Once you decide to step on to the path, you must have the desire and determination to follow the path with consistent diligence. Staying on the path when the going gets rough takes commitment and discipline. Your Middle Self, acting through your sub-personalities, will try to turn you back or distract you from your goal. Your Survivor Self will subtly try to convince you to get you off the path. The only way to break this pattern is to reclaim your personal power and delete, erase and destroy autopilot and all the programs and sub-personalities driving it.

We all have the choice to create what we want in life. The only catch is; are we willing to recognize that choice? Through our countless decisions during each day, we choose which path to take. Through karma, we place ourselves exactly where we are. We cannot control or affect another person's life path directly. We can only be models for others to observe, but those in denial and illusion will not be able to see your example. In fact, they may object to your intrusion and accuse you of trying to manipulate them. You can only change and heal yourself. However, you can help those who are willing to face their issues. Again, it's their choice.

Many people will go through many lifetimes before they recognize that they're not even in kindergarten yet, but in preschool. They tell me they don't have a choice, that they didn't choose their life circumstances. However, this is *victim consciousness*. In truth, it's all up to you. Nobody is going to make the choices for you. I was there at one time, and change looked like an insurmountable mountain range, but I just kept on, knowing that I'd get to the top. After twenty years and much physical pain, I did, as have many other survivors. We just keep on keeping on, and know that we'll succeed. You, too, can do what I and many others have done, and reap the rich rewards. When I set out, I didn't know that, once you reclaim your personal power, transformation is instantaneous. According to my beliefs at that time, this was inconceivable. Now I know it to be so.

Traps await the unaware, however. You may think it's a long, tough journey and never take the first step, or you may live in the *illusion* that you're on the path but are not. The truth will always show itself to the aware observer. The main obstacles to transformation are denial and illusion, but you won't see them until you let go of the illusion that your life is all right. Another common trap is when other people point out to you that you're in delusion, and you in turn accuse them of judging you.

After two decades, I've finally found a path that works for me and many of my clients and, in these pages, I share it with you. If you come up with something that works better for you, please let me know and I may include it in future revisions. If I find a better mousetrap, I will use it.

Part One

In The Beginning,
We Must Start
Somewhere

1

Recovering your Direction, Finding the Path

In the beginning, we knew who we were. We had no mission or anything to prove because we were sparks of light. As co-creators of the universe and aspects of GOD, we were members of the Brotherhood of Light. We were at the Godhead, with no lessons to learn as we were one with GOD—the highest level we could achieve in our beingness. We were in oneness with our soul. In fact, this was where all souls begin their existence. There are no "old souls" or "new souls" as we all came into existence at the same time. One soul was not better or had more knowledge than any other.

At some point in our existence, we decided to separate from the White Brotherhood and the Presence of GOD (or Source Consciousness) and move out into the universe. We had a desire to explore experiences in physical bodies, but since we'd never before entered dense physical reality, we didn't understand what it was all about. It looked inviting, so we decided to try it out. The Lords of Karma warned us about what we might encounter in this foray into the physical world, for example, that we could get caught in the desire body and personality selves, which would cause us to lose our connection with GOD Source. Nevertheless, we had free choice and decided to take this trip into the physical world anyway, knowing the chance we were taking.

We took our first incarnation into the physical world, and although we enjoyed the physical experiences, what the Lords of Karma warned us of happened and we were drawn into the mire of competition, manipulation, control, judgment, and justification of our actions. As a result, we began to experience anger, fear and separation from self. We lost contact with our souls so we were without a rudder to guide us.

As we immersed ourselves more deeply in our body's animal needs and desires, we lost the directions back to our Source. Having lost the road map, we tried to navigate life as best we could. Unfortunately, the farther we moved away from our Source, the more we got lost in fear, further losing our sense of balance. Each time we incarnated, we had to go before the Lords of Karma, who reminded us of how we separated from self, and the lessons we had before us that stemmed from that separation. They said, "We warned you of the perils of entering a physical body. We will assign a teacher to you to make sure that you keep your commitment and help you back on the path to enlightenment. "Are you willing to live with that responsibility?" Of course we said, "Yes."

They also gave you a variety of possible parents who would fulfill your needs for the lessons you had to learn. You checked them out and made your choice. You had the counseling support and help to file a flight plan for your journey into the physical world. So, the words you had with the Lords of Karma became flesh, and you found yourself in a body with the family you had chosen. Unfortunately, on the flight into the body, you lost the flight plan so you had no directions to navigate this new life. You lost contact with your teacher and became unplugged from your higher self and your soul, so you couldn't communicate with your Source.

An inner shadow or veil was placed between you and your higher self so you were denied its guidance, and were isolated from any other support. The rest is history. Without the flight plan and soul's guidance, you became hopelessly lost. After a few forays into the physical world, you had created a situation in which you would have to reincarnate many times to find your way back to Source.

The challenge of each lifetime is to consciously carry into your new life the memory of the instructions and directions contained in the flight plan you filed. Unfortunately, most people don't remember the contents of their flight plan, nor do they even know that they've lost contact with their soul's guidance. Few know what the requirements are for each life and the entire cycle of lives, and nor to they know what they must do to return to Source. This has many implications.

One implication is that most people confuse the vehicle with the driver, so parents treat their children as physical bodies, not knowing the consciousness *in* the body that's driving it is different from the actual body itself. We are *not* our bodies or minds; we simply take on a body and mind as focal points to learn physical plane lessons, but most parents don't understand this.

Parents also assume the baby cannot understand what they say, so they talk carelessly to children or about them. Many parents don't recognize or fulfill a child's need for love and support, so the child feels rejected and abandoned. (Many books explore the effect of childhood mistreatment, neglect, and abuse. For example, see my book *Your Body Is Talking; Are You Listening?* or books by John Bradshaw and many other authors.)

Another common misconception is that a child doesn't need to be actually abused by someone in order to develop dysfunctional behavior. Simply the child's *interpretation* of how it's treated can trigger the same problems as actual abuse. Programming and beliefs may cause a child (and adults) to interpret an innocuous situation totally wrongly. Then, we will react to our *understanding* of a situation or remark rather than to what is actually before us. The challenge is to dispel the illusion and denial that cover our reality and cause us to misinterpret that reality.

Owning our own personal power is one of the main lessons we must learn. Walking through "the valley of the snakes" without looking down is a real test. Hold your head high and know that nothing will bite you unless you allow it. This book talks extensively about claiming and owning your own personal power and taking total responsibility, for this is the way out of the illusion and denial.

There are no victims, but only people who allow themselves to be victims. To really understand the base cause of a person's behavior, we must go back to the Akashic Record. Over many lifetimes, we accumulate a personal history that directs our basic path in life, but the presence of GOD within us gives us a process to clear the records ourselves. The only catch is that we must know exactly what information the records hold. Once we know the content of the records, all we need do is claim Grace and release all previous karmic contracts and agreements. When we understand the lesson, we can forgive and love the person and/or the situation by claiming Grace. This will release the lesson and, in recognition of our accomplishment, the Lords of Karma will remove the lesson from the files. Countless volumes explore this subject and teachers all have their own account (see my book *Opening Communication With GOD Source*).

As students in the mystery school of life, it's our responsibility to recognize the lessons. No enlightened beings are going to rescue us from our pain, trauma, and errors that we have created in our lifetimes. We knew before we entered this life that *we* are the Christed beings who are to bring in the new millennium. Fortunately, some us are now recognizing that there'll be no second coming of Christ to wipe the slate clean, and that *we* must learn how to turn on the presence of God within. The next ten years will be the most critical years of the last 2,000 years.

Many false prophets will be sprinkled among genuine spiritual leaders, and we must discern the truth and appropriate action for ourselves. Many people claim to be teachers in various mystery school traditions, but guidance tells me that this is not something you can self-proclaim. Based on training and ability to present the material, those already in the White Brotherhood decide who will be teachers.

From now on, your true identity will be apparent to people who have the eyes to see and the ears to hear. There will always be "true believers" who are looking for the panacea to spiritual enlightenment and someone else to show them the way. Eric Hoffer's book *True Believer* describes well the various mass movements and their followers, who will follow any guru or teacher who claims to know the way, but often never finding it. Again, ask if teachers walk their own talk. Do they exemplify peace, joy, happiness, harmony, and unconditional love and acceptance in their own lives? And do they empower followers to reclaim their personal power? Or do they steal it to empower themselves?

As in everything, the final test is how your life evolves over time. With a true teaching, you will experience more peace, happiness, harmony, and joy in life, along with unconditional love and abundance. The final outcome is always in the application in your life of your understanding of universal laws and spiritual principles. It's all an inside job. Nobody can give you joy, peace, happiness or harmony from the outside, and if you think they can, it's an illusion for you're being driven by need, and the final payoff will always elude you because you see yourself as a human *doing* and not as a human *being*. You don't have to "do" to get. All you need is to "be" and you can have all that life offers. The challenge in this is that you must let go of your security and control, step forward, and risk stepping into a new reality.

When we make that leap to claim our own personal power, we will be tested to see if we're really committed to the journey. The vulnerability of being an "open book" brings up fear in many people. The only way to change is to summon up your commitment and let go of the need to control your life and those around you.

It may seem odd that you must let go of control to advance in life, but the need for control is a sure indicator of fear. Where there's no fear, there's no need for control. Without fear, you can venture out into the unknown trusting that, "Good things will happen even if my life is out of my control." However, if we're driven by fear, it will be obvious to others even though we cannot perceive it ourselves.

Many people believe in a great spiritual hierarchy, with the path to transformation being governed by laws and rules. Most people are addicted to following rules because then, they don't have to make decisions for themselves. For example, the Hebrew nation has always been governed by rules, and they have been trying for thousands of years to find the safe path back to God. One of the most adept teachers from the White Brotherhood chose to incarnate into their midst to teach them that the rules are in their hearts and not written on parchment, yet they would not accept him. Apollonius of Tyana or Jesuwah Ben Joseph, (or Jesus Christ, as the Christians call him) taught only one law: "Love yourself, God, and your neighbor with all you have. Accept people as they are. Love and forgive everyone." That same law has been handed down over the centuries but, today, few Christians practice the actual teachings. Even though this is a fundamental spiritual principle and universal law, it has little influence on today's violent and materialistic society.

Fifteen years ago, I sponsored some workshops for Neale Donald Walsh, who would go on to write the *Conversations With God* books. At that time, he'd just written a little booklet entitled *Hitler Went To Heaven*. The introduction explained that the book wasn't about Hitler at all, but about our unwillingness to forgive Hitler and everybody else for what they'd done in the past. My own sources tell me that Hitler was, in fact, simply playing a role in the vast evolutionary plan in our society (as we all are), and that what people do ultimately makes no difference, for the GOD Source *always* forgives them. The GOD Source has no negative reference point from which to judge anybody. It's our fear that causes us to blame and seek revenge. No matter how terrible an act may be, without exception, the person must be forgiven, for we are all in lesson.

Many valuable tools are available to those on the path at this time, such as the specific steps in this book. The books that comprise *A*

Course In Miracles also clearly explain the need for forgiveness and how to come to peace with it. The steps may not work for everyone, but we must start somewhere. So, let us go back to the beginning and the early mystery school teachings on the subject. Many historical teachers offer clues on opening up the treasure chest of our lives. For example, Madam Blavatsky and her successor, Anne Besant, were master teachers, and more recently, Dion Fortune laid out an intensive course, with self-discipline at its heart.

In Summary

Most people are like ships floating aimlessly in a fog bank, having lost their charts and forgotten the course they mapped out before they incarnated. But being trapped in the fog doesn't matter because they don't know where they're going anyway. Without a course based on spiritual principles and guidance from contact with our souls, most of us are hopelessly lost. Feeling powerless, we fall back on stealing the power of those weaker than ourselves, and amassing "the most toys" before we die. How do we live with this? By burying our insecurity under layers of denial and illusion so that we hide our predicament even from ourselves so that we can avoid taking responsibility for our spiritual growth.

The history of your life up to the present, and how you plan to achieve your goals for the future, will indicate how successful you are in handling your life. If you do not discipline yourself and take responsibility, the past will become the future as the cycle of return brings you back to the same lessons over and over until you "get" them and release them.

Constant peace, happiness, harmony, joy, love, and acceptance are within our reach, but the illusion that "all is well" keeps them from us, leading to such ploys as blaming others for the obstacles in our lives, or accusing them of not cooperating with our needs. Only when we can honestly acknowledge and let go of our needy state, and realize that everything we need to evolve spiritually is already within us, will we discover that transformation is, indeed, instantaneous.

2

In The Beginning Was The Word

The Gospel According to St. John begins with: "In the beginning was the word, and the word was with God and the word was God." He goes on to list all the things that he was to do, especially bear witness to the true light that illumines every person who comes into this world. The text continues with: "We were born not of the blood, nor the will of the flesh, nor the will of man, but of God. And the Word was made flesh and dwelt among us."

John seems to be the clairvoyant writer of the Bible. Most of the other biblical contributors wrote letters to someone else describing their travels and experiences, but not John. He was in direct communication with the Source. Interpreting the first paragraph yields a good description of who we are. John clearly knew who he was and what his mission was, yet few people understood him. The same feels true to me today, in that few people are open and willing to understand who they *really* are, and what their true purpose is. Today, we're still as confused as people were in John's day, but at least some of us are waking up and are willing to commit to become "the bearers of the light," as John described his mission. His purpose was, and still is, to get us to recognize that *we* are also bearers of the light.

If we are to understand what he wrote, we must recognize our mission so that we can support the evolution of this planet for, if we don't take that responsibility, the planet will evolve without us and begin over. Whether we like it or not, this planet is on an inexorable path to a higher evolution and we can become part of this transformation, but only if, as John stated, we become Bearers of the Light.

9

As the Bearers of the Light, how have we done? Let's just say that we're doing better than we were. John also said that, "We were not born of blood, nor the will of man or the will of the flesh." We must accept that we are first and foremost spiritual beings who incarnated in this world to take on a body, but we are not that body. The physical body is a focal point and a means to learn lessons on our path back to our source and to be true nature-bearers of the Light of GOD.

John further explains [3:21] what the path is, and that we must be reborn because we got off the track. That which is spirit is spirit; that which is flesh is flesh. If we attach ourselves to a form of the vehicle, we are of flesh. If we can release and let go of our attachment to form, we can be reborn.

Even if we have fallen into darkness and condemnation, we're still offered the opportunity to be reborn and return to the light. Some people are attracted to darkness, and we can do nothing about that except forgive and be Bearers of the Light unto them, without judgment. We can only evaluate our *own* behavior and make whatever adjustments are needed to put us back on our *own* path to enlightenment.

Each of us must do the work ourselves. If people ask us for help, then, yes, we can step in and help, but we cannot intrude on their path. They must see the light themselves. If they claim they are enlightened, and we perceive otherwise, we have no right to push our observation on them. We can state our viewpoint and offer our opinion, but must not push our opinion because the path they are following may be *their* truth, even though we can see that they're heading down a deadend road. They will remain in the illusion until they see the light for themselves. We cannot change people against their will and must let them go their own way—a most difficult task if they are close friends, relatives, or family members. If their light is dimmed and they cannot see the path, that is not our problem, and we cannot simply flip some switch for them. However, we can maintain the hope that they will do it themselves at some point.

Our responsibility is clear—to understand the spiritual principles and universal laws that govern ascension—and this book shares the understanding that has come to me in my quest. Some would call it "channeled" material, but I regard it as tuning into our Source. It takes commitment, concentration, and discipline yet, with the proper training, we all have the ability to do this ourselves. All the records are available. Everything is known, and all we need to do is discipline ourselves to ask questions and listen to our Source, free of the constant chatter of self-talk.

3

The Path to Enlightenment

In our Holographic Mind, we all know what our mission is; the challenge is deciphering the directions. The question is: "How long are we going to continue bumping through life, unfulfilled in our mission?"

Since most of our parents could not relate to anything but physical form, we picked up from them that a physical form was all we were. But when we identify solely with the body, we decide that that's all there is and walk away from the truth of who we really are.

Transformation can take one second or a hundred lifetimes; it's our choice, but to transform, we must transcend the boundaries of physical form. So, ironically, we took physical form in order to transcend it. It's almost a "Catch 22," in that we must have the form, yet must detach from it. When viewed from the physical level, this is a paradox, but we must let the old form die to be reborn, yet remain in form with the vehicle, but not attached to it.

If we can get far enough back, to the point where we're not attached to the form, then we can see our illusions and misconceptions, and let them go. But we must get to that point where we know who is really making the decisions in our life. Who is the spokesperson that's doing the talking for us? Our higher consciousness? Some sub-personality deep in our Subconscious Mind? Or a whole committee of sub-personalities? And how can we find out?

When we reconnect with our soul, we'll know the path we are to take, for the soul has the directions we lost when we identified exclusively with our personality self, thus losing contact with our guidance.

So often, I have heard and read of people believing that somehow their soul has become lost and that they must "find" it because it has lessons to learn, or that it has become "fragmented," or that we must retrieve it and make sure it learns the lessons so that we can become whole again.

The truth is that *we* separated from our soul; it did not separate from us. It is not in any way lost, fragmented or splintered, so we do not have to recover it. It is *us* who are lost. The soul has all the answers, so it has nothing to learn. It holds a clear picture and understands what we must do in our life to get on the path and recover our lost self. We need to let go of the personality self and identify with our soul and higher self, for *they* know the way back to the Source because they're in continual contact with GOD Source. *It is our responsibility to recover our fragmented lost self.* This is something I cannot stress enough. In fact, I'll be repeating this throughout this book so we really get the message.

~~~

Now, we live with two types of vibrations:
- A lower form, which is the personality self. It can have a high or low vibratory rate, but it's usually unbalanced.
- A higher form, which is the soul, and has a high vibratory rate and is balanced because it's not attached to the body.

Doctors prescribe drugs for people who are operating from fast energy vibrations so as to slow them down. In higher form, the body produces its own chemicals to speed up, slow down, and handle intruding viruses, etc. In the lower form, we react to viruses, bacteria, allergies, and myriad other things, and resort to outside chemicals to control reactions.

Becoming a spiritual being involves transcending the duality of physical form. And when you're not attached to physical form, that form is unaffected by physical world problems. The only way to recognize your degree of evolution is to note how many emotions, diseases and other ailments to which you react, for your body can respond effectively if you're able to function from a high level of consciousness When we become a spiritual being in a physical body, we *use* the body to navigate through the lessons that are presented to us, but since we are not *of* the body, the ills of the physical world do not affect us.

Another paradox is that as long as we are in a physical form, we're subject to the operating frequency of the physical world around us. Now, the Earth has a characteristic resonant frequency, and our body must function at that frequency or it will begin to malfunction. Our consciousness can increase in frequency, but our physical body cannot, so this puts us in a duality that can be tough on your body. To rectify the situation, we developed the Body/Mind Harmonizer (see Appendix), which allows your body to function at the Earth's frequency of 12 – 20 Hz, while the enlightenment process functions at a higher level.

In today's stressful times, most people's bodies vibrate at 220 – 380 Hz, which is extremely hard on the endocrine, immune, circulatory and neurological systems. Over an extended period, this can cause adrenal insufficiency, which is the same effect that diabetes has on insulin, the only difference being that there are no drugs to correct adrenal breakdown. Doctors prescribe antidepressants or other drugs that change body chemistry, but they don't get to the root of the problem. However, within 7 – 10 days of beginning to use the Harmonizer, this problem rectifies and the device rebalances the whole system without drugs.

Once you're free of limiting boundaries that block you, you're on the path, but we all set conditions and limitations on ourselves. In order to become a "meta-human," we must take total responsibility as the creator of all the experiences in our lives.

We invite into our life all the situations that cause our experience, yet most of us deny our role in this, and resort to control, blame, and manipulation. When we release the denial and end the illusion, we can begin the process of transformation.

The challenge is to see the truth. The title of Wayne Dyers' book, *You'll See It When You Believe It*, tells us that, whatever beliefs you hold, you will experience a reality that conforms to them. The deeper that you're in denial, the more illusion your beliefs will contain, and the harder you will defend your illusion. Not only do you need to believe something in order to see it, you must embrace the truth of: "My only belief is my discernment."

Belief System Rework

By virtue of the assumptions we live under, and the conditions and limitations we place on ourselves, we are actually imprisoning ourselves in a cage. Harry Brown's book *How To Be Free In An Unfree World* offers a good description of this syndrome.

People believe what they do for a variety of reasons, and hang on to those beliefs that provide some kind of payoff, but often a particular belief does not support the person. And it may even prove harmful, as when the members of a cult practice mass suicide.

The first step in belief system rework is to scrutinize all your beliefs to see if they support you or hinder you. But can you detach from your cherished beliefs long enough to objectively evaluate them? During this process of re-evalution, you are vulnerable, so it's important to give yourself support, approval and validation. Because you are essentially a spiritual being who took on a body, can you make the *Word become flesh and make it work in your life?*

Some people believe that we can meditate our way into higher realms. That may be possible once we have achieved mastery by assuming total personal responsibility for our physical plane lives. However, although we *are* spiritual beings, we chose to take on physical bodies to work out our earth plane lessons, so meditation cannot be used as a mean of avoiding those lessons. But it helps us greatly to work swiftly and effectively through them.

We cannot stress enough that once we arrived on the Earth plane, we "forgot" our true spiritual identity because we were "brainwashed" by our parents and others. Of course, they did this unknowingly because they, in turn, were brainwashed by the generation before them, and so on throughout time. And by identifying with the "false" self of personality, we let autopilot and Middle Self take over. Fortunately, as if waking from "mass amnesia," many of us are beginning to remember the true identity that we all forget when we incarnate, and are ready to make the quantum leap. However, specific universal laws and spiritual principles stipulate that we either work through the lessons without judgment or, as we will see later, invoke Grace to release them.

We all want peace, happiness, joy, harmony, acceptance, approval, validation, and unconditional love in our lives, but it seems that these qualities elude us except for rare moments. If we're truly honest with ourselves, we must look denial and illusion in the face and commit to take responsibility. When we accept the fact that *we*, and no one else, are responsible for our own well-being, we can achieve self-esteem, self-worth, self-confidence, and self-validation. These are all earth plane lessons that we must master before we can move up to the spiritual plane lessons. *Fortunately, when we know that we can have all of these qualities in our life all the time, we will achieve this level of enlightenment.*

Contrary to popular belief, self-esteem is not a learned quality. We are all born with the positive self-supporting qualities of self-esteem, confidence, validation, acceptance, worth, love, and approval. We're also born with the ability to experience happiness, joy, harmony, and inner peace, and to understand adult language. But as we grow up, our perceptions and interpretations begin to fashion our beliefs and view of reality. We lose our self-esteem and sense of well-being by allowing others to control our feelings.

As children, we formed our beliefs based on the way our primary caregivers treated us, which is regrettable since most of us come from dysfunctional families. In turn, we as adults perpetuate the cycle by unknowingly teaching the young children around such negative traits as self-rejection, disapproval, blame, shame and peer pressure. I have found that children are so sensitive to what we say that we can program their lives for failure or success just by how we treat them. As a result of negative treatment, children give their personal power away to others and begin to reject themselves.

By their third year, children set up their life path to become either self-supportive or self-destructive, which determines whether they are able or unable to accept love, respectively. As adults, if they're unable to accept love, no matter what strokes, praise, support, and recognition they receive, they will be unable to recover their lost self-esteem and self-worth. They may discount and reject other people's validation of them because they feel they are not entitled to it. Fortunately, children will accept remedial therapy better than adults because they have less negative programming to overcome.

When we evaluate approaches for self-empowerment and recovery of self-esteem, we overlook the fact that our Subconscious Mind has awesome power. My research has revealed that most people put honest effort into changing their attitudes and behavior to reclaim their self-esteem and self-worth, but many seem unable to succeed, so they become further discouraged and disappointed. Our Conscious Mind may buy into the goals but the Subconscious Mind must also accept the validity of those goals.

Both minds must be aligned to the task, or the Middle Self will sabotage the effort by controlling our actions without our conscious consent. Being concerned with only the threat that change promises and not the result, our sub-personalities will act out the programs they believe will protect us from any threat. However, if we can invoke the awesome power of our Mind's transformative energy, we can accomplish everything we set out to do. This means training ourselves to create new programs for effective, supportive behavior. In computer language, our bodies are the "hardware" and are not the cause of the problem; that lies with the dysfunctional "software" programs. Two of my books describe the causes of dysfunction and the reprogramming of the mind to attain clarity. This book presents processes for turning self-rejecting, self-depreciating, lack of self-worth behavior patterns into "alrightness" patterns of self-esteem, self-love, and self-worth.

In 1992, my experiences motivated me to find a safe path to ascension. In response to my questions, the GOD Source had told me earlier, "No one can ascend in a 'dirty body,' " but I didn't understand that term at the time. Now, I know that they meant that we must clear all our earth plane lessons before we can work on the spiritual plane lessons. This was made painfully clear to many people in September 1992, when a few attendees at an ascension celebration proclaimed they were enlightened and ascended beings. Unfortunately, they had not gone through the proper preparation, so they left their physical bodies behind, and ended up trapped on the astral plane in panic because they couldn't get back in their bodies. (They discovered they had not ascended, but had left by way of the solar plexus chakra, a one-way door that you cannot reenter.)

My personal experience was with a young woman who claimed to be a highly enlightened being. Unfortunately, she was in denial of her actual level of personal enlightenment. When she left her body, she became trapped outside it and couldn't return. Her soul left for the spiritual plane and is now back on the cycle of return, from which she will need to start over in another body back at the same level.

Both emotional and physical structures cause us to become too attached to them, and the purpose of this book is help you detach from these structures. If you feel you cannot get along without that physical plane "something," your teacher will work with the universe to bring you a lesson to reveal your attachments and remove the objects of them from your life. Your soul and Holographic Mind have all the answers.

Part Two

Recovering
Our Lost Self

4

Crossing the Threshold From Denial to Reality

In 1987, the Wellness Institute, our bookstore/counseling center, was forced out of business by the activities of a group of people who we trusted. We had invited them to join our business venture in 1986, and after working with us for six months, they proceeded to try to take over the business and push us out. Susie, my wife, recognized this but, because I was so caught up with enthusiasm for my newfound success having finally begun to receive recognition as a therapist and speaker, I didn't listen to her. She described our new business partners as "spiritual flakes" and said she no longer wanted to work with them.

"All you ever think about is the center and have forgotten about our personal welfare," she complained, and took an outside job, leaving me to handle the center's business and deal with our partners. However, my lectures and healing consumed all my time and I didn't notice that the business was being mismanaged. When the group felt they had the confidence of the board of directors and enough votes, they issued an ultimatum, saying that all the subtenants of the Wellness Institute would leave en masse if Susie and I didn't hand the Institute over to them. Worse, we received the ultimatum on the afternoon of December 24. Needless to say, Christmas 1986 was devoid of cheer for me and my family.

To pay me back my investment, they offered me limited use of the center's facilities, but when they discovered that I'd invested over $200,000 in the Institute, they changed their offer to giving me a one-year option to lease my office back from them on condition I used it only in the evening. Apart from that, I was barred from any other presence in my own Institute. They also told me that, when the year was up, I would have to find alternative premises. We declined their offer, outraged that Susie and I had invested our entire life-savings and three hard years to start the center and husband it into a flourishing business, and were now having it stolen in front of our very eyes.

While all this was going on, the landlord complained that the group had paid only half the rent for the last three months, claiming that the Institute was in the process of reorganizing and would make up the balance in January 1987. The group had assumed that Susie and I would accept their offer and pay the back rent for them. The landlord demanded payment, giving us three days to come up with the money. On the same day, our partners folded their tents and slipped away in the night. And worse, we couldn't even pay the rent because the Institute's bank accounts had been frozen for nonpayment of taxes. My wife and I had to close the center and pay the back rent and taxes from our own already depleted personal account.

After they left and we were able to untangle the mess, we discovered that, by manipulating the books, the group had embezzled over $30,000 from the business in less than a year. Also, they had written themselves huge year-end bonus checks that had completely cleaned out all the bank accounts. Three times that Fall, I'd asked to see the Center's books but had always been met with one excuse or another and, being busy with my practice, I'd never really followed through.

These were professional people with degrees and licenses, and proclaimed themselves "spiritual," but obviously didn't understand the laws of karma nor what would befall them for their misdeeds. We have met some of them in the past few years, and karma has certainly taken its toll as they pay the high price for karmic misdeeds. Even though she hadn't directly participated in the theft, the mother of one of the partners had manipulated the books to cover up the embezzlement. She, too, incurred karma just as did those who actually took the money and goods. It seemed that these people just didn't understand that "what goes around comes around."

In retrospect, we might have been better off to have just given them the business and gone on with our lives, starting over somewhere else. We would then not have been personally liable for the huge debts, but we didn't because of "the principle of the thing" and because of our attachment. We were outraged that our partners and supposed friends could have been driven by greed to the point of violating their ethics and integrity, and learned many hard lessons from the experience. But Susie and I paid dearly for our education.

Physical plane lessons are a two-edged sword, as everyone involved has a lesson to learn. My lesson in that situation was that I was looking for validation from outside of myself. The Wellness Institute was my identity. People were telling us how great it was that we provided such a spiritual center for the community and how wonderful all its services were, and I got all my validation from that. I also supported the cost of operation for the first year from my own savings and income to get it going. In the third year, I was again doing that as many of our office renters left. We tried to downsize the business and limit it to a small center for our own use, but we were still not getting the lesson. Eventually, we ran out of money and had to close it down altogether. We later realized, of course, that none of this had been about money. Acceptance, happiness, peace and joy were the real issues.

It took us a while to understand the lesson that caused all of our life savings to disappear in 1986 – 1987. We have recovered now, but it took us 13 years to get back to where we were before we began our journey with the bookstore. We lost our home because we couldn't make the payments, and the engine went out on one of our cars so we gave it away because we had no money to fix it. We were even evicted from the house we were renting because the bank had foreclosed on the owner. We tried to purchase the house but the bank wouldn't accept our offer and just wanted us out. However, we did find another house to move into and bought it with a $2000 down payment borrowed from my mother. The owner, a real estate broker, let us pay $200 a week because were afraid that if we didn't pay weekly, we might not have the full $800 at the end of each month. This all happened in a three-month period at the end of 1987.

Owning that house, however, proved to be nightmare and another lesson in taking our power back and standing up for what's right. The seller's game was to sell a house to a family in financial trouble, make it hard for them to make the payments, foreclose on the house, and keep as much of the buyers' money as possible. He had done this four times before, but he'd met his match in us. We did not give up and run as had previous buyers.

Further, the seller had misrepresented the house to us and it could have been red-tagged as unsafe by the county building inspector. Fortunately, the inspector realized our plight and worked with us to get the house to conform to code. We could have given up, but we had no place to go nor the money to even make the move so, for the next five years, we fought it out with the real estate broker from whom we'd bought the house. In the ensuing protracted court battle, we went through three lawyers, one of whom misrepresented her ability in real estate and almost lost the case for us. This attorney even double-billed us and we had to go through the State Bar Mediation Service get her off our back.

Our third attorney told us, "If you'd had proper representation in the beginning, you'd have been able to get the real estate broker's license pulled plus a settlement of $250,000 for the five-year battle and damages. Finally, we managed to get the title cleared but at a cost of over $30,000. In the end, it proved to be a good investment as the house is now worth three times what we paid for it, and we are back on track financially after a 10-year uphill battle. The moral of this story is that life will deal you the lessons, and the growth lies in how you interact with them.

Quite often, we do not recognize the "dark night of the soul" until it hits us hard. In our case, we found ourselves in a downward spiral with few resources to pull ourselves out of the tailspin, but eventually we did.

The period 1987 – 1997 was a real struggle for my family. Due to the scarcity of funds, we were limited in what we could do, and suffered hardship, but not severely. We never wanted to admit that our living standard had dropped considerably, and we tried to convince ourselves we could get along with what we had. We considered ourselves a functional family and, from the outside, it appeared that we were. We heralded each New Year as a new beginning, but when we looked back at year's end, we saw that we'd simply been spinning our wheels for another year. Of course, there had been good times when everything had gone right, but I had a nagging feeling that something was sluggish and holding me back.

For 12 years, we'd lived under the illusion that we understood and practiced unconditional love, yet it just didn't seem to manifest in our lives as we expected. In our illusion, we tried to make it happen but unconditional love just wasn't there, despite my fervent claims that I was teaching the subject. We did not realize that our illusion was still operating, nor its depth. Then, in 1992, we resolved to remove the denial. What a watershed year it was! We finally saw the light at the end of the tunnel.

I find that most of my clients, including my family, live under illusory beliefs about "the way life is supposed to be," which conflicts with the beliefs held by the Subconscious Mind. When the Conscious and Subconscious Minds are not aligned, it is the subconscious beliefs that control our life, whether we want that to happen or not. Occasionally, I'll find clients with sufficiently strong will to overpower the existing subconscious programs, but that puts them in a double-bind and is so physically draining that they may experience emotional, physical, or mental breakdown, or suffer from unexplained depression.

In my case, intense physical pain forced me into close scrutiny of the current and past events in my life in order to uncover the denials. I had become aware of this in 1978, but by 1990 had had only marginal success in clearing it up. If you honestly attempt to face your denials and illusions, your Conscious and Instinctual Minds and your Middle Self may put up a real battle. However, my family and I discovered that the reward for perseverance is crossing the threshold to a new life of peace, harmony, love, joy, approval, and acceptance.

Self-esteem, self-worth, self-approval and self-acceptance are qualities we all want, but I now understand why living a life of unconditional love as a reality takes so long. In my case, I appeared to be self-confident and exuded all these qualities, but this was a façade I was hiding behind to protect myself. Self-examination proved to be the key and, in the period 1995 – 1999, I succeeded in deleting, erasing and totally destroying the last of the façade. After a 20-year battle, I no longer needed to hide behind anything and was finally in control of my life.

The final challenge in erasing denial is control and authority. If we were to give up control and authority over everything in our life, would we be able to function effectively? My family said "Yes," but we did not give it up. Many people are so addicted to control that they will drive others away and not even recognize the cause.

The need for control and the subsequent rejection involved will cause major problems in life. Control as a form of security will destroy friendships, marriages, relationships, and businesses, and will almost always lead to rejection. But, until we face the truth and commit to letting go of the need to control, our denial will stop us from recognizing it.

There seems to be a set of sub-personalities that fit the personality type, be it controller, codependent, or victim. Each type operates from a different set of programs:

- Controllers will usually have manipulator, authority figure, judger, self-righteous, and justifier sub-personalities.
- Codependents will have internal controller, confuser, indecisive, resenter, rescuer, savior and empathizer sub-personalities.

- Victims will have internal controller, procrastinator, confuser, indecisive, avoider, disorientor, blamer, resenter, struggler sufferer, insecurity, feeling sorry for self, and refusal to take responsibility sub-personalities.

In my case, the denial and control were so subtle that I didn't even recognize them. Now I've worked through them, I am sensitive to them and can spot them a mile away, such as when one person tries to monopolize a conversation. These people try to dominate conversations by talking over others, raising their voice, or running an incessant monologue without pauses. Seldom do they listen to other people or allow them to get a word in. And even if someone does manage to have their say, monopolizers do not listen because they're thinking about what they're going to say next, and impatiently waiting to regain control. If the opportunity to speak doesn't come naturally, they will simply butt in and talk over whoever is speaking. There are varying degrees of this annoying trait, of course, but it is one I observe in a great many people.

These are all illusions we operate from to cover our fear and anger. Quite often, we find parents who live through their children's success or achievements because they feel that they themselves did not succeed and are insecure in their life. Look at the little league baseball or soccer games where the parents get into heated battles over the players and the games.

One of our sons was not doing well at school, yet our family illusion was: "We don't control our children, or inflict our beliefs on them." I assumed that the boys were functioning effectively in their lives, but that was a major denial that enabled the failure one of my sons in school. We acknowledged his life decisions were not our failure, and told him, "We are not going to be hurt by your nonperformance in school and you can work at JiffyLube for the rest of your life if you wish."

When we stopped enabling him and made it clear that his scholastic career was his responsibility, he made a 3.0 grade point average. Furthermore, he set his goals, and received a grant and a scholarship to attend a vocational college. He finished an accelerated course, and was offered four jobs on graduation. He has gone on to follow his path because he wanted to be a diesel/heavy equipment mechanic. He had done well in his chosen field, had an excellent position, earned a good wage, and bought a house, all by the age of 25.

He has continually moved up and speaks his mind when he feels he is being treated unfairly. For example, in a dispute with his foreman, he tried to make peace for over a year, but management wouldn't see his side of the dispute. Other people were also unhappy with the foreman but wouldn't support my son, so he quit. Four years later, at age 29, he started a new job at a much higher salary as a field mechanic with a large heavy construction company that treats him very well.

As with my son, you succeed when you feel entitled to the success. Your life will reflect exactly how you feel about yourself. If denial or illusion is operating in the mind's "computer," you will receive exactly what you programmed the computer to do, based on the value you place on yourself.

If we'd been living our life through our children and believed that we were successful only if they succeeded, then we could have insisted that he go to college. But, as parents, we saw that his success or failure was not our success or failure. Overly protective parents cripple their children, and their attachment can be disabling to young adults because they cannot express themselves as unique individuals. Youngsters need to break clear of parents and set their own agendas at least by age 16. Most of the time, they will make appropriate choices if we will let them and, even if they don't, do we have the right to control their destiny? As parents, we found that we had to walk our own talk.

We had an easier time with the second boy because we had practice. He achieved a 3.5 GPA in high school and was a regional officer of the Unity Church youth group. In college, he achieved a 4.0 average, had a good job to help him through college, and handled relationships well.

In 1988, prompted by the John Bradshaw TV series, my wife and I decided we wanted to understand recovery, so I attended three conferences for professional recovery therapists. My understanding of Bradshaw's material began by realizing that we'd been dealing with these concepts for over ten years. Even though we knew the concepts from our work with Paul Solomon and my psychological training with Fritz Perles and Virginia Satir, and although I was teaching the principles, we were not applying them in our lives. In other words, we were not walking our talk.

We discovered that we were deeply attached to the material/physical world and were really deluding ourselves about our self-esteem and self-worth. Once we faced how we denied and suppressed our fear, anger and other emotions, giving up our attachments came easily, but more difficult was breaking through to our suppressed childhood pro-grams. However, after dealing with that aspect of our lives and being willing to give up everything, we discovered that we could have it all.

We set our intent and committed to taking total responsibility, be-ing consistent and following through in every aspect of our lives. This turned out to be the greatest gift we could give ourselves, for it brought the exhilarating liberation of the freedom of joy and happiness. We had lifted the bondage of fear and separation.

We found that we had to recognize the denial before we were able to see it, and that strong denial gets pushed into denial-of-denial. It's then hard to believe something that doesn't fit your concept of reality. Getting the total picture of what it meant to be a "no limit person" and really stepping into our personal power took us about six years, but when it finally happened, the experience was really exhilarating, and we would like everyone to find this peace, freedom, harmony, joy, and happiness in their life.

Looking back over the last 20 years, we can see how we broke through the barriers and how, as we did, our children did, too. We may have started out as a dysfunctional family, controlled by our parents' programs that we had blindly accepted, but we broke free of that pro-gramming and committed that we wouldn't inflict the same behavior on our children. Since we'd deferred having children until we were in our thirties, we had a chance to grow up and shed our parents' patterns.

We committed to raising our children other than how we'd been raised. It worked and we now see the result—two well-adjusted young adults—so the vicious circle can be broken in one generation. Looking back, we can see the result of working out childhood difficulties to become a functional family that gets along well.

Susie and I had planned to sell our home and move into a motorhome so that we could travel and promote my books. Recently, however, my older son found a new position near us, so he his wife sold their house in Reno, Nevada, and moved in with us. Once again, we are a family in transition. Our younger son is going back to college to earn his teaching credential and also lives with us. Fortunately, the house is large enough to accommodate five people but, nonetheless, I am pleased that we can all live in great harmony.

What's our recipe for success? We have found that we must be hon-est with ourselves as well as others and tell the truth, be ethical and act with integrity. We must follow through with committed, disciplined work, and with focused intent. Without these qualities, you will not get there but, instead, may wallow in procrastination, confusion, avoidance and denial. Transformation *is* possible; we proved it. You can, too.

A Spiritual Being Having a Physical Experience

Releasing attachment to the material world can be tough if you have a controlling Middle Self that will play games with you until you threaten it by committing to take control of your life. It feels that it plays a major role in your life, and interprets any attempt to wrest control as an attempt on its life.

Most people, including the experts, use the term "Ego" for the controlling self. This is a misconception. Ego is actually only the Subconscious Mind's file manager, secretary, or librarian. If we threaten it or attack it, it will shut down, and nothing then gets into or out of the file system. Short-term memory is disabled, affirmations don't work, and patterns that we don't like continue. As long as you blame Ego for any aberrant behavior, Middle Self will stand back and let you attack Ego. Meanwhile, Middle Self's autopilot has free rein, with sub-personalities running the autopilot programs. As long as you don't know who is running your life, Middle Self will not inform you that you're mistaken because it likes its role as unseen controller.

In 1991, a teacher I didn't know very well asked me, "You're always saying that your ultimate goals are peace, happiness, joy, harmony, acceptance, approval, abundance, unconditional love, but that the only problem is that few people really have this in their life. Do you have those qualities in your life?"

"Not all the time," I answered.

"Well, if I can give you those things, would you go with me?"

"How?" I asked.

"To obtain all those qualities, you would have to give up everything: attachment to your family, house, cars, and everything else that you might be attached to in the physical world. All you could bring with you would be the clothes you're wearing."

I thought long and hard about this, and my response was, "That's very limiting. You're asking a lot of me, and I don't know if I can do that. It sounds very much like the ancient mystery school approach."

He replied, "Well, if you want to take this path to the next level in your enlightenment, this is what is required. It's your choice. You *will* have to do this at some point, so why not now?"

I engaged my Conscious Mind, my Middle Self's committee of sub-personalities, my Ego, and my Subconscious Mind. None of them seemed to object, so I assumed this was the right path. After making this basic commitment, I also began to look at my commitment to be a spiritual being having a physical experience rather than a physical being having momentary spiritual experiences. I meditated on this and it did seem the right path to take. Getting organized to make this step took three months, and when I next saw him, I said, "I'm ready and willing to go along with the concept, so what's next?"

He surprised me by saying, "There is no *next*. If you truly have made the commitment, it will soon show up in your life. Your teacher will contact you to check out your intention."

About three weeks later, I had a dream in which I heard a voice say clearly, "It is all over."

I asked, "What is over?"

"Your life."

"You mean my life as it is today?" I asked, quite perturbed at the assertion that my life was over.

"Yes, your life as it is today is over."

"But I have responsibilities to my family and my clients," I protested.

"So what?"

"How can that be?" I asked, beginning to panic. "This can't be the end. What should I do?"

"There's nothing you can do," the voice said with finality.

"You mean that this is the end of my life, and I should just die without lifting a finger to stop it?"

"Your life as you've known it ...," the voice corrected me.

"You mean there *is* a way out of this?"

"Yes, there is."

"How and what do I do then?" I asked, relieved at maybe having a second chance.

"You need do nothing," the exasperating voice said.

"Look, that doesn't make sense. You said my life is over, yet I don't need to do anything for it not to be. Could you please explain?"

"As you have discovered, you have decided to let go of attachment. Even to your life."

By now, I was totally confused. "You mean I *am* going to die. What if Susie wakes up in the morning to find a dead body in bed?"

"So what?"

"You seem pretty callous. So I can walk out with no responsibility for what may happen tomorrow?"

"That is not what I said," the voice remonstrated with me.

"Explain then," I asked.

"You must look at the big picture, not just this life. You must evaluate the flight plan you wrote before coming into this life, what you have accomplished, and what unfinished business you would leave behind. Would it not be better to finish all your priorities before you leave?"

"Of course, but if my life is over, then I cannot attend to unfinished business," I pointed out.

"You're missing the point," the voice said. "What have you been preparing for over the last few months?"

"Dropping attachment," I said, "but I didn't know this was going to happen or I might have chosen differently."

"Why is that?" it asked.

"Well, if I'd known that my choice would cost me my life but chose anyway, I wouldn't have been very smart."

"You're still not getting the point."

"Why not. It seems pretty simple to me. You, whoever you are, are telling me that my life is over and it's because of the path I chose. Am I supposed to believe this, or is this just a bad dream?"

"You're still not getting the point, and now you're beginning to come from fear."

"Just what am I supposed to think? You just keep telling me I'm not getting the point and need do nothing. I don't understand."

"Are you asking a question? If so, I'm not hearing it."

"What am I supposed to do?" I asked, emphatically and impatiently.

"You're doing it now. All you need do is let go of the fear."

"You're telling me I'm going to die, and should let go of the fear. There is much I still want to accomplish yet it seems that it's not going to happen now. What's next?"

"You're still not getting the point of this conversation."

"Then what *is* the point of this conversation?" I asked, just about ready to give up out of frustration.

"You have it now. This is the point of this whole discussion. You have made the commitment to let go of attachment and the need for outside validation. What you are going through is a seventh door initiation. The reason we came to you was to see what your intention is. Are you really going to walk the talk?"

"You mean *that's* what this is all about?" I asked, beginning to see a chink of light.

"You wrote in your book *Journey into the Light* that you would be watched over and supervised after you went through the seventh door. Do you believe what you wrote? This is our first visit with you. If you follow through with your commitment, you will do some amazing things in the next ten years. This is just the beginning. You will become an author, a major speaker and will accomplish many other things."

"I'm not sure this makes sense to me. First, you tell me my life is over and I'm going to die. Then you tell me I need do nothing. And now you're telling me I'm going to make great strides. Who is going to provide the money for all this? In this life, or am I going to start over in another life? You say all this is going to happen but it's not clear to me how."

At this point, the dialogue with this Source ended and I had to use self-hypnosis to put myself back to sleep because of the fear that I would never wake up again. When I did wake up and recalled the conversation, I pinched myself a few times to see if I really was in a physical body. I then understood that transformation is all about losing attachment, and have since let go of attachment to anything, life included. I therefore no longer have any fear around dying.

Thus began the most dramatic transformation in my life. I assumed that if this Source was right, then I'd better get on with it. I began to actualize this commitment and follow through with my decision to let go of attachment, until a life-threatening illness arose to challenge my survival. I've always been a survivor, and would normally push through any illness or situation. I'd always been able to do this in the past, until this day when I just couldn't seem to pull through the illness, no matter what I did. It began one Sunday morning when I was working out at my health club. I felt really good after the workout and went home. I was reading the Sunday paper when, about four hours later, I began to manifest symptoms of six illness syndromes in less than two hours. The pain in my chest became so severe that I couldn't breathe without going into coughing spasms. I had heart palpitations and aches throughout my body. I felt as if I had a combination of asthma, emphysema and pneumonia. On top of that, I developed symptoms of chronic fatigue and Epstein-Barr syndromes, as well as alternating intense chills and sweats. From being active in the morning to being unable to move in the afternoon was quite a contrast, and it was getting worse. I then realized how people feel who are on the losing side of a battle with a life-threatening disease.

I recognized that my Middle Self and the committee of sub-personalities—a formidable opponent when you're down and with few resources to fight back—were battling for survival. I was blaming my poor Ego for leading the battle, but the ringleaders were a group of sub-personalities led by the autopilot. I then realized just how powerful our mind is when we try to take control back. At that point, I realized that I was a physical being who wanted a spiritual experience, but did not have control over my body.

The Middle Self's committee really doesn't care whether you're in on the committee meetings, for their dialogue continues without your awareness. With the control sub-personalities chairing the committee, they can make decisions that affect your life without your permission. In fact, they would prefer you not be in on their decisions. If you're threatening their control, they will try to sabotage and derail you, as they did in my case. It was a battle for control.

Any "normal" person going through this would have ended up in the hospital, because of the serious nature of the symptoms. However, if I had gone to the hospital, would I have survived the battle? We'll never really know. Fortunately, Susie and I understood the crisis I was going through and, with her help, I recovered in about three days. I healed myself in two weeks with no lingering effects but, even eight years later, I was still clearing the sub-personalities and the programs that were residuals of that battle, with denial-of-denial programs still surfacing even today.

An ongoing battle for control rages inside of each one of us, but most people don't recognize it because it's disguised as addiction, ritual behavior, depression, illness, physical breakdown, and other various sabotages that "happen" to us. We blame it on something outside ourselves and continue to live in the illusion that we're not the one causing this debilitating dysfunction. If we're living in denial-of-denial, we see nothing wrong with blaming it on outside events and other people. We further evade responsibility by making insurance claims, going on disability and bringing lawsuits, so that we can continue to blame and justify not taking responsibility. The decision to take control of our life and assume responsibility requires that we reclaim our personal power, walk through the door of blame and resentment, and let it go.

We have recently discovered one more glitch, and that is control sub-personalities hidden in the denial files that Middle Self can access. These are so powerful that they can cause people to actually pass out when they try to confront an issue which has associated programs.

When you give up the will, your mental programs could actually kill you. It happens all the time, but we don't recognize this as a cause of death, and nothing about it appears in the medical literature. However, in my practice, many of my clients are literally killing themselves. Some actually succeed if they have "I want to die" programs but, most of the time, we manage to pull them back into life once they can release the cause that's driving the dysfunction. I have had clients given only weeks to live pull back and resume a normal life. Rewriting the programs can be an ordeal, but it can be done. Recovery is always possible.

Transcendence to a Spiritual Being

We are not a body/mind having a spiritual experience. We are spiritual beings that take on physical bodies to learn lessons. Contrary to the common religious belief that we have only one life on earth, many people are waking up to the facts that reincarnation is a reality and that we cannot violate universal law and spiritual principles without consequences.

The reason why most people do not know that they are soul first and human being second is that, since birth, their parents and others have told them that they were only bodies. But the more we identify with our body/mind rather than our soul, the more we separate ourselves from our Christ/God-self. We allow inner shadows to block us off from our Higher Self, our "telephone operator" to the Akashic Record (see my book *Opening Communication With God Source* for more details on this aspect of self).

As a result, our personality becomes isolated from our soul, which then has no voice or any way of communicating with us, so we lose our source of direction and our connection with our flight plan. We become blocked from our Higher Self and God by an overshadow. As a result, we lose the presence of God within, thereby blocking ourselves from our source of love. By closing the door to the spiritual self, we give our power away, get lost in the mire of the physical world, and allow the Middle Self's sub-personalities and autopilot to run our life.

Most people are having too many problems just dealing with their day-to-day lives to realize that they're flying blind into the storms of life. The terminology that we use in this book is a foreign language to them. Those of us who embrace the spiritual journey and its concepts are disparagingly called "New Agers," people who have lost the "true path" taught by the Bible and organized religion. It's no wonder that people looking for a way out or someone to blame for their lives would steer clear of the spiritual principles embodied in this book.

In my spiritual searching, I saw the qualities of unconditional love and abundance all around me but, for forty plus years, had not been able to attract them into my life. I observed those people who seemed to have them but they couldn't tell how they'd obtained them. Many of the highly touted speakers on financial and business success will give you formulas, but when I talked with many of their students and advocates, I found that they were simply willing themselves through life, creating double-binds as they violated their mind's programming. Money does not create happiness and joy. It may create an *illusion* of happiness but, as soon as some crisis comes along to rock the boat, the bubble bursts and they're back to square one. Granted, you can bully your way through life with sheer personal power, but does bullying work in all areas? And does it bring the peace and harmony that many people desire? Those of us using the principles described in this book know that they work well in our lives, but we cannot force our concepts on to people who refuse to see the light.

In my own inner quest to find inner peace, something was always missing. I knew that illness, disease and dysfunctional behavior didn't exist on the spiritual plane, but how could I get back to where I was before I lost my way? To do this, I had to recognize that the body is a vehicle for us to learn lessons and play out our life scripts. I had to accept that we are spiritual beings having physical experiences, but even though I knew that, I was still unable to make the necessary shift.

We can go through life assuming we're making this shift in consciousness, but this may be a delusion to the point that we fool ourselves. The only true test is: "Am I walking my talk?"

If any form of judgment, justification or defense arises in any thought, conversation or interaction, you're still locked in the physical/mental plane. It's a simple test. If you're claiming that anything outside you is causing you pain, you're identifying with the body/mind. I realized that the only way I could break out of this was to confront my fears, which are all illusions on the spiritual plane.

Now, any of us can choose to move out of pain anytime we desire, but you must back it up with consistent commitment and follow-through. Otherwise, you will have only fleeting spiritual experiences. Spiritual teachers advocate many ways to reach this spiritual ascension, but few recognize the physical plane lessons that must first be overcome before this spiritual shift can take place. You cannot skip over the lessons; they must be learned in order make the shift.

Claiming Dominion over Your Life

To make this transformation, you must let your old illusionary self die. We live in a reality of an *illusory* self that is not our *true* self but, once we can live a reality based on that true self, we find that it does, in fact, provide the peace and happiness we desire. When we release the illusionary self and get down to what makes us happy, we can let go of our physical and emotional plane fears.

Few of us have actually moved out of duality. We may occasionally rise to the spiritual plane until some fear, rejection or conflict pulls us back to the body/mind on the physical/emotional plane. For fleeting moments, we may feel how it could be to live in bliss, but we continually re-identify with pain and fear rather than love. If we could keep our consciousness functioning on the spiritual plane, we could see our way back to the path.

What we perceive that makes us happy is usually something outside of ourselves. We gather together in groups, clubs and business or fraternal associations, drive expensive cars, and build lavish homes, all to show our success in the external world but does this create inner happiness?

When they wake up enough to evaluate their lives clearly, many of my clients have found that material success is empty. Many have had to go through the trauma of a financial crash or a life-threatening illness to force them to wake up. And what about all those millions of people who are unable to get off the treadmill of barely making a living? The same principles apply. It makes no difference where you are or what your station in life is. It's all about recognizing that your life the way it is now is simply not working.

Once you accept that your life is not working, the next crucial step is to commit to making changes by seeking help or counseling to sort out the pieces that are not working. You can do much of this work on your own with the various tools that we provide in our books, but acknowledge that sitting down and taking an inventory of where you are now will take some time. Be aware, too, that as Middle Self senses that it's about to lose control, it may try to distract you, or provide detours to deflect you from your purpose. Procrastination, confusion and indecision are common ways to block you from making the decision to set goals and plans to move forward on your spiritual journey. Staying on the path in the face of all this opposition takes considerable discipline and commitment. And the further you are from the path, the harder it will be to discipline yourself to get back on the path and stay on it.

Many of my clients have functioned on autopilot for so long that they can't even remember how long they've been wandering with no direction in life. Years may have gone by with no recollection of what's happened in that time. One client had been operating from multiple personalities for over thirty years, and he had only fleeting memories of that time. But rather than berate themselves, these people must forgive themselves for the lack of direction and wasted years, and commit to taking control back.

Other clients, who know the universal laws and spiritual principles, refuse to act on them or take their power back and get on with their life, or claim that they just don't have time. *It's all about discipline, not time.* People who say, "Oh, I want to do it but just don't have the time" are procrastinating. They're willing to just coast along life's detours with excuses and justifications. We can find all the excuses and justifications we want. In fact, our mind has a whole library of them that it can activate to deter us from the path.

In the past, I was like everyone else, and couldn't describe or understand what "taking responsibility" was all about. So I learned what all the experts said about reclaiming your personal power and was able to help many people to reclaim their power and take total control over their life. Quite often, though, clients wanted to take control over their life but were unable to. They seemed to be in a void where I was unable to help them. Many pleaded with me to find what was blocking them, but I couldn't even find that. I felt that it was an inner decision one had to make, but I didn't know how to make it happen.

The mind is very cunning when we try to get it to reveal the tricks it uses to retain control. You must ask just the right questions with the proper wording to unlock the program files. When we're on autopilot, twenty basic sub-personalities run our lives. We can delete, erase and destroy them from the file, but they will reappear no matter what we do to block them if we don't simultaneously take control of, and responsibility for, our life.

For a long time, I couldn't find the cause for this, or how to stop the mind from recreating the sub-personalities. Then, in April 2000, I had a breakthrough. I broke the code and could get into the file on responsibility. The breakthrough came when I was working with a client who was trying desperately to get a handle on his confusion, indecision and procrastination. We found what amounted to an "inner watcher" that monitored every interaction he had with other people and how he responded. It also monitored his thoughts and feelings about how he was handling his commitments to the lessons and responsibilities that he had to accomplish each day.

Until then, I was unaware that we have an Inner Middle Self and an Inner Conscious Mind that watch our behavior closely to see if we are taking responsibility for every aspect of our life. If you're unable to deal with your daily responsibilities, and use procrastination, confusion, disorganization, indecision and justification to avoid taking control of your life, then Inner Middle Self and Inner Conscious Mind step in, install sub-personalities, and simply take over. But, if you can take control of your life and demonstrate effective results for a given time, this Inner Mind will back off and let you have your life back.

Discovering this inner aspect of the mind provided me with the tools and understanding I needed about how we can take control of our life. All those whom I have since helped to clear this hurdle have said, "It's interesting to be on the outside looking in and watching people out of control, in confusion and indecision." After I worked with them, they would say unanimously, "When I was unable to take control of my life, I couldn't even see the confusion I was in." That's because, when you're surrounded by the illusion, you can't even see it, just as a goldfish in a bowl can't see the water it's swimming in.

This new awareness has also allowed me to explain what we must do to take control of our life. We must *constantly* monitor our actions, reactions, responses, feelings and thoughts to recognize when we are getting off the mark and losing control by blaming, judging or being afraid. It is not about controlling anyone else in any way. It is about how you react to sensory input from another person or from your own thoughts and feelings. In any interaction, therefore, ask, "Am I giving my power away to the situation or person? Am I going into fight or flight?" Every day presents countless temptations to see if we will respond in an effective or a dysfunctional way.

Our Middle Self does not like unfinished sentences or questions, so it will complete them for us and, more than likely, not how we would have done, so we must be very clear as to our intent. If we change our mind and decide that we don't want to do something, then we must close off that avenue of action, and acknowledge that fact to ourselves. If someone says something disparaging about our behavior and we feel that they're wrong, we must cancel their statement and acknowledge that it's only their *opinion*, not our *reality*. If you let the erroneous statement go unchallenged because you don't want to confront the other person, your Subconscious Mind will record the statement exactly as it was said, and you will register, "I am not all right," or, "That person does not like me."

During a typical day, your mind will take a position on countless attitudes and interpretations. If you continue to avoid taking responsibility for your feelings and actions, and place great stock in the opinions of others, this will create programs that run your life. This Inner Mind views itself as your protector and savior, and will justify its actions as being for your benefit, at least until you reclaim your personal power back and take control of your life. If you do, Inner Mind will gladly hand the reins back to you, for it really wants *you* to run your life.

There is a great danger here that it's important to know about. Do not begin to take control and then back off and relinquish control again. Once the Inner Mind hands over control to you, it does not like to have to pick up the pieces and resume control. It will give you a second chance, but if you drop the ball again, you have a battle on your hands. The Inner Mind will make it progressively hard for you each time. Before it will let go a third time, you must show it that you really mean business. When they tried to reclaim their personal power, I've known clients who reacted by feeling nauseous, and having cold chills and hot flashes, and other painful symptoms as their Inner Mind put up a fight to prove to them that it was unwilling to pick up the pieces again. If you've given up in the past, do not try again until you really mean it.

Making Friends with Your Ego

When you were born, your Ego was ready to respond to your environment, as it was designed to do. It was fully functional at birth and it set itself up in what it felt was the best pattern to work with you. Your Ego is one of the most important players on your team, for it serves as the internal telephone operator, file manager, secretary and librarian for your mind. Its primary role is to work with the brain's switching network to transfer information between the Subconscious Mind's files and the Conscious Mind, without tampering with the context. When we blame Ego for all kinds of behavior that it has not participated in, then we make a big mistake, for it's actually the Middle Self that causes problems, not Ego.

To help you survive childhood, Middle Self and Ego worked together. If you were brought up in a functional family by caring, compassionate parents, your Middle Self accepted that it didn't have to protect you from these big people. It accepted that love and approval were the norm. It assumed that all it had to do was set up and file the programs that you transmitted to it.

If the family was dysfunctional, however, your Middle Self perceived threats to your survival and went into survival mode to protect you. Now, your Middle Self was working from its *interpretations* of incoming sense data in order to create a picture of the reality "out there," interpretations that were often in error because your Critical Parent sub-personality was identifying with your feeling that you were not "all right." And since nothing told you differently, you believed the conclusions. The interpretations seemed reasonable, so you identified with your autopilot's sub-personalities and they began to run your life. The Inner Child sub-personality tried to protect you from these big people, but its conclusions were also inaccurate.

To reclaim dominion over your body/mind, you may have a battle on your hands. Your autopilot and the sub-personalities that are driving it will react only if they feel threatened. *But if your life is operating on a comfortable illusion, you won't confront those sub-personalities*, and they will run your life on autopilot.

Most people in the psychological field, eastern religions and students of *A Course In Miracles* describe the Ego as an enemy that has covertly destroyed our life. After almost 20 years with the Course, I began to question this concept. I decided that God created every part of me and wouldn't create an enemy within me to destroy its creation.

After many losing battles with what I theorized was Ego, I decided to reexamine my view of Ego. I reasoned that if I could make friends with it and come to terms with what it really is, then it could make friends with me, too. At first, I didn't feel up to the task, so I continued to fight it, but eventually gave up, feeling that it was sabotaging me all the time. A few years ago, I discovered that all I had to do was recognize Ego's role in my life, tell it that I was no longer going to attack it, and forgive myself for the harm and trauma that I had blamed on it. When I acknowledged, "Ego, I now know that you are my Subconscious Mind's file manager, secretary, and librarian," I had no more problems with it.

Ego has no agenda to conflict with you or control your life in any way. It has no programs that would allow it to do anything to affect your life. The only action Ego can take is to shut down, and if you attack it, it will do just that. As a result, access to all the files is denied, except for the survival operating system. My experience is that if you have not made peace with Ego, a shift cannot occur, as Ego is the key to the Subconscious Mind. When I realized that my sub-personalities were my real enemies and were causing the inner battles, I'd taken a major step forward in understanding how to correct the situation. The sub-personalities were sitting on the sidelines watching me blame Ego, yet *they* were really in control of my life.

I finally grasped that *all* parts of our mind will work with us once we decide to claim control over our life. Ego is not the only one we must make friends with. When we claim dominion over our mind and truly prove that we're not going to fall back into confusion, then *all* parts of our mind will work with us.

Many people have tried to use affirmations to no avail. This is because Ego, the file manager, is not installing them in our mind's computer. If Ego isn't working with you, nothing goes in or out.

The affirmation to make friends with Ego took less than five minutes, and is the key to accomplishing this shift quickly and easily. This affirmation changed my views of how the mind operates. I realized that each level of the mind has an operating system that we can reprogram to work with us, a process that proved simple once I understood the programs that drove the levels of mind, for they, too, have an intelligence that allows us to work with them. However, if you go on the offensive and attack them, something in their operating system shuts them down.

The following are the affirmations to reprogram Middle Self and Ego. These two affirmations will rewrite the protocol that Middle Self and Ego operate under, such that they will then cooperate with you and file any program you want them to from now on:

> "I recognize now that I have to make peace with my Middle Self. It is my responsibility to reclaim my personal power. I want you to know, Middle Self, that I am taking my power back now. I know I gave my power to you when I was a child because I was not able to handle

my life very well. I did not realize at the time the consequences it would have. I am not taking your power. I am only taking back the power that is rightly mine. I have no intention of damaging or destroying you because you are an important part of my team. I know I must take my power back and take responsibility for my life now. I know you did the best you could with the programs you had available at the time. It is my responsibility to be the programmer of my life. It is my responsibility to install all the programs now. I am committed to taking control of my life now. I thank you for your help."

"I want to you to know, Ego, that I am committed to making friends with you now. Due to false information and a misconception, I felt that you were the villain and the enemy. I realize this is a false and erroneous misinterpretation. I know now that you are the file manager and the secretary/librarian for my Subconscious Mind. I recognize my mistake now. I am giving myself full and total permission to forgive myself for any harm and trauma that I may have inflicted on you in the past. I need your help since you are an important part of my team. I am loving you and forgiving you since I know you did the best you could with the programs you had available. I am loving and forgiving myself. I am installing these programs in the file now."

Releasing the Duality of Life

Making the transition to the spiritual plane requires letting go of physical/emotional plane duality, and letting the "old self" die, something few of us actually accomplish, preferring to identify with the illusions of pain, rejection, and fear, rather than love. Reality is black-and-white, in that you live in either love or fear. Which one do you choose? Fear holds us on the physical plane, even though we may claim we've chosen to move to the spiritual plane.

We can make all the claims we want, but things always come back to our behavior. As Emerson said, "What you are speaks so loudly I cannot hear what you say." When we accept the power of unconditional love and of our mind, and know that love is our inheritance, and accept that we're entitled to it, we have made the first step in transformation. The problem is that, by living in the duality, we are constantly pulled into believing that we cannot overcome obstacles in our life. We give our personal power away to self-pity, or we let others control us. But if we use our power, we can overcome anything. The lessons continually play over and over, like soap operas, until we understand that we can claim Grace and overcome the past. If we can keep our causal consciousness functioning on the physical plane, we can heal the separation and then get back on the path of peace, happiness, harmony, acceptance, and unconditional love. Once we heal the separation, we can live in love rather than fear.

If we can keep the spiritual aspect of self operating on the physical plane, the dysfunction will not return but, if it does return, that tells us that we didn't learn the lesson. When we accept unconditional love as our inheritance, we keep open the pipeline to GOD Source via our Higher Self. When we fully comprehend and can access the spiritual aspect of our being, we have made contact with our Source. We have then recovered the directions and the rest is easy.

The Higher Self is the "telephone operator" for you to connect to the Highest Source of your being. Many people feel that the lines are hooked up, but they can be disconnected very easily. You must constantly check and monitor how you're feeling. A simple check with Kinesiology will indicate if you are being blocked (see *Your Body Is Talking; Are You Listening?*). Until you hook up the phone line between Holographic Mind and the Higher Self, you cannot access the soul's files. You access the God Source through the highest source of your being, the phone operator and file server for the Akashic itself.

If you function at the physical level, it is hard to make contact. When you release the duality and live in the spiritual level, you are in contact all the time.

5

The Path to Recovery

The Spiritual Journey, a spiritual path and spirituality are all quite different, yet few recognize this:

- The Spiritual Journey is an all-encompassing path covering all aspects of body, mind, and spirit.
- A spiritual path is one discipline that may or may not lead to spirituality.
- Spirituality is the result of the quest, and is attained by working through the lessons in each area of the Spiritual Journey.

Most people in the spiritual field assume that they're on the path so they can jump over the physical and emotional lessons. Unfortunately, that's a fallacy. Why did we incarnate on this planet in the first place? To clear karma and learn the lessons we simply can't learn as pure spirit. We will continue to make field trips to this planet to clear the lessons we created in the past when we were in our downward spiral.

Many people I meet in the spiritual field shun the recovery process and twelve-step groups such as AA, ACOA and CODA because they feel recovery is for people who have emotional problems and don't feel good about themselves. However, those in recovery groups understand and accept that they have a problem. The so-called spiritual people have the same challenges, but they choose not to recognize them. In their delusion, they overlook their problems/challenges and assume they can skip over the lessons. But it doesn't work that way. All bodies are the same, all minds are the same, and they react and respond the same way but, just as with computers, it's the person at the keyboard who makes the difference.

With enough support, commitment and will power, we can control addictive, compulsive behavior patterns, but does that mean we'll be able to release the root cause of the compulsion? Many learned professionals feel that a person cannot overcome any addictions or dysfunctional behavior patterns without eternal vigilance. Many therapists are convinced that you will have to fight your addiction for the rest of your life. This is patently false. All addictions are simply attempts to avoid taking responsibility for a lesson. The belief that you may be able to control the compulsive behavior but not release it is also false. This may be true in some cases, such as if the person is in denial-of-denial but, believing that if you let your guard down, you will fall right back into the dysfunction causes additional fear and stress, and may even discourage you from trying in the first place. The best way to help those in recovery is to give them hope of total remission. Fear and stress may also cause a person to trade substance addiction for addiction to a support group or person for security or safety.

When you uncover the original cause and the programs that are driving addictive compulsive behavior, they can be cleared. You no longer have to fight it, which gives you time to focus on other situations and lessons.

Bradshaw and others have described the results of abuse and how dysfunctional families cause children to react. Bradshaw's TV series on families touched on the way negative emotions lock themselves in the body, and some enlightened therapists recognize the need to release these emotions as the most important part of the recovery process.

The Subconscious Mind is located not only in the brain but in every cell of our body. Each time we go through an experience, positive or negative, a record is created. Positive experiences are recorded in the mind's memory files, but negative experiences are also deposited in the body's cellular memory. Each time we encounter the same experience and handle it inappropriately, we reinforce the program, which ultimately becomes a habit. Then, each time you're in a similar situation, your Middle Self's sub-personalities step in with self-talk and instructions on how to react. Your mind has now recorded a program and a pattern of instructions. Each time you repeat the pattern, you reinforce it. A point may come when the body/mind memory file is unable to contain any more data, which causes a dysfunctional breakdown such as stress, sickness, illness, or disease. Eventually, the habit pattern runs your life automatically (like a robot), because you don't know how to break out of the program.

We often wonder why we sabotage ourselves, when we know on a logical, intellectual level that it isn't working. In his book, *Real Magic*, Wayne Dyer states, "You can never get enough of what you don't want." Many of my clients are addicted to substances, situations and relationships that don't meet their needs, yet they continue pursuing what they despise, thinking that if they get enough, it will somehow meet their needs.

I find that many people acknowledge a desire for, or even claim they are in, recovery. The real test is whether they need to control, use authority, or otherwise defend or impose their views. Those seeking self-empowerment must constantly self-evaluate the causes of their reactions for, if we can tell the truth about how we feel at all times, we can and will empower ourselves to overcome our fears. It is our faulty perception and misinterpretation of situations that cause our fear and anger. So we must recognize what we're projecting on to others—such as wanting them to be a certain way for us—so that we can control them. And due to faulty interpretation, we may falsely perceive rejection or invalidation from others.

Our life is played on stage with as many acts as we need. We must develop the courage to take center stage, even if the lights are too bright. We must brave the glare and come to truth. When we see that truth is nothing to fear, and that we're not going to be discredited or rejected, we can come out. We are the scriptwriter, producer and director of our life play, but many people let their sub-personalities run their show. As a result, we don't appear onstage as we'd like to. We must take back the lead role in our play and stop playing our soap operas. The sub-personalities can be supporting actors, but they must recognize our lead and not try to upstage us.

I try to show my clients how they are operating out of behavior patterns that no longer work for them. They must then decide for themselves which is more painful: staying in their rut or changing. This often creates chaos for them since staying in the rut they know seems safer than climbing out of it, even if staying is more painful. Clients are often afraid of confronting their own sub-personalities, which would prefer that the client stayed in denial, so they can continue their masquerade. They can be very convincing in their dialogue because they know your weaknesses and will use them to their advantage. You may even believe that *you* are making the decision, yet a sub-personality has taken your personal power and made the decision for you.

In Neuro/Cellular Repatterning (N/CR), we can locate programs created by sub-personalities and release them, allowing clients who have been in conventional therapy for years to break out of their defeating patterns in as few as five sessions. We've seen thousands of people who have completely recovered from many self-defeating compulsive/addictive behavior patterns, and reclaimed self-esteem and confidence, which opens the door to harmony, love, and joy in their lives. We have observed the body heal itself of disease in a matter of minutes to weeks, the only variable being the client's willingness to accept, own, release, and forgive old behavior patterns and negative programs.

6

The Doorway to
Self-Empowerment

Throughout this and my other books, I emphasize that transformation can be instantaneous, although many of my clients say, "I've been working on personal growth for over ten years, but still haven't attained any of my goals. Why do I always seem to miss the mark?"

The answer lies in facing your denial and illusion, and being honest with yourself. Our Subconscious Mind's programs must be aligned with our Conscious Mind's beliefs, and our Lower Self must agree with our Middle Self. Also, the committee of sub-personalities must be in total agreement with our path or they will sabotage us, thinking they are protecting us. And Ego, the file manager and secretary, must be open to working with us or we cannot rewrite files.

The simple truth is that we cannot venture into the realms of the Higher Self and the spiritual path until we have built a solid foundation in the physical world. You can either build the steps as you ascend on the path, or you can build an elaborate illusion that will convince you that you have built the steps. But, one day, you'll discover that there's nothing there to walk on ... and it could be a long fall without the safety net that we should have built on the way up.

As we mature in our journey through life, we allow our perceptions and interpretations to set limitations on ourselves. How we are treated causes us to expand or contract in the way we perceive the world around us. Ideally, our experience will be happy and balanced, so we try to see the world like that, but if abuse, fear, and dysfunctional family patterns began to form as a child, our survival-self and Instinctual Mind take over and we sell out our power to the Middle Self. So the next step is to master our own mind and the awesome power that we possess.

Most people use less than 5 percent of their mind's capacity and less than 20 percent of their body's abilities. It's mind-boggling to realize that, with our vehicle, we experience only a tiny fraction of the physical world's possibilities. What would life be like if we could access more than 25 percent of our mind, and 50 percent of our physical body capabilities?

Divine intelligence has no limits. The dimension of thought has no limits. When we transcend the limitations (boundaries of form), transformation happens instantaneously. When we live each moment of our life as if we have total control in that moment, we are there. The observer-self now becomes the director, scriptwriter, producer, and director of our life. We do the same things we did before, but with a different slant, unattached to the outcome, for each moment brings a new response.

Many clients have described their experience with my work as, "I can see my life shifting in a way I've never experienced before. The illusion is gone since the denial has been released. I can see how I was operating out of denial-of-denial because I couldn't even see the truth. Now that I can see the mistakes I made, I can see how unclear I was. But, I didn't know it at the time because I couldn't see it under all the illusion that covered the denial. It's all so clear when you get over the blocks that cause one to be unable to see the truth. Now that I have clear sight about my life, I'm on the other side looking in at people. I can see now what you meant by, 'When the observer-self is clear, you can see other people's dilemmas, but they can't perceive their own illusion and denial.' I know I was there myself, but it's so clear now. I can see why people will not listen when you describe their situation to them. It's great to be on the other side now. I can easily handle situations that were uncomfortable in the past. But now I don't take the bait and get hooked. There's no need to fight or run away anymore, as I can handle every incident without worry, anger or fear."

Thought is our connection to the invisible universe. If we fill our thoughts with worry, fear, anger, and feelings of separation, how do we connect? We must first let go of judgment, control and manipulation. We want others to fit our pictures, so that we can feel comfortable and secure, but our need for control can become an addiction. When we rise above the need for control and manipulation, we can begin to address change.

Change is not transformation! True transformation happens in an instant, when we recognize that we no longer need to hold on to a specific behavior. When we drop attachment to that behavior, suddenly it is no longer in our life.

Since we're the creator of all our thoughts, we create all our experiences. We also invite all the situations and other people into our lives. No boundaries or conditions block our transformation, but our *perception* of these conditions and situations causes us to put ourselves into little boxes and cages. What we think and what we speak springs to form. Replaying the old soap operas of the past holds us in the past. Running away from lessons doesn't make them go away. They may change how they appear next time, but they do not go away.

When we get up the courage to confront boundaries and release limitations, we can begin our transformation. We will not push limits or test possibilities, however, until we're willing to move out of our comfort zone. In transformation, we go through gates where our past behavior is no longer in our reality. If a lesson crops up again, it hasn't been completed. As we transcend the form, any limitations that the lessons held over us simply fall away. Recovery is just the decision to release denial, end the illusion, and move on in the spiritual journey.

To be a "no limit person," we must let the old self die, close the book on the past, and begin writing a new book of scripts for the present and future. There are times when you can rewrite the past to change future outcomes, but it is better to let them go, close those chapters, and archive the book in the history section of your mind's files.

7

Are You Taking Responsibility for your Life?

Many people ask, "How can I recognize responsibility and how do I know whether or not I'm being responsible?" Having a job, taking care of self and family, and paying your bills are obvious forms of responsibility, and those who can't respond at that level usually feel like victims. At a deeper level, taking responsibility means responding appropriately in every situation, without judgment, blame, manipulation, justification, or the need for control and authority over anyone or anything.

We know we are acting responsibly when we address whatever comes up spontaneously and without judging it as "right or wrong." When we instinctively know the appropriate behavior or response without having to decide how to act, but can instantly evaluate what we see and hear. When we respond without fear or the need to defend, inflict hurt, seek revenge or hold on to resentment. When we accept that we respond to any situation to the best of our ability at that time. If we make a mistake, we forgive ourselves, make amends, and move on to the next challenge without blame, loss of personal power, self-esteem, or self-worth. We do not experience indecisiveness, confusion, disorientation or victimhood.

When we recognize the need for change and strive to make the change without fear or the need for control, we are on an integrated path to transformation and recovery. However, few people can operate at this level all the time. For instance, if you read this chapter's opening sentence and said to yourself, "I'm doing that already," you might be tempted to say, "It doesn't apply to me," and skip this chapter. If you feel that way, it's perfectly all right. But, you must recognize when your Middle Self is feeling confronted by the fear of change. Your

Middle Self may be running your life and, because it fears losing control, it will do all it can to divert you from recovery and transformation.

In any conversation about recovery, one question always comes up. "Are you willing to change and become vulnerable to the lessons you're facing?" The word "vulnerable" scares most people, especially if their Middle Self is running their life, or they are in denial and illusion. It's not possible to enter transformation or recovery until you can make rational decisions and take responsibility. If you're in illusion, you will justify your underlying behavior and believe your own illusion is the truth.

Change is an unknown that causes the fear of loss of control. Until you can understand what the term *taking responsibility* means, you will always retreat to the safety and security of what you believe, even if it's uncomfortable. At this point, you must recover your lost Self, your inner child and all the disowned sub-personalities that your Middle Self has created to help you navigate in life. Before you can be open to change and move into recovery and transformation, you must find out who you are and stop letting your sub-personalities masquerade for you. *This is not the real you.* If you feel you're complete and whole as you are, that's your truth at this time. Nobody is going to change your opinion, until *you* decide there's a need for change.

The first question I always ask of my clients is, "Do you have peace, love, happiness, harmony, acceptance, approval, self-esteem, self-worth and "alrightness" in your life most of the time? If you can answer, 'Yes,' then continue on your path. If you honestly answer, 'No,' are you willing to leave your comfort zone and wake up?"

An abundance of love and happiness awaits you when you become honest with yourself. But moving from pain, fear, and anger into love, happiness, recovery and transformation takes great courage, for waking up is a process fraught with pitfalls and rejection.

Resistance to change stems from fear of the unknown, of failure, inadequacy, intimacy, rejection and abandonment. However, most people cannot even recognize their fear, let alone confront it. These fears in turn all stem from the inability to give yourself love or receive love from others. *All disease, illness, and dysfunctional behavior patterns are caused by the inability to give or receive love.*

There is a way out of this downward spiral, however. N/CR is a process that reveals the patterns and issues of the mind that have left an imprint in the body. This imprint stores memories in the body's cells, which then builds up enough energy to create a program. Basically, N/CR involves listening to the dialogue between your body and mind in order to recognize and release the dysfunctional patterns of fear and anger.

Most of us lost the ability to love ourselves during childhood because we were told by our parents that we were not all right. By the age of three, children have decided to be either self-supportive or self-destructive but, unfortunately, most parents don't know that. However, the lesson here is one of loving and forgiving our parents, knowing that they did the best they could based on their understanding and experience. As children, however, we bought into our interpretation of who our parents told us we were, often assuming in the process that we were not all right. We began to build a life pattern of thinking that other people victimized us. When we decide to wake up to the fact that *we* are in control, reclaim our personal power, and take responsibility, then we will cease blaming others or viewing ourselves as victims. Until we make that decision, however, this dysfunctional pattern will continue.

The first step in any recovery process is to recognize the problem or challenge. The most difficult part is being honest with yourself and evaluating your life without justifying or deluding yourself, for recognizing an illusion is impossible if you don't believe you're in one.

So, the challenge is to be honest with yourself and *tell yourself the truth*. You can't release an addiction to pain until you drop your denial and delusion. You can't find your lost self and your own truth until you tell the truth, acknowledge that you've made mistakes, and forgive yourself. When you get out of judgment, justification, attack, and need for control, you can move into recovery and transformation. The temptation is to blame others, run for shelter, or eliminate from your life all the people and things who threaten you. But denial results in stuffed feelings of fear, of rejection and abandonment, and a fear of intimacy.

There are two types of people: victims and survivors. Survivors seem able to handle the lessons of life more easily because they can avoid, or recover faster from, victimization and move on. Victims seem to go down for the count as a way of life, and can't see past their punishment/persecution complex. In both cases, their life runs on autopilot until they take responsibility and move into creator mode. Middle Self is an uncanny creature that can't make logical rational decisions, yet we sell out our personal power to it sometime between birth and the age of three.

When we disassociate from our feelings, we move into denial of self and lose the ability to recognize the image that we're projecting as our self. In childhood, if we become a wounded child, we may retreat into a magical/fantasy inner self, where we can hide from trauma and pain. As we grow up, our Middle Self will create sub-personalities for protection and we can escape into them, but this only causes disassociation from the real self.

This dynamic is rampant in today's codependent society and, as a result, people are trying to extract love externally from one another, not knowing that *they are the source of their own love*. A codependent places all value on the other person and acts through self-pity, always taking the blame. A counter-dependent is inner-directed and must have authority and control, and is self-centered and blames others. Both will manipulate to get love from outside of self.

The control sub-personalities create their own identity, eroding your true identity, self-esteem, and self-worth. If negative sub-personalities are in control, they will starve us of positive feedback or love. Middle Self needs limits and must be taught how to respond positively to work with us. We must do what our parents were unable to do and give the Middle Self parameters, boundaries, and define what we want it to do. We must assure our Middle Self that we do not intend to destroy it, but instead make it feel safe and secure. If we don't let it know that *we* are in control, however, it will continue to sabotage us because it has known what control feels like, and doesn't want to relinquish it. Our inner child and all our sub-personalities have our Middle Self masquerading behind them. If we buy into the projection, we become a personality controlled by the sub-personalities. *The real self will emerge when we let go of the illusions with which we cover ourselves, and face the truth of who we are.*

Of course, there will be tests, temptations, and lessons, but you will see them clearly. You will understand the lessons behind them when you realize that you are a manifestation of GOD Source. The presence of GOD Source will manifest in you when you accept and demonstrate your personal power. You will then be able to tell your body what you want it to do, and it will perform as commanded.

To control your mind, you must recognize its infinite power. You are not a body but a spirit manifesting in a body to learn lessons such as detachment. No one can make you do anything unless you give them the power to do so. The emotional sub-personalities are not the YOU of you. The true you isn't self-righteous, controlling, authoritarian and will not attack anyone. *The true self is pure love and acceptance and does not need to defend itself.*

To get our inner selves and ourselves to understand the meaning of responsibility so that we can practice detachment, we use a kinetic process. To achieve this, write out in longhand the following responsibility affirmation, 21 times a day for 21 – 40 days. This will impress upon your Middle Self and sub-personalities the basics of responsibility in your life. (If you're speaking directly to another person you can substitute "you" for the plural forms such as anyone, other or anybody).

The responsibility affirmation is as follows:

> "Middle Self, I want you to know I am taking responsibility for myself and the way I feel. I am taking my power back now. It is no one's responsibility to make me feel accepted or loved. I do not need other people's approval to be all right; that is my responsibility and I accept it now. I know that I am loved and will be loved all the time, consistently, whether another person loves me or not. I would like everybody's love, but it is not required for me to be all right. I love you unconditionally as you are. I am not going to make anyone else responsible for my happiness. That is my responsibility. I know in the past that I based my self-esteem on other people's approval. I blamed others and projected my responsibility on them for my "alrightness." I am now responsible for how I feel and I know I am acceptable, loved and all right."

8

Concept versus Reality

When we have a goal clearly in mind, we would like to think that all we need do is to set out and accomplish the goal. However, reality sometimes finds us thwarted in our results; everything seems to be in order, so why do we fail to achieve the end result? Many people put honest effort into striving for the goal, trying to change behavior, attitudes, methods and approaches, yet some of us seem sabotaged and frustrated, unable to solve our problems. If it's an illness or disease we're trying to overcome, failure can be devastating and sometimes worsens the situation.

Your reality out-pictures in the events in your life, creating the events that you actually experience. However, if your life isn't happening as you would wish, it could be because you don't want to recognize and see "what is." Take inventory of your past successes and failures:

- Have you actualized and accomplished your goals?
- What do you desire most in life?
- Do you need another person to validate you and make you feel as if you're somebody?
- Do you look outside yourself for love?
- Do you have the relationships you want?
- Can you be alone without feeling lonely or separate?
- Are you using an addiction to hide from yourself?

The programs recorded in your Subconscious Mind cause and create your everyday reality. The programs will play out in your life, no matter what your beliefs are about of certain expectation. As long as your Subconscious Mind's programs control you, you will operate according to those programs until you become the scriptwriter, producer and director of your play. Your Middle Self with autopilot, Subconscious and Instinctual Minds will control the cast of characters until you become the computer programmer and operator. When you take full responsibility for control of the cause-and-effect results in your life, you can begin to operate in the conscious, rational, decision-making mind. A new reality blossoms when you commit to change, out-picturing the change in your life. The biggest challenge is making good on your commitment.

Taking inventory of your "I'm okay" qualities reveals who you are and how you're operating in life. To compile a "self-worth inventory," read each of the following statements and decide whether you agree with it:

1. *Self-esteem:* "I feel good about myself with no need for external validation or approval."
2. *Self-love:* "I honor, support, respect, trust myself, and take responsibility, knowing I'm all right without outside support. I am kind and caring towards myself, and follow a wellness program such as exercise, eating properly, and listening to and respecting my body."
3. *Self-confidence:* "I accomplish my goals and take responsibility for doing so."
4. *Self-approval:* "I need no one's approval or validation to know that I am all right."
5. *Self-acceptance:* "I am happy without another person's love, support or acceptance."
6. *Self-validation:* "I can function without external stimulus or encouragement, knowing that my actions will be right for self-determination."

The above are what I call the "alrightness cluster qualities." They're never separate in that, if we have one, we usually have them all. We seldom find a person with only one of these qualities, with the possible exception of self-confidence but, even then, it's usually a cover for insecurity, and a control sub-personality is running the program. I call this the "car salesman" personality for it's a learned trait used for survival.

We cannot give people these qualities; they must claim them for themselves. We can support children in showing them ways to claim them, but they must do it themselves. All we can do is make it a win-win experience for them so they can see that they're all right and will succeed. When we show them how to lift self-rejection and "I'm not all right" from their minds, they will claim their self-worth and self-esteem.

We are born with these qualities but most of us begin to lose them in our first year. However, some children and adults still have them because they were raised in functional families that supported them with love, approval, recognition, and acceptance, and fostered their self-worth. There was no competition, jealousy, control, or need for authority. The children's behavior was separate from them as human beings. When there is no rejection, emotional put-down or competition between parent and child, children have the freedom to be who they are without masks, cover-ups and facades. Self-esteem and self-worth are not demeaned or attacked.

In my own family, we raised our children with love and support for them as individuals. We made it clear when their behavior was unacceptable, but did not punish or discipline them as people. We never tried to change or discipline their behavior by force. We always made it clear that we were not rejecting them but only their behavior. We always stressed that we loved and accepted them as they were. We knew that they understood the parameters and rules of behavior in the family.

When they were small children, we realized that getting sick was a cry for attention or indicated we had broken a commitment with them, so they felt rejected and abandoned. When we located the cause and corrected the situation, they would recover in hours. We were able to forgive each other and release anger. We feel we were, by and large, a functional family and the results proved us out. Both of our sons have high self-esteem and self-worth. We did not have to teach alrightness self-worth qualities to them, so our family managed to avoid the vicious behavior circle and not pass on the dysfunctional behavior that our parents bequeathed to us.

In my therapy practice, I have found that babies are so sensitive to rejection that the slightest indication that mother is not giving them the attention they want will cause them to feel rejected. In many so-called "primitive" cultures, mothers breastfeed their babies and carry them everywhere they go for two to four years. The result is no dysfunctional behavior patterns at all and perfect bonding with the mother. These "primitive" people existed for centuries with no problems until corrupted by "civilization," with its fast food, guns, and crime. Now that we have made them dependent on us for protection, food, and clothing, dysfunctional patterns are endemic in these cultures.

In the past, if a birth mother gave up a child for adoption and signed the adoption papers, that was it. She had relinquished all rights to the child. Nowadays, however, a new law allows a birth mother to reclaim the child up to six months after adoption, and some of the legal battles for "ownership" can drag on for two or three years. This totally denies the child's right to safety, security and trust. After three years, the child knows only the adoptive parents, but a court can order the child removed from the adoptive parents' home and placed back with the birth mother, a total stranger who has already rejected the child once. According to many court-appointed psychiatrists, this will not cause any damage to the child. This is patently false. *This totally disastrous conclusion completely ignores the child's feelings.* The child has enough problems with identity from the adoption. This new view of seeing children as collateral material without rights to their own control erodes their self-image to the point that they don't know who to trust or who they are.

Many of my adult clients who were adopted as children feel unloved, abandoned and rejected, even though the adoptive parents did everything they could to love, trust, support, protect, and bring the child up in a secure environment. The rejection and abandonment programs are still installed in the Subconscious Mind until the client and I remove, delete and erase them.

The statistics about birth traumas caused by rejection are a sad commentary on our society. Based on the reactions from my clients, only 20 percent of their mothers wanted children, even though many of them did not turn out as good mothers. Another 20 percent had children even though they did not want them, and made the best of it. Many times, this caused major problems in the children's lives and, as adults, their lives were not working very well. A further 30 percent did not want children yet felt forced into it by religious or societal pressure, unexpected pregnancies or mistakes. This caused disasters in these children's lives. These dysfunctional families are the causes of much of the crime in today's society.

I can trace back all the problems in an adult's life back to childhood. Another 30 percent of mothers did not want to have children and opted for abortion despite pressure put on them by religion, parents and society. Many of them ended up with medical complications resulting from the abortion. Often, my female clients suffer from severe PMS and endometriosis stemming from programs that told them they should have children. Once we released these religious or society-based programs and they made a commitment not to have children, the symptoms completely disappeared.

Some children have many encrypted pre-birth programs about rejection because they sensed that their mothers didn't want them in the first place. Clearing the resulting abandonment program is difficult but essential if the child is to grow up and not create another dysfunctional family. It's hard enough for an adopted child with supportive parents to succeed, but virtually impossible if the baby is bounced back and forth, treated by the courts as property to be traded at will. About 95 percent of these children will not succeed as adults.

Pass a child around like a used car, and you guarantee a dysfunctional adult with no self-esteem, self-worth, self-confidence, self-approval, ability to validate self, and worse, lacking self-love. Such adults feel they have no value, so they go from one unhappy relationship to another with partners who validate their low self-esteem.

With the advent of the computer age and dotcom millionaires, parents are farming their children out to the point that they rarely see each other. Until about ten years ago, this was an isolated problem, but from what I have seen in the few cases I've dealt with, we are going to have serious behavioral problems with an entire generation of children.

In my case, my mother rejected me before birth by trying to abort me. I was not put up for adoption, however, but experienced all the other childhood miseries. I have finally succeeded in forgiving my mother and rewriting all the rejection programs in my Subconscious Mind that drove down my self-esteem, self-worth and self-image. I was driven to find the causes and developed a process to release them. But I still don't know how to reach all the people in denial-of-denial who don't realize the depth of the illusion in which they live.

This leaves us with a sad statistic that three out of five children are rejected before they are born, and one in five is rejected after being born. This leaves only one in five with a successful start in life. I also found that maybe one in fifty comes from a functional family. However, I'm unlikely to meet those people from functional families in my practice because they don't need my help.

Where you are on the path makes no difference if you have not faced these issues in your life, and maybe don't even know they exist. I have found that more than 85 percent of the clients I work with who claim to be on the spiritual path have yet to actually step on to the spiritual journey even though they think they have, for their childhood programming is blocking them. *Again and again, I emphasize that we must build a foundation before we begin to build our spiritual home.*

~~~

Like a huge central computer and its memory banks, it seems that our Subconscious Mind has no compassion about our mental, emotional, or physical pain. It cannot make rational decisions, but works only on stimulus/response based on stored patterns and programs laid down by our interpretations of incoming sense data. Middle Self, on the other hand, controls the multitude of feelings of emotional sub-personalities, such as the feeling self, critical parent, inner critic, pleasure seeker, justifier, and the inner child. But denial of the illusion can also block feelings and, if those sub-personalities control your life, they can wrap you in illusion that blocks any change.

Many people live "in their head" and block their feelings totally. In the "thinking versus feeling" mode, the intellect is afraid of emotion so it controls, justifies, suppresses, stuffs and blocks emotions. If we live in a purely "mental world," we are in illusion and denial. On the other hand, people who live out of their emotions and feelings let those emotions control them, so they bounce between "fight or flight" patterns. Both groups of people are on autopilot and are controlled by their Middle Self.

I now realize that what I once thought was Ego is another aspect of the mind. The Instinctual (or Survival) Mind operates similarly to what I thought Ego was, in that people in this mindset are also on autopilot, but with a very different focus. *Those on autopilot will block getting in contact with the causes of their frustrations, stress, blocks and disappointments, and are victim-oriented.* Middle Self's sub-personalities are in total control of their behavior.

I once believed that Ego was the driving force behind autopilot, but now see that the Conscious Mind is a very powerful source of control in life. The Conscious Mind is divided into three separate operational modes, all operating out of Middle Self :

- The automatic level is the *Instinctual (Survival) Mind.* Brain researchers describe it as the *limbic mind.* When we operate out of this mind, we cannot make quick decisions or learn easily. Memory recall is very hard. Healing seems to drag on with no progress at times. In this mode, people appear to operate and function effectively, but are frustrated if they try to take on responsibilities beyond their abilities. They are single-trackers and cannot change their focus of attention without conscious effort. Most are kinesthetic learners and must take notes and write information down, for the Instinctual Mind has no understanding.

- The next level is the *rational decision-making mind*. Most of these people are multi-tracking. They comprehend, learn, understand and operate effectively out of this level of mind. Most of those in this mode are auditory learners.
- Inventors, artists, writers, scientists and those at the forefront of new changes in the world, operate out of the *free-associating mind*. This mind operates like a computer and comprehends extremely quickly. Many of these people have photographic memories.

What I described as Ego in the past are actually the controller, manipulator, authority, judger and self-righteous sub-personalities. Your Ego (file manager) and Subconscious Mind are fully operational before birth, and pick up and file in the body's cells whatever is said, thought, and felt by not only the mother but anyone else in the vicinity.

If you're not at the helm of your life, your Middle Self will take over without your knowledge when you are born and will do whatever it feels is necessary to keep you protected. Unfortunately, it still has access to all the material you filed away as a fetus and baby. Another problem is that when it gets a taste of power, it doesn't want to let go. However, we now have techniques that can access all the files and reprogram them to release all the childhood trauma.

Many people operate out of the Instinctual Mind, without realizing that they are. Their challenge is to reclaim their personal power and take responsibility for making their own decisions. Most of these people are not even in their body, and getting them in is often a real challenge for me during a session. When emotional or physical pain gets too hard to handle, they tend to run away, and not take control over their life. Or they can "gray out" as one of my clients puts it. More recognizable, and more dangerous, is the "brownout" or even "blackout." In these states, people are barely conscious of their behavior, forget what they're doing, and act out psychotic or dysfunctional behavior without knowing.

For twenty years, I have helped clients reconstruct their childhood, when they're blocking painful or traumatic experiences. (In my case, I was blocking everything from before age ten, and have only recently recovered memory of my childhood, and it's not at all what I expected.) Pre-birth rejection annihilates self-worth before you're even born. Then, if you didn't bond with your mother at birth, you have another strike against you. If your mother put you in daycare soon after you're born, that's a third strike. If you were adopted, add a fourth. If you're from a broken home, there's a fifth, regardless of whether the breakup was in the best interest of the family.

To avoid a devastating experience of rejection, children must bond with their mother by age two, and with the father by age seven. Letting children cry themselves to sleep or denying them direct contact with their mother results in the trauma of abandonment. For this reason, careers and motherhood simply do not mix. At least one parent must be with the child during the first five years, preferably the mother until 18 months, and thereafter, either parent. One of the reasons my children became successful in their lives was that, for the first eight to ten years of their childhood, Susie and I took turns working and parenting.

When children begin to associate with other children and break away from parents between ages five and seven, they need less parental contact, as they're beginning to establish their independence. However, children who have no one to trust or depend on in the first five years may take much longer, and may never break their codependency on the parents without therapy to help them understand their feelings. In adulthood, such people transfer this addictive behavior pattern to their partner, employer or whoever will let them. They select partners who will allow them to act as children, thereby recreating mother/son or father/daughter relationships. Children born to these parents have nothing but problems growing up.

The Prognosis

In many ways, life is like a football game. We're given a set number of "time-outs" on each lesson, and when we've used all our time-outs in a particular lesson, we must go for the goal. If we're on the two-yard line and we sabotage ourselves by not going for the goal (avoiding the lesson), the lesson flares up in our face. If we still refuse to recognize it, we will get hit with it full force, which can be anything from an auto accident to physical illness, or a mental or emotional meltdown. If we still don't get it by this time, it will appear as a life-threatening event. The challenge is to recognize the lesson while it's still a feather touch rather than a two-by-four.

With children, it's much easier than with adults to help them release the self-destructive behavior and the negatives created by loneliness, rejection, frustration, discouragement, disappointment, invalidation, humiliation, and fear. First, we don't have to back out a lifetime of victim programming. Second, children grasp new behavior more easily, unless they have been severely abused or have no support at home. An unsupportive home environment or a dysfunctional family defeats whatever success we may have in therapy or the classroom.

I have found that, with adult clients, if they can recognize their behavior as dysfunctional, we make much faster progress than with clients who do not. Commitment, willingness to change, and knowing how to change affect transformation progress. Knowledge is important because if you can't understand the problem, you most likely will not admit that it exists. Even if clients recognize the situation, they can resist change if old patterns have created sub-personalities that are ingrained or locked into denial or denial-of-denial.

There is hope. Recovery is possible if we will commit to change. To begin the spiritual journey, we must have built a good foundation and, no matter how we work on our transformation, we will not succeed until that foundation is built.

Transformation is instantaneous when we can step out of illusion, and detach from the need to justify, judge, control or have to have authority.

9

The Truth Always Releases You:
Are You Living in Illusion and Denial or Reality?

Telling the truth should be easy. If you're all right with yourself, have developed self-esteem, self-confidence, self-worth and feel adequate in yourself, it's not a problem, especially when speaking the truth means that we can avoid getting caught in compromising situations. People who are not in touch with reality live in denial, but deny that they are, hence their denial-of-denial. The disparity is always *interpretation*. If you're communicating what you *think* is the truth, which part of you arrived at that conclusion? Your Middle Self's sub-personalities? Do they try to justify what they say or project blame? And according to whose truth?

Everything rests on what you believe is truth. If you need to be in control of everything in your life, the truth may prove a hard nut to crack. If you feel threatened, your need to control will force you to fight for your truth at all costs. If you need to justify your position to maintain your alrightness, your truth is dogmatic because, "I know it's the truth, and that's that."

To divine *what really is the truth*, we must look at how we arrive at our truth, at what we believe. Did we accept another person's word or did we logically deduce it for ourselves? Many people assume if the source of the material is from inner self or a "higher source" outside of self, then this must be right. Unfortunately, we often receive information directly from our Middle Self or an alien entity or discarnate being without recognizing that it's staging a deceptive masquerade. Are you able to distinguish between your sub-personalities and a Higher Source that you identify as *the* Source? If you're in recovery and not in denial or illusion, is your accuracy proven over time? Can it be validated with verifiable results?

Most people accept some theory because it fits their needs or desires or feels comfortable and isn't threatening. If a powerful enough authority figure, or a large enough group proclaims something as the incorruptible truth, it then follows that it is THE TRUTH. But the question is always, "The truth according to whom?" The word of GOD or a church leader, a guru, a teacher, healer, or spokesperson for a powerful group?

Many religions, cults, and groups rule with fear. If you're a member of one of these groups and you don't accept the group's TRUTH, you will suffer whatever sanctions are meted out to those who disobey. At this point, you give your personal power to the leader. The GOD Source does not want you to give your power away to anyone else or to use an incarnate person as an intermediary between you and the Source. You came here to be a *master of your life*. Claim your personal power and do it now.

We must look not at the world picture but the impact of our environment on us. Are we willing to live our lives unthreatened by anything? Can we detach ourselves from emotional reaction, denial, or illusion to the point where we can allow ourselves to be vulnerable enough to tell the truth?

Honesty and integrity are crucial. Are we going to face ourselves and honestly evaluate each situation without the delusion of being threatened, or do we feel we must protect ourselves and run? Can we be honest enough to know that we can be vulnerable and not get hurt, or will we be rejected or isolated for our opinions and statements? If we feel our opinion is inaccurate or unacceptable, we will automatically feel rejected by ourselves. If we are in integrity with self, there's no need for defense.

On the other side of the coin is anger (i.e., loss of control and an attempt to regain it). Anger covers up fear and in turn causes people to be aggressive, controlling, and manipulative. When we think we're going to lose something, we will use every trick in the book to manipulate everything and everyone we can to gain the upper hand in a situation.

With most people, arriving at this point comes down to this: Are you willing to love yourself enough so that you don't need acceptance and approval from anyone other than yourself? If so, no one can threaten you. When you get to this place in your life, you have no problem in telling the truth or being honest with yourself. You know it without a doubt and it releases you from all the pain of emotions. No one can hurt you or reject you; only *you* have that power. If, however, you believe you can be rejected or threatened by anybody, you will defend yourself whenever you feel anyone is unloving, non-accepting or disapproving of you. It all boils down to the one question: "Do I need the love, acceptance, and approved of others, or do I have my alrightness, self-esteem, and self-worth in me?"

If you don't have those qualities installed in yourself, other people can steal your self-esteem and cause you to feel rejected and abandoned. It may seem that others are "doing it to you," but you're doing it to yourself because *you're* the one who's trying to get love and acceptance from outside yourself. Nobody can love you for you! Only *you* can decide whether or not to love yourself.

The blocks to love take many forms, and they will always elude you until you decide to commit to yourself that nobody can hurt you or reject you. Until then, you will accept love substitutes that you will misinterpret as love coming from "anyone who acknowledges, respects me, or lets me know that I am all right." It only makes a difference to you.

In some people, self-worth degenerates to the point that the only time they are feel loved is during sexual activity. As a result they become sex-addicted, which can lead to aberrant behavior patterns. Contrary to popular opinion, we have found that rapists are not sex addicts. They are angry at women, often in reaction to a controlling manipulating mother, and their aggression is a display of power and control over women.

Today's society puts so much focus on sexual performance that concern about not being able to measure up causes many people to feel inadequate. Drugs to increase potency proliferate and are advertized daily in the media. Many people try to downplay the influence of this issue in their lives, but I find self-doubts in this area to be a major factor with my clients.

I also notice another interesting dichotomy. Before marriage, women may be sexually active with a strong libido, but it often wanes after marriage. Many of my male clients complain that women's sex drive diminishes as they get older, and many of my female clients complain that men think about little other than sex. Men seem to view sex as an inner-directed need that must be satisfied, while women seem to want to satisfy their partner as well as themselves. For many women, if sex were simply to vanish from their lives, they wouldn't miss it at all. The exact opposite seems true for men. However, when men advance on the spiritual path, they will come to a point where sex is no longer a driving need, and will plateau out to the level of drive experienced by women.

You will not recognize the lesson or the master teachers in your life until you decide to move out of self-pity and martyrdom. When you commit to move from victim to cause, people will recognize your love. It will seem as if you went through the very stone wall against which you've been beating your head for a long time. The pain and agony of lack of love, hurt, and rejection will disappear, and you start to detach from emotional reactions, can accurately discern what is before you, and make sound decisions.

As you recognize the teachers and the truth in all lessons that are presented to you, you can then release inaccurate interpretations of other people's intentions. If you feel that someone treated you unfairly, you can take responsibility and communicate with that person in unconditional love and forgiveness, and clear the situation up. If the other person is unwilling to understand or see your explanation, that is perfectly all right, too. You used your "response-ability" and the situation is cleared up for you. You will now have a direct awareness; the lesson is finished because all emotions or feelings are released, and there's no need to judge the person or talk about the situation anymore.

When a person is caught in the illusion of misinterpretation, then judgment, control, justification, defense, blame, attack, fear, manipulation, and authority become a way of life. Control sub-personalities in autopilot now control your life, making all your decisions for you and you may not even be aware of it. Autopilot has no morals, ethics, or integrity, nor does it see any reason to be honest or tell the truth. It works out of the survival self so, with an attitude of "anything goes," it protects itself as it sees fit. It has no concern about your health or well-being because it sees itself as separate from you.

The Middle Self likes to hide the truth, and will do that by censoring your listening ability. It actually reinterprets what you're hearing to the point that if other people ask you what they said, you may have heard something completely different. Your Middle Self will go into justifier-mode, and defend what it has let you hear or not hear, and you'll buy into it as *your* interpretation, *your* understanding. You may find yourself making statements you later regret or feel guilty about, and will constantly find that you're self-righteously defending yourself from others who you feel are damaging you. You feel that you're taking right action because you perceive that others are defaming you or some person you respect. You justify with, "They're not seeing the truth; they have an ego block in ethics or integrity."

The only problem is that, by projecting blame, you may be doing exactly what you're accusing other people of. When you accept the fact that there are no rights or wrongs in life, and that everything has a cause, it's possible to move away from the illusion. When we step out of the illusion and into forgiveness, life becomes abundant with prosperity and love.

Accepting that there are no mistakes, and that everything happens according to the lesson we must learn requires considerable understanding. If you succumb to the temptation to judge, justify, defend, or manipulate your actions to feel all right, *you have just created karma for yourself, and you are set up for a lesson replay*. A mistake is a lesson that was presented to you but you failed to learn. It will be presented to you again and again in different ways, so that you may not be able to recognize it. It is your responsibility to recognize the teacher and the lesson.

Once in the eighties, I had soundly criticized a person because I didn't like what he was doing or his professional ethics. The following day, I had two earaches and was stone deaf on the third day. This persisted until I understood the lesson. Once I did, I wrote to the person and admitted my mistake. Slowly my hearing returned, but full recovery took over a month. This painful lesson shut down my practice and made my life miserable, but sometimes we just need a blockbuster to get the lesson.

Autopilot will act as if it's separate from you, doing what satisfies its needs even if that is diametrically opposed to your conscious desires or values. Not only will it justify its behavior to you through self-talk, it will convince you to accept its explanation. The main fuel for this control and manipulation is anger and/or fear, and its tools are attack, justification, self-righteousness, arrogance, contempt, blame, condescension, criticism, and a host of other negative emotions that it can use to stay in power.

People operating in this mode see themselves as justified in spreading rumors if they feel they have been attacked or treated in some unethical manner. In most cases. they do not recognize their inaccurate perceptions, what they are doing, or the effect they are having on other people. Unfortunately, they are setting themselves up for a karmic lesson which will be replayed with the same consequences rebounding on them unless they clear the lesson.

For those trapped in this mode, autopilot is in total control of the situation, so they will deny being in illusion, rendering any rational discussion of the situation virtually impossible. They will interpret any comments as criticism or judgment because they need to protect self at all costs. In their view, *they*, not you, are acting in integrity, honesty, and truth. Their autopilot is unconcerned about outcomes, as it considers itself always right, no matter what the situation. For these people, any perceived threat is met with counterattack. Of course, the opposite is true: "If I defend myself, then I am attacked" (*A Course In Miracles*, Lesson 135).

If you counterattack, can you evaluate your own behavior without deluding yourself? Highly unlikely. More likely, you will feel angry or guilty, place blame, judge, justify, or get upset at yourself or others.

The average person processes 50,000 or more thoughts a day, so we're talking to ourselves 70 percent of the time, and the Ego and Middle will chatter among themselves until we take control of the dialogue. Depending on who's in control of your mind, self-talk can yield much valuable and useful information but, if your autopilot is in control, it may feed you with irrational information that's detrimental to your health and well-being.

When you recognize the illusion, the sub-personalities that masquerade behind all the disguises and facades will be revealed to you. As you let go of the illusionary self that your Middle Self has created, you move into the role of cause/creator self that is endowed with unconditional love. When you reclaim your "alrightness," self-esteem and self-worth follow automatically, and your life will then be full of the abundance to which you're entitled.

Part Three

Rewriting Your
Life Script

10

20 Critical Factors to Overcome in Self-Mastery

Examine each of the following statements and decide if and how much you agree with it. Be honest in your evaluation with yourself. The only person you can fool is you. If you're in denial of your true reality, you may not be able to recognize whether or not these are your behavior patterns. The spiritual journey requires that you not live in an illusion, so use your introspection and evaluate your answers with honesty.

1. I lack self-love, self-worth, or self-esteem.
2. I mirror what I see in others.
3. I have no personal power.
4. Most of the time, I live in fear and anxiety.
5. Everyone else is to blame for my misfortune.
6. Other people are constantly "doing it to me."
7. I need to be right so much that I strive to make others wrong.
8. I must be in control and power to protect myself from others.
9. My beliefs and prayers do not manifest in my life.
10. I hold high expectations about what life should be like, but it seldom works out.
11. I feel depressed about the future with very little I can do about my situation.
12. My constant confusion about how to act paralyzes me into procrastination and inaction.
13. Fear of failure and/or success causes me to create failure to block my goals.
14. My goals and values are not aligned with what my experiences have been in life.

15. I refuse to accept things as they are and prefer my own reality, even if it is an illusion.
16. I have no concept about my purpose or path in life.
17. I constantly devise new masks, facades, or ways to deny and cover up my feelings.
18. I feel indecisive. As a result, I refuse to take responsibility for my actions.
19. I feel rejected and abandoned since nobody accepts, respects or cares for me.
20. Life is a struggle because I do not have financial abundance.

Even if you agreed with just one of the above statements, then this section is for you. However, you're not alone. Most people live as victims, believing and feeling that someone else can make them happy or sad, loved or unloved. However, the mind is intended to be used creatively, productively and with purpose, rather than operating most of the time on autopilot. *Ideally*, you're in an alert and active state, constantly proactive in life, and undergoing experiences that accelerate the development of your consciousness. Your Subconscious Mind and Lower Self run the routine functions of your body as they are programmed to do, but *you* consciously run your life.

Your thoughts, beliefs, attitudes, perceptions, and others' opinions or perceived judgments about you create your feelings and emotions. As with a computer's hard drive, your Subconscious Mind/Lower Self records everything in your memory, and either *you* cause and create your own reality, or you let others do so by programming your "computer." Are *you* responsible for how you feel at all times? Are *you* the master of your emotions and circumstances in your life? Are you responding to life based on *your* thoughts and attitudes? Or have you handed over this awesome responsibility to someone else?

The challenge associated with the above "20 factors" is misalignment between the viewpoints and interpretations of the Conscious/Middle Self and the Subconscious/Lower Self. Conflicting interpretations cause stress and tension in the body and loss of emotional control. Most people operate out of the Middle Self's sub-personalities which in turn use the Subconscious Mind/Lower Self's behavioral "database." This causes conflict in your life because your sub-personalities are making decisions based on existing programs. Middle Self operates from the database using sub-personalities to control mind functions if one is on autopilot. If autopilot controls Middle Self, it will always win and you will be a victim of your own emotions, possibly without knowing why.

For any permanent success, the Subconscious and Conscious Minds must be aligned with your larger purpose, or else your Middle Self and its sub-personalities will strive to take control and sabotage your success in attaining a desired goal.

We can find an untold number of reasons for not confronting our fears and an equal number of ways to justify to ourselves why we shouldn't. Sometimes, we insulate ourselves so well from the actual truth of our reality that we can't differentiate between truth, fact and illusion. We will rationalize and justify to ourselves and others why we do the things we do, and why our behavior is perfectly acceptable. We may be on autopilot so completely that we cover up our feelings to the point that we can't even recognize that we are in denial.

We can make all kinds of claims about what we are going to do, but our *actions* indicate whether or not we are in integrity with our stated purposes. Further, we often identify with the created physical self to the point where our actions begin to affect our bodies with illness. We may become complacent in a comfortable rut, resisting change because it's fearful, but the inner conflict may manifest as a disease with no known cause. The real cause is our failure to take responsibility for our life and keep the commitments we made with ourselves. We will continue in a downward spiral until we listen to the inner dialogue and clear the anger or fear.

On the other hand, you can be master of your life, totally detached from the illusion of believing the false self to be real, accepting everything and everyone as they are, not making judgments, and free of the need to justify yourself or wield attack thoughts. With no need to be top dog or an authority figure controlling everyone and everything in sight, you're not threatened and can relate effectively with everyone about who you are and what reality is for you. Life becomes a choice rather than a series of uncontrolled knee-jerk reactions.

The real question is: can you evaluate yourself honestly without self-delusion? You may come up with, "I like myself. That isn't me. I don't say or do things like that." Even if you don't justify in this way, it could be worthwhile to evaluate your life from the standpoint of how much abundance, joy, happiness, harmony, true peace, unconditional love and acceptance are in it.

Many people live in delusion within their own illusion. Understanding and accepting *"what is"* in your life is crucial to getting to the base causes of any conflicts or problems in your life. If you will be honest with yourself regarding the choices you're making about your communications and relationship with yourself and others, then you can honestly assess how you respond to each of the 20 factors above. This will reveal what factors are your resistance and blocks to growth in your life.

We have found that most people don't want to admit to themselves that these resistances exist and are the panic buttons of their life. Resistance t o growth is characterized by fear of the unknown and will always correspond to a belief that has been programmed into your Subconscious Mind during this or a past-life. Lessons from your flight plan that you must learn will reoccur until you recognize them and learn what they have to teach you for your growth.

Buddha summarized it as: "It is our resistance to life that causes our pain. What you resist, you draw to you. As long as you resist something, you're locked into it, and you perpetuate its influence in your life."

What You Resist Persists

Nonresistance is the willingness to accept what is "as is," and look at changing circumstances in your life as valuable information, rather than as problems or catastrophes. This universal law is the first step to transformation. When you decide to take responsibility for your actions and emotions, recognizing they are your *perceptions* and not facts, you can move quickly through lessons, knowing that the real blocks on your path stem from the resistance in your life. The problems and roadblocks then become challenges that you can overcome.

Limitations exist only in your mind, so do not concentrate on the answer to the question or justify the "why," but look for the cause in you. Don't project blame on someone else. You set up the lesson, even if your interpretation makes other people seem wrong. It's not your duty to impress upon them that it's *their* lesson. You may be right, but trying to project your interpretation on others causes you to fail the test, because you really set the lesson up for yourself to learn from. You will be tested until you recognize the lesson and let it go. It is our resistance that creates problems. If it wasn't your lesson, too, you wouldn't even be involved. When we let go of our attachment to holding onto our position, determination or attachment, the challenge is met and the situation goes away.

Your Middle Self's "critical parent" control sub-personality will always tell you that you are right. But if you are a master of life, you accept what is and go on to the next lesson. Awareness that you're acting out these factors or the attitude that "I'm working on them" won't change your behavior until you know the underlying cause. When you have identified the cause in yourself and recognize this as a challenge (rather than a problem), then you've made a major step toward transformation. The process of reprogramming can then begin and you can release yourself from emotional reaction.

Successful reprogramming requires the three "D's—Desire, Determination and Discipline—and the four "C's—Context, Commitment, Concentration and Consistency. Your willingness to evaluate your attitudes, thoughts, perceptions, and interpretations, and become forgiving and nonjudgmental of others will also be key to your metamorphosis.

Once you're able to release the fears behind your reactions and confront your comfort zone by going through your fears, you discover that the fear was not valid but just an illusion, or False Evidence Appearing Real. You're then able to experience real peace.

Conflicts are simply illusions that we bring to reality with our minds. When you let go of the created self you think you are—the product of your own and others' mistaken perceptions of who you are—you then come to the point where you can let go of insecurity, need for validation, and self-imposed limitations. At that point, the *real you* emerges, your self-image becomes clear, and you can take responsibility for your own love and acceptance. You no longer need validation from others. You appreciate their love and acceptance, of course, but having a successful relationship with anyone is no longer a requirement or a need. Your own love is a working relationship in your life.

When you gain a sense of "alrightness," self-worth, and self-esteem, you won't be clear of these reactions from others, however, but you will recognize the reactions as "other people's stuff," and you can detach and respond in a way that serves you in a positive, peaceful, loving way. Your positive self-image now is visible. People will recognize your confidence and treat you with due recognition and acceptance. Then, the negative reactions and emotions of others won't throw you off-center or push your buttons. When they do react, you will know that any negativity on their part is really a cry for love, and you can heal them with your love and support, since you have plenty for yourself and can now channel it out to others.

They may not allow in your love and acceptance, of course, but it's not important to you that they do. However, it will be there for those who *are* willing to receive it, but you place no conditions for performance or behavior on any relationship or your willingness to share it. It just is. You are teaching love and it excludes no one, as love cannot be given in part. It has no boundaries and is always unconditional in the moment.

11

Are You Living in Love or Fear?

Fear: F-alse E-vidence A-ppearing R-eal

There are only two polarities in this universe: positive and negative. Similarly, in every life, there are only two energy polarities: *Love* and *Fear*. The opposite of Love is Fear, manifest as rejection or indifference. One or other of these polarities controls your life, and there are no gray areas. You are either operating from Love or Fear. The intensity, degree or level can change, but the only way you can change the form is to take total responsibility in your life.

Love is kindness and caring, and acceptance without judgment, conditions, manipulation or authority. Love leads to wellness and healing, to expansion, understanding, growth, rebirth, support, approval, peace, happiness, joy and harmony in your life. Fear, on the other hand, is contracting, restricting, debilitating, judging, controlling, manipulative, authoritative, self-righteous, indignant, contemptuous, and demanding. It causes you to run away from yourself and to feel hurt, shy, guilty, self-loathing or self-pity, worry, anxiety and tension, rejection, depression, confusion, and hopelessness. This leads to chaos in your life, and can cause emotional and physical illness and disease. When you lose your will to live, your instinctual mind will take over and install "I want to die" programs that can manifest a life-threatening disease.

There is never a lack of love; we just separate ourselves from it. All we need do is open to it and let it in. Love is our innate natural state, but few of us know what it really is, and we can't give what we don't feel we have. We must recover and rewrite the love program that most people lose before they're three years old.

As we've seen, three out of five children were rejected by their mothers before they were born. As a result they have never felt what love is and may not have a love program in their files. In twenty years of practice with thousands of clients, I have seen this repeatedly.

If your parents didn't give you a model of what love was, usually because they themselves didn't know or couldn't express love, your "database" won't contain the "love program." However, this can be remedied with an affirmation (see my book *Your Body is Talking; Are You Listening?* for the process). Clearing all the programs that have caused emotional trauma and the resulting breakdowns may take some concentrated therapy, however.

Due to childhood rejection, most of us turned love off, and all we need to do is reclaim it by rewriting the program that originally negated our love program. We were born with the love program and, since our bodies are made of love energy, it's an intrinsic part of our being. We must accept love in order to fill up the vacuum when we release fear. If you're on autopilot, controlled by your programming, you must locate the program that falsely misinterpreted a situation and denied love. A child can interpret any form of attention as love, even physical abuse if this is only form of attention the child receives.

If fear is in control of your life, to become effective, you must choose love, but not merely at a conscious intellectual level but also subconsciously. You must address the defective programming in all mind's files—the Conscious and Subconscious Minds, Middle Self, back-up files, time-line files, and denial and denial-of-denial files. Each file must be deleted and rewritten with new programs. Otherwise, we can assume we have created a positive image for ourselves, but when we go to our denial files, we can find that we have overwritten the programs in the Conscious Mind/Middle Self, but they still exist in the Subconscious Mind's denial files. Of course, we can use sheer willpower to push ourselves through life, but it drains our energy and taxes our physical health.

Such fear eventually becomes debilitating to the body through stress, depression, emotional trauma, illness and disease. You can blame such outcomes on someone or something else so that you don't have to take responsibility, *but you create it all*. The lesson is to detach from the feeling and recognize what's going on. Blaming never ever works at any level. It's a delusion. We create every situation in our life without exception. People may play into our games and soap operas but *we* are the scriptwriter and lead actor.

At any point in your life you can choose love and change the outcome. Once you're operating from love, however, you're open and vulnerable to life, handling whatever comes up. You may stumble but you always catch yourself and move on. All you need to do is move from fear to love. *So, when are you going to choose love and heal your life?*

If you're living in love, then accepting people and situations, and expressing unconditional love to yourself and others is effortless, but if you're not there yet, the transition may look like an enormous challenge. Illusions about love await the unwary, based on all the varied interpretations about what love is and what it is not. Most people confuse love with sex. Relationship addiction can be confused with love. An immediate electric attraction that lights a fire emotionally can really cause confusion. Love is a building process, not a sudden event.

Of course, the most prevalent and erroneous interpretation is to confuse sex as love. The media bombard us with depictions of sex, passion, attraction, and infatuation, and call it love.

Now, sex can obviously be an aspect of love, assuming total acceptance and appropriate feelings but, otherwise, it's an addictive satisfaction of an animal need. Sex is not love. True love exists in and of itself, and we cannot create or erase it. We cannot give what we don't understand. Conversely, we cannot accept love if we don't know what it is.

Many "love substitutes" evoke reactions in partners such as, "He can't, doesn't or won't say he loves me," "She doesn't make me feel loved when we make love," "I need this person in my life because he/she makes my life complete" "Sex is like the fourth of July. I can't live without it. I need this person in my life."

Or you find another person who needs you and the chemistry is right, and suddenly you're attached and codependent, hooked on the adrenaline rush of relationship addiction that we mistake for love. "I can't live without him/her" can result in serious injury or death if one of the partners considers the other to be "medicine." Crimes of passion are caused by the irrational feeling of "If I can't have him/her, then nobody will." The result is often a murder/suicide.

You can't be addicted to something that nurtures, supports and expands. The definition of an addiction is being attached to a need for something that is not healthy or causes you do something in excess to satisfy a need. However, many people confuse bodily or emotional reaction—a passion reaction or attraction—as love. The paradox in an addiction is "getting too much of what you do not need." That does not apply to love. You cannot get too much love.

If you're committed to experiencing all situations with unconditional love, forgiveness and acceptance with no judgment or control, you can achieve total wellness.

When you're coming from love, taking advantage of anyone wouldn't even cross your mind, but if you're not taking responsibility, you won't see anything wrong with manipulating or taking advantage of others.

The attitude of, "I am not responsible for your behavior. I can say anything I want to. How you react is your responsibility" also gets people in trouble. It's untrue, because what you say may affect other people in a negative way if they are suggestible. Few people have their life in order to the point that what other people say doesn't affect them. What we say *can* cause another person to experience pain, fear or anger. If we mistakenly believe that we are not responsible, we may feel we are off the hook for the pain we cause, but we must operate from an ethical standpoint at all times. No matter how angry we are or how rejected we feel, we must come from a neutral place and treat people fairly.

Addictions indicate that you're acting out dysfunctional, even self-destructive, behavior. The medicine of addiction will never satisfy the need for love.

In examining your life, the main questions to ask yourself are:
- Do I have an authority, power, and/or control need with other people?
- Can I release my need for control and, if I did, what would happen?
- Do I let others form my reality for me?
- Am I sensitive to what others think and say about me? If so, why?
- Do I give away my power and rely on others as to whether I feel okay?
- Do I make other people responsible for my happiness? And if so, why?
- Could I set aside my beliefs, value systems, judgments, and preconceived notions about the way I am currently living? And if so, am I willing to evaluate my direction in life?
- Am I willing to open myself up, becoming vulnerable to the things that currently seem threatening to me?

If you can evaluate your life without deluding yourself, without excuses, control or justifications, you're ready for recovery. Otherwise, ask yourself why your secrets are so painful or repressed that you're unwilling to look at them? Are you choosing pain instead?

If you're protecting patterns in your life that justify or defend your alrightness the way you are, you may be blocking yourself from an abundance of love in relationships, business, financial, joy, acceptance, and happiness. Is it always the other person who won't cooperate with you or accept your ideas? Does that ring a bell?

If you must have control, life will continually deal lessons that seem to put your goals out of reach. Most people make insidious statements to themselves, subconsciously trying to justify their behavior or the situations they're faced with, such as, "I'm not supposed to do that or get this," "I want your love but on my terms," "You don't understand my needs so I have the right to attack you," "Don't expect me to love you if you don't love me first," "People use me or take advantage of me," and "No one gives me acceptance or recognizes my love."

What Love Is: Kindness and Caring

Love is:
- Communicating that you matter to me and that I desire and appreciate your presence in my life.
- Making a positive difference rather than detracting or needing control.
- Opening the path to your own feeling-self by opening the door to your own heart.
- Committing to be a person who gives unconditional love and enhances life through serving.
- Recognizing value without demand, need or judgment.

Understanding and Acceptance

Understanding is the most sought after facet of love. Many times we try to be understanding and understood, yet our need to control causes rejection. We lose the effect of love by not listening and accepting people as they are. Understanding isn't an intellectual function, nor does it flow from logical thinking. It operates through *compassion*. If I forget about myself in the moment and focus my attention totally on you, listening creatively without planning what I'm going to say next, I will understand and be aware of your needs. *Creative listening* is a quality that must be established in your relationships to let other people know that you're interested in what they're communicating. Most people can form what they're going to say as they speak unless they're "single-trackers" who cannot focus their mind.

Acceptance is unconditional. If I don't approve of your behavior and say so honestly, it will not affect my love for you. I may say, "I love you as a person, but some of your behavior is unacceptable to me." This way, I'm not rejecting the person.

Understanding and acceptance build trust and security, for I will not be honest with you unless I trust you. I accept you as you are, without trying to change or control your personality or behavior. If I place any conditions on how I am going to accept or approve of you, I may *call* it love but, by placing conditions and values on it, thus making it conditional love, I am rejecting you. No conditions can be placed on acceptance because, by definition, it must to be totally unconditional with no reservations.

Service

Encouraging our loved ones to be and do the best they can, with no judgment causes them to aspire to their highest level. Supportive challenge isn't hostile or attacking. You can serve others by giving them support to free themselves of self-sabotaging behavior patterns. If you're hesitant because you fear rejection by them, you won't support them. Conversely, you can observe a situation and discuss the incident honestly without judgment. However, do not let a need for validation drive you to support failure or resistance so that you "look good" in comparison.

When you can discuss other's behavior openly, free of attack, control, criticism or justification, you're allowing your unconditional love to support and expand their horizons by creating trust. If any one of these factors is missing or withheld in a relationship, then love is incomplete and will cause conflict. If you can confront your fears openly and honestly, expressing how you feel, you're on the path to transformation.

What Love Is Not

Most people want to believe that they're operating in a loving way, yet many are living behind walls and masks so that no one can see who they are because they live in a fearful illusion. The game is, "How can I stop people from knowing who I really am because, if they really knew me, they wouldn't love me."

If resistance, justification or unwillingness express themselves in any situation, truth is not there.

Love substitutes wear many disguises:

- Supporting the actions of others because you love them, even if they're dishonest. Unwillingness to call them on their unethical behavior.
- Possessiveness, requiring undivided attention from a person for fear of being rejected.
- Allowing leeching or jealousy to control another person. Attempted ownership stems from fear of loss.
- Attachment or manipulating to get love. Being codependent.
- Strong attraction, causing intense passion, relationship addiction, infatuation of emotions and sexual feelings resulting in attachment you call love.
- Martyrdom in which you put the needs of others before your own.
- Flattery, building others up, and giving them attention so they will validate you and not reject you.
- Devaluing and rejecting yourself because you feel you do not match up.

Classic martyrdom lines include:

- "Will you love me if I put your needs ahead of mine?"
- "I will let you abuse me because I need your approval."
- "I can live my life through you."
- "You give me all my value in life because I am making you feel I love you."

However, at some point, clinging codependency will lead to rejection because the burden on the other person becomes so great that he or she flees.

12

Your Ego: Friend or Foe?

W hy do some people behave irrationally, and seem unable to control or handle crisis in their life? Recent psychological research concludes that the body/mind communicates with itself about every item of sensory input received. We perceive only a fraction of the information coming to us from our environment, and store that in something that can hold over 200,000 times the capacity of any computer made today. This huge "computer" is a network that operates in every cell of our body. However, Middle Self is a partner in this amazing mental computer we call the mind, and can, therefore, tamper with the files without our knowledge.

Until recently, I thought that Ego was the villain, controlling our thinking and the Subconscious Mind's programs. A few years ago, however, I discovered that Ego is an innocent "file clerk"—the file manager for your computer, a secretary, and a librarian for the Subconscious Mind. It has no agenda to control the mind, or to tamper with any programs or sensory data. It doesn't make or cause you to do anything. This revolutionized my ideas about how the mind works, and I feel it's a major step forward in understanding how the mind processes information. Therefore, I am intent in getting this message across to everyone, and you will see this repeated in all my books.

Brain research seems focus on how the brain interacts with the body's neurological system, but I have discovered that what we call "the mind" is located not just in the brain but in the whole body network, in which every cell is a tiny computer connected by a sophisticated network, similar to the phone system. Ego serves as the phone operator of this system, keeping the Conscious and Subconscious Minds in synch. It works with the brain's switching network to transfer sensory input from the Conscious Mind to Subconscious Mind's memory and retrieving the appropriate information from the Subconscious to the Conscious Mind when action is to be taken. Middle Self is the program manager that we work with to install programs that are then forwarded to Ego to put them in the appropriate file.

Over the last 15 years, medical science has proven without any doubt that communication in the mind/body is not through the neurological system. Neurotransmitters send electrical messages to muscles and the functional aspects of our body. They are the energy links that cause our body to function. The actual messages are transmitted by chemicals produced by the endocrine glands in the brain and other parts of the body. Researchers have found that receptor points are even on leuko-cytes, the immune system's disease fighters. The main chemicals are neuropeptides and cytokinins along with 20 more minor chemicals.

Now, if you're in control of your mind, have reclaimed your personal power from your Middle Self, and made peace with your Ego, then all this happens smoothly and easily. Sensory input comes in and Ego simply files it, and/or retrieves information for you to act on without tampering with it. Unfortunately, many people allow their sub-personalities to interpret and tamper with the content as it's filed and retrieved, overlaying the information with context, so we blame Ego for problems that are actually caused by our sub-personalities. But why do we create these sub-personalities?

As a child, you often needed help with a difficult situation, so sub-personalities were set up to help you. Operating out of the Survivor Self and Inner Child, they kept you on track and protected you. If you were raised in a supportive, caring, cooperative loving family, your Middle Self created loving, supportive sub-personalities. But if you were raised in a dysfunctional family (which accounts for 95% of the population), your sub-personalities took (and still take) a defensive posture, reacting in a survivor mode with stimulus/response. Of course, they feel they're protecting you with their defensive interpretations of situations but, unfortunately, those interpretations are not usually in your best interest. They cause you to take a defensive or attack action when it's unwarranted, tell you that *you're* not all right, or subtly control you through autopilot. And most of the time, you're not aware of their insidious takeover, as it happens over many years.

If you sold out to the autopilot's interpretations when you were a young child, your sub-personalities in autopilot are still probably running your life now. Most people assume they have control of the direction in their life and deny that anyone else controls them, but every client I work with is controlled by hundreds, maybe thousands, of sub-personalities that erode self-worth and self-esteem without his or her awareness.

Parents simply don't recognize their child's sub-personalities, or the extent to which they are interpreting the child's world and forming its habit patterns. Since few parents know anything about these sub-personalities, they don't see the need to give the child any form of mental training. So, the sub-personalities are left alone to protect the child and interpret reality for it, many times in an illogical manner.

A child cannot evaluate a logical, rational decision. It assumes that what it thinks it perceives "in here" is what's really happening "out there," and creates more sub-personalities to deal with the perceived situation. When the child matures into adulthood, it does so either with supportive or defensive, fearful, or angry sub-personalities that continue to control the adult's life.

Few people in the medical, health, psychological, or religious fields understand how the mind works and how it interacts with the body/mind. The sub-personalities are very shrewd manipulators and, most of the time, can think and act faster than your Conscious Mind. They use the Subconscious Mind's memory banks to store the patterns and programs that they create. They use the Conscious Mind's ability to program, operating beneath your knowledge if you don't monitor your self-talk. By using your intuitive sense, they predict your future actions before you do, and can set up disguises and masquerades, making your actual behavior very real and believable to you. If you identify with and condone the behavior of your sub-personalities, you allow them to set up autopilot programs that further control you. They set up the illusion, and fool you into accepting it.

As a result, sub-personalities are controlling your mind, and you have no dominion over your Subconscious Mind's scripts. A ship piloted from the engine room with no one on the bridge will eventually crash on the rocks, but your sub-personalities see nothing wrong with that. In fact, they like crashes because they can seize more power. When you lose control and move into fear or anger, you give the Middle Self carte blanche to take over and run your life. Its sub-personalities operate by interpreting incoming sensory data and acting only for their own survival, quite often at your expense. Their only concern is self-preservation at all costs, with no concern for the effects of their actions on you or anyone else.

Five basic sub-personalities in the Subconscious Mind control your life: the child, the adolescent, the critical parent, the survivor self, and the adult. These five come in hundreds of disguises to deceive you into thinking that they're acting in your own best interest.

By manipulating and interpreting incoming data, and screening possible alternatives, your Middle Self's sub-personalities control you. Suppose, for example, you're in a situation and twenty possible responses exist, yet your Middle Self gives you only two of its own choosing. Who is in control? By censoring your possible choices, your Middle Self has effectively seized control of the situation, yet you still feel you have free choice because you have two options.

You may not even be aware that you're participating in the reaction because your Justifier sub-personality deludes you into thinking that a self-righteous reaction is appropriate. However, this reaction may appear totally irrational to a bystander. You're often unaware that the autopilot is in control, for it has fooled you so well for so long that you really believe you're in control. In fact, if the bystander suggests that you're under the control of your sub-personalities, you would probably defend and justify your actions.

Many people I work with get upset when I tell them that they have no basic control over their life and must reclaim personal power from Middle Self. Fortunately, all the functions of the Mind can easily be reprogrammed with affirmations.

The first step to liberation is realizing that your sub-personalities manipulate you much of the time, and then becoming watchful for it. When you feel judgment, justification or defensiveness creeping up, you know the controller is retrieving the wrong habit patterns. You must take control of the situation and tell your sub-personalities that you're taking over. It's important to quickly stamp out any sub-personality justification or defensiveness.

Your mind processes all forms of sensory input by rationally evaluating its significance. A sub-personality, on the other hand, makes no rational decisions. It takes a black-or-white stance, assuming the person or situation is either supportive and accepting, or rejecting and attacking. Other people are seen either as sources of help or as obstacles to become angry or fearful about. Thus, they can justify any action to make you feel you're doing the right thing. So watch yourself for any self-righteous denial or unwillingness to discuss a situation.

Ego does an excellent job of filing away sensory input information received from the environment. The only problem is that if you're not controlling the filing process, your sub-personalities will impose their own interpretations and put those on file. As a result, most people are unaware of the content of many of their files. Dysfunctional behavior stems from not knowing what patterns are operating.

However, understand that, as you demand control back, you may be in for a fight. If you have a powerful controlling Middle Self, then it could be a real knockdown, drag-out battle. I have found that strong sub-personalities don't understand that winning the battle for control could kill its host and itself also. Middle Self always feels that if it gives up control, it's finished. It believes that as you transform, you will want to kill or destroy its sub-personalities. And it's right; you *do* want to delete, erase and destroy their control. This committee will appear to operate as a separate being, unconcerned with your welfare

Reclaiming your personal power requires you to convince your Ego that you don't want to take its power, but that you want it to use it more constructively. It requires that you understand what the Ego's original role was. Your Ego has a contract with you, as it was designed to be the secretary of your mind, moving information back and forth between the Subconscious and Conscious Minds.

Concepts about what Ego is in the psychological field and *A Course in Miracles* clearly portray the Ego as the enemy, something also echoed in many religions. However, Ego isn't the enemy but, if you attack it, it won't defend itself; it will either run and hide, or shut down. If it shuts down, nothing gets in or out of the Subconscious Mind. If that happens, no amount of affirmations will have any effect on your life because they simply don't get filed.

Your mind cannot function without an Ego, just as a large corporation could not operate without secretaries. Nor could a library function without librarians, or a computer function without a file manager. You must help Ego by telling it, "I know understand your importance, and I love and forgive you. I was operating with false information, so I viewed you as the culprit that was manipulating me. I'm not blaming you, and I know you did the best you could with the programs you had available."

This releases the Ego from the guilt. It also heals your separation from God when you realize that Ego had nothing to do with creating the separation. Ego then feels free to operate as it was designed to and to work with you.

We must recognize that Middle Self is of the body, created by the mind and does not, itself, have a spiritual aspect. We must teach it that it won't be killed or relegated to oblivion if it begins to cooperate. It really isn't giving up its power but is working with you to form a stronger unit. It's part of the team, and you need help from all aspects of your mind. When it agrees to its new assignment, you can help it reprogram your mind so that it's free of interpretation, and functions more effectively.

Ego, on the other hand, has no agenda to change or manipulate the files in any way. If you have a poor memory, you can be sure your Ego isn't working properly and isn't filing incoming information in an organized, logical way. As you regain control of your mind, you will regain an excellent memory. The librarian will once again be performing its duties properly.

13

Making Friends with your Ego: The Next Step in Transformation

In the preceding chapter, we saw that your Ego is your Subconscious Mind's filing clerk, and files all incoming sensory input in your Subconscious Mind's memory. Your Ego performs another equally valuable task—that of retrieval librarian.

The Ego likes this job title, which solves a dilemma for my clients who are beating up their Ego. Furthermore, this task is invaluable to you because it governs your memory. Because you need memory retrieval, Ego realizes that it's indispensable. (In my case, I couldn't remember my childhood and found that I had shut off everything until I was ten years old and filed it in the denial-of-denial section.) However, my life changed dramatically once I was able to use my Ego's ability to restructure my childhood, rewrite most of the files that I had misread, and set up new programming.

In addition to assuring your Ego that you recognize its value, you must get Middle Self to recognize you as the scriptwriter, producer and director of your programs in life. Since Middle Self is the program manager, it has been writing the programs and installing them. When it recognizes you as the operator and programmer, you must show it that you can perform the task, otherwise, its sub-personalities will try to fill this role again by default and you may be left powerless. If you take responsibility and make conscious choices all the time, your Middle Self will fall into line. When you have some win-win experiences, it will support reclaiming your personal power.

Ego doesn't want to control your life in any way, so Middle Self had to take over by default most of the time. Use the following affirmation to reclaim your personal power from your Middle Self:

"I must make peace with you, Middle Self. I must reclaim my personal power now. I recognize I gave my power to you when I was a child. I know you are the program manager and did the best you could with the programs available at the time. I am taking my power back now, but that does not mean I am trying to take your power or destroy you. I just want my power back now. I know we must work together because you're an important part of my team and I need your help. From now on, I know I must be the computer operator and programmer and I'm going to do that now. I thank you for help."

Use this affirmation to make friends with your Ego:

"I know I must make friends with you, Ego. I know that that through a misconception and false interpretation, I assumed you were the enemy and the villain that was fouling up my life. I recognize you have no agenda to foul my life up. I know now that you are the file manager, secretary and librarian for my Subconscious Mind's computer. I know we must work together because you are an important part of my team and I need your help. I am giving myself one hundred percent permission to forgive myself for any harm and trauma that I inflicted on you from my misconception. I know you did the best you could with the programs that were available to you. I thank you for your help. I am forgiving myself and loving myself now."

Both your file manager and program manager work in conjunction. These two affirmations rewrite and reprogram them. They must work together as they both manage the input from your Conscious Mind along with all incoming sensory data. Prior to reprogramming them, any affirmations you may have tried to use would not have been filed since both program manager and file manager were in the way. In my case, very few affirmations had any effect at any time. In all the clients I have worked with in 20 years, only three people had working managers.

If you don't at least understand the beginnings of personal power, you cannot reclaim your self-worth, self-esteem and self-confidence. In my case, this was a valuable discovery. When I began to reclaim my personal power, I was fighting with my Ego, assuming that it was the enemy. I beat it up all the time and blamed it for my problems. I accomplished nothing in this battle except to shut it down.

Once I realized that the sub-personalities were my real enemy, I assured my Ego over and over and that it was a valuable part of my life and that I wanted it on my team but, initially, we made no progress at all. I was about to take a different tack when I discovered that sub-personalities were responsible but letting me believe that Ego was the villain. I also realized that I was still allowing many of my old programs to run my life.

If Middle Self has to run your life because you're on autopilot, you have to prove to Middle Self that you're capable and are going to take responsibility for the job. If it feels that you will not take control of your life, it can resist you, and act almost as a separate mind over which you have no control. I had quite a battle to understand how to take control and rewrite the programs. With perseverance, however, I found the key. Today my Middle Self is free of fear, and my Ego is working effectively with me.

Realizing that you can tap into the awesome power of your mind can bring up some fear. If you're afraid of the controllers in your mind, then they know they have control. This is quite common in clients who have not reclaimed responsibility for control of their mind. The more you assert control over your life, the more your Middle Self will overtly try to seize it back. That's why it's important to tell your Middle Self that it has a new role in your life. If it feels valued, it will go along with almost everything you ask of it.

As we've seen, most of the trouble in my clients' lives stems from programs laid down in early childhood. Many children are so sensitive that sub-personalities will blow a simple rejection out of proportion. This can cause feelings that erode self-worth, self-esteem and self-confidence. They interpret sensory input, and decide how the child will react to future situations. And since children usually don't know how to use their Conscious Minds to script programs, sub-personalities have free rein.

Unfortunately, up to fifteen years of age, autopilot takes over, and will cause the child's self-worth and self-esteem to be threatened. Critical Parent is seen as a monster that discredits the child and misinterprets support, making it look like criticism. If you're from an abusive background, it will convince you that you're not acceptable, that you don't fit in, that you're not all right, and that it's all your fault. Middle Self's self-talk in your mind will tell you, "They don't really mean what they say. They're telling you something that isn't true; they don't really mean it. They're trying to manipulate you."

In early childhood, my programs actually interpreted the words of well-meaning people in this fashion. My controller sub-personalities saw themselves as my champions, out to protect me from disappointment and pain. As a result, they tried to keep me from being rejected or hurt, so they tended to view people as adversaries. A child will base a belief on a false interpretation that is quite real to the child. Trying to convince the children that the belief is incorrect is extremely difficult, and calls for establishing trust. Next, we must ferret out the base cause for the false belief—the experience or the core issue that caused it. Then we can begin to turn the belief around. Winning children's trust requires great caring and unconditional love but, if we succeed, they will open up and reveal what led to the false belief. My experiences as a child make it easier for me to work with children. Because they recognize that I understand their situation, establishing their trust and confidence is easier.

This process goes more quickly with children from families that are not severely dysfunctional, because they will trust us more readily. When they can accept our caring as unconditional love, we can support their self-worth and self-esteem.

Adults, however, have years of building programs and patterns, something that appears to work for them when, really, they are submerged in illusion and denial-of-denial. I first help them recognize they can escape this behavior. Then they must see the denial. If that's not possible, they will continue in the delusion that their life is working even though it clearly is not. The challenge is always the commitment to change. Knowing that we can rewrite a new life script and delete the old programming from the file allows us to eliminate the behavior and substitute a new pattern in its place.

Two common problems are, first, that many people fear change because it's uncharted waters and, second, their denial sub-personalities prevent any recognition of the denial. They justify their behavior and talk around any suggestions to the contrary. Some kind of emotional and/or physical crisis may need to occur before they recognize the denial.

Many clients describe times when they didn't seem to have control over much of their behavior, and they said or did something completely out of character. When we're on autopilot, we react according to the programs that drive our behavior with sub-personalities, so the behavior is perfectly aligned with the programs, and something that alarms bystanders is fine to the client.

Ironically, everything is working as it was set up to do. We cannot blame the Subconscious Mind, for it's functioning exactly as it should, and if we want to make changes, we must change the programs, not vilify the Subconscious or Ego.

Conclusion

We don't have to teach people about self-esteem, self-worth, self-confidence, self-approval or self-validation. All we need to do is recover their original program that lies buried under all the later programming that got written over it. We were all born with those attributes and all we need to do is reclaim them. But if we teach people how to do this without determining what caused them to overlay programs that are blocking them in the first place, they may cover them over again.

Some of my clients had been in traditional therapy for 10 to 30 years and felt that they had attained what they thought was balance in their life, only to see it crash when a crisis arose. All four levels of the mind must accept change for it to become permanent, otherwise internal conflicts may occur.

Contrary to most sources, I now know that Ego is a "file clerk" and our memory retrieval librarian. It doesn't influence our behavior at all. The word "egotistical" is a misnomer and cannot be applied to Ego at all. The real villains are the fearful or angry controlling, confronting and manipulating sub-personalities.

In the Middle Self, when we remove the programs and sub-personalities from the file, we can get people to take control of their behavior, which results in getting control of their life. The Catch-22 here is that everyone must recognize they have total control of their life. We create all the situations that happen in our life. Intention, self-discipline and commitment controls every facet of our life. When we recognize that the Ego is just an operating system in our mind that makes no decisions about our direction or behavior, we will have more peace, happiness, harmony and joy. When we reprogram file manager to work with us, we can understand that all it is an operating system in our mind. I have found that often, if we've made considerable progress in enlightenment in our life, Ego will discount our attitude toward it and accept that our belief about it is a semantic misconception. Either way, it makes our life much more controllable and much easier to function in.

14

Responsibility Affirmation for Mastering Emotions

Like most people, you probably assume that you correctly perceive what other people are saying to or about you, but you could misinterpret what you perceive and suffer unnecessary hurt, rejection or lack of acceptance. This affirmation will help you to detach, to claim your personal power, and to begin to respond positively in all situations. You must reinstall the program manager and the file manager program, however, before you use this affirmation process, so that Middle Self and Ego will work with you. This will stop the Middle Self from making negative interpretations or judgments and sabotaging you.

After consistent, disciplined use of this affirmation, you will be able to distinguish your *interpretation* from people's attempts to *intimidate, manipulate* or *control* your responses. You will be in control of your behavior and can choose how to respond rather than reacting blindly. Instead, you will recognize and disconnect from others' attempts to control or intimidate you. In time, you will become detached, so you will recognize the hook and bait, and won't automatically buy into controlling behavior.

When you accept that *you and only you* cause your reality, you will be able to release yourself from knee-jerk emotional reactions. This affirmation will help you break the chain and stop the tapes from playing when you run into control attempts or other uncomfortable situations. Becoming detached, nonjudgmental, accepting, loving, and forgiving of all actions will inevitably lead to transformation and metamorphosis.

We must realize that *no one does anything to us*. We send out radar-like signals to other people that announce: "This is my self-image and how I want to be treated." If you consider yourself a victim of someone's behavior, accepting this may be hard, but it is the law of neurotic attraction. We attract people who match our needs, yet most "victims" have no idea that they themselves are inviting mistreatment and abuse.

This meta-communication telepathically broadcasts to those around you exactly how you want them to react or respond to you. It makes no difference how you feel consciously or if the person is in direct contact with you. Your unspoken broadcast invites and invokes their treatment of you, but most people do not realize that *you* are programming how they should feel towards you, because they do not understand what meta-communication is or how it works.

Without knowing it, we interact with each other on a subliminal level all the time. Our Middle Self sends out telepathic signals that others intuitively pick up. We cannot stop this broadcasting so we must remove all the files and programs that put out negative messages such as, "I am not accepted, respected, recognized, acknowledged," or, "I am not all right." People pick up these programs without knowing why they're reacting to you the way they do. Likewise, before you say anything to anyone, you must engage your Conscious Mind and review your reaction or response.

Positive mindset and the mental image are vital aspects of healing our separation with self. The challenge in doing this is that you must clear all the programs and sub-personalities that cause you to operate from a negative mindset. If you don't, the only way you can override a negative mindset is with sheer willpower, but this will not last long unless you keep pumping yourself up.

My experience, and that of many others with whom I've worked, is that keeping up the pumping is hard without an occasional seminar so that you can work with the group energy. But I noticed that when I went to a seminar, I'd feel pumped up for a couple of weeks, but then my energy would start dropping. When I finally cleared most of the programs that negated my positive feelings, I noticed that the energy never dropped again. Many others have reported the same feeling.

Each time an emotional reaction happens between two people, an instantaneous chemical chain reaction causes a change in both people's bodies. Neuropeptides transmit a message to each cell in your body based how you react or respond to the sensory input from the interaction. If it's positive, the message causes an enhancing, supportive effect in you. If it's a negative, angry or fearful interaction, it triggers a damaging effect on your immune and endocrine systems.

Each time you let the interaction happen, you create a new pattern on top of the original program, which reinforces it. The more it happens, the easier it is for you to repeat the reaction. You have no choice; you *will* react according to the program without your conscious control. This becomes cellular memory. If it continues, it will eventually create pain in your body. This message tells you that you must take control and correct the reaction, provided of course you can understand the message. More information on this theory and the processes to correct the programs will be given in my forthcoming book *Mind/Body Medicine Connection: PsychoNeuroImmunology in Practice* (to be published in late spring 2001).

At this point, your Middle Self's autopilot has control and you will be under its authority until you recognize the programmed reaction. If your soap opera has a payoff for you, however, you may not want to recognize the illusion, and you will interpret the emotional interaction as love, attention, or approval. The sooner you're willing to see and own your dysfunctional behavior, however, the sooner you will move through transformation.

You must stop and recognize the situation immediately, for it has already triggered a chemical change in your body. Once you know how to detach from your emotional reactions, you have thirty seconds to stop them and choose to detach from them. If you cannot recognize or stop the reaction, you will create another blockage in your body/mind.

Therefore, each time you react to a sensory or emotional stimulus, it becomes easier for your Middle Self's sub-personalities and autopilot to take control next time and repeat the same reaction. Repeated chemical changes affect the body, depressing your immune and endocrine systems, eventually causing physical or emotional pain that will result in illness or disease. Remember, you will remain a victim until you recognize that something isn't working in your life.

If you're unable to see a problem, it doesn't exist for you, so the first step is to recognize and own your denial. If you can't do that, you won't see the need for change. If you're unwilling to discipline yourself to do something about the problem before it reaches a crisis stage, the inner dialogue will continue until it causes a dysfunction in the body and/or the mind.

This is the concept behind Neuro/Cellular Repatterning (N/CR), which finds the source and original cause of dysfunctional behavior. N/CR also reveals your reaction and the instructions your Middle Self and autopilot gave you for the behavior pattern that resulted from the abuse or action.

I find that most of my clients respond out of fear or anger, and project it out on other people, who then become their victims. N/CR works on the contention that clients can recover from the results of these compulsive obsessive behavior patterns by recognizing that they did the best they could at the time based on their then current interpretation and understanding.

Most people will react to establish control of a situation, or to protect themselves against attack or loss of control. It may only be a *perception* of attack, but if people feel fear or anger, they will react no matter whether it's real or imaginary, right or wrong. At the point of reaction, they're not thinking about the final outcome, but only their feelings in the moment. The counter-dependent (top dog) will attack. The codependent will cave in to abuse. But rather than point blame, we must forgive them, love them unconditionally and release them completely.

Forgiving everyone in your past and giving them the opportunity to forgive themselves releases you from the bondage of the past. Also forgive yourself and love yourself for letting it happen. Taking responsibility for your actions puts you completely in control your life.

Just as we broadcast a negative self-image, when we claim our personal power, others will respond accordingly. Showing others that we feel all right and love ourselves will signal that to other people, who will then acknowledge our all-rightness and treat us accordingly. The key is the committment to taking responsibility and then disciplining yourself to follow through every time. If you fail to anticipate a situation or make a mistake, do not berate yourself, but simply forgive yourself, knowing that you will see it next time.

One of my clients, Bob, was really being put to the test. He had made the commitment to watch his feelings and be aware of his sensory input at all levels and at all times. His intent in doing this was to respond in a positive manner to every situation that came up. His first test came when he was in a bar with some friends and felt outside of the group. His interpretation was that the women they had met would not be interested in talking with him. His past behavior had been to shut down and get drunk to deaden the rejection and the "I'm not acceptable" feeling.

When the same feeling came up on this occasion, however, he did not allow it to take over or make him hide behind alcohol. He sat back and observed his feelings and the emotion that came up. He didn't yet know how to counter the feeling and step out of the downward spiral, but at least he managed to go into his observer self and stop it from taking over. In his next session with me, we cleared the childhood trauma that was behind his feeling left out. Since we knew what the catalyst was, backtracking to the cause was easy.

The next test came the following week when Jim, his supervisor, began to berate him for no reason. Again, Bob went into observer mode and decided he wouldn't take the bait and simply let Jim unload. He noticed that he was not feeling attacked, rejected, or not all right. Nor was he reacting in any emotional manner. When Jim seemed to have finished, Bob calmly asked, "Are you done unloading your anger?"

This put the stop to Jim's dialogue immediately. Bob then asked, "Did unloading like that make you happy?"

Jim was speechless, for he couldn't answer the question in any way that wouldn't negatively implicate him. At that point, Bob asked, "How would you like to end this in a win-win situation for both of us?"

When Jim nodded, Bob said, "It's already a win for me because I didn't feel upset nor did I enter into the argument with you. We can make it a win for you by understanding who upset you so much that you had to find someone lower in the pecking order to unload on. I'm not the office chicken in the pecking order and nor do I appreciate being dumped on."

Jim then apologized and regained his composure.

"Who did make you so angry, Jim?" Bob asked.

"My wife just called me up and chewed my ear out. She does this all the time. I can't say anything back or she just gets more intense. When I go home tonight, though, she'll have forgotten all about it."

"Sounds like she needs a therapist to help her find out what's caus-ing her anger," Bob said.

"I've suggested that but she denies that there's anything wrong."

"Well that ends that then. You need some help yourself, though, so you can learn how to deal with how she makes you feel so that you can become non-reactive like I was. Now you need to forgive your wife for her behavior and forgive yourself for unloading on me."

After Bob showed his boss how to do that, Jim felt much better. Bob gave him my number, but will he seek help? I doubt it. He never called me, anyway. But at least Bob no longer gets tested on these situations, as he passed the test with this encounter.

There are only two types of people: *survivors* and *victims*. Survivors understand that they must keep going regardless of the odds, and push forward through any pain. Victims do not take responsibility and cannot therefore have control of their lives. Somebody or something always seems to be standing in their way.

There are only two ways to live in this life: *love and peace*, or *fear and anger*. There is no lack of love in the world, but many people cut themselves off from this source of love. It's our inheritance and we're entitled to it, but we must forgive ourselves and give love to ourselves.

Quite often, we're drawn into a conflict because we feel we must defend ourselves, but there's no need to take the bait every time. Suppose a person is unloading on you, as with Bob. Just listen and know that it's a call for help. When the person appears to finish, ask, "Are you done with your monologue or do you have anything more to say?" If he or she is done, ask, "Did what you just said make you happy?"

Because there's no way to answer this question positively, the person is pushed to reevaluate what he or she said. You can add, "This could be a win-win situation for both of us if we can discuss the matter in a reasonable manner and come to a resolution as to why it began."

Verbal conflict is usually about controlling the situation or conversation, or feeling you have been put down so you have find someone lower on the pecking order.

Never engage in an argument, as it solves nothing. It's just a power play to gain control. You may be defending on principle, but it turns into a no-win situation. If you are the power controller, you must look at why do you need to be right all the time. If you're on the receiving end of someone else's power play, ask yourself why you engage in these emotional forays? Arguments will always degenerate into heated emotional exchanges in which there has to be a winner and a loser. To make it a win-win situation, excuse yourself from the interaction or just listen passively as did my client.

Affirmations for Mastering Emotions

The conceptual pattern for the process is:

1. I accept that I am a new person and am releasing the past. I now live in the moment. I create my life by what I say to myself each minute of every day.

2. I create my own reality. I let go of denial, control and justification. I am honest with myself and others. I walk my talk. I alone am responsible for how I feel. I do not blame you for my feelings now or in the future.

3. I am beginning a new life. I am allowing the old self to die and pass away. I am being reborn and intend to be a different person. I want you to notice that and recognize that I have let go of the past. Do not hold me in my past; I am a new person. I now recognize emotions as attempts to take control, manipulate or justify my behavior. I am committed to detach from that behavior now.

4. I recognize my own love as an individual. I do not depend on you to love me and accept me. I will not act or think less of you nor give you less attention. My commitment is to love you more and accept you as you are.

5. My independence does not mean I reject you in any way. I now love more. I am committed to our relationship. I am willing to be interdependent with you. I am willing to support and be with you but not cripple you.

6. I am committed to establishing my own self-worth and require others to recognize and respect my self-worth. I do feel guilt when you feel neglected, although I would like to know your feelings and will care and adjust my life so that our relationship can succeed. I will not allow anyone to be codependent on me for love. I will care with unconditional love and respect and will contribute all I can to our relationship, but I will not accept any guilt or blame for improving my relationship with myself. My goals are to establish healthy self-esteem and self-worth. If you choose not to participate, I will understand that. I will not feel rejected if you choose another path. I will continue to love you.

Affirmation for Taking Responsibility (Long Form)

"I want you to know that I am taking responsibility for myself and the way I feel. Making me feel accepted or loved is not your responsibility. I do not need your approval to be all right; that's my responsibility and I accept it now. I know that I am loved and will be loved at all times, consistently, whether you love me or not. I would like your love, but it's not required for me to be all right. I love you unconditionally as you are. I am not going to make you responsible for my happiness. That is my responsibility. Nothing you can do will make me unhappy or hurt; that is my responsibility. I know in the past that I tended to base my self-esteem on other people's approval. I have blamed you and projected on you my need to feel all right. I am now responsible for how I feel and I know that I am acceptable, loved and all right."

Affirmation for Taking Responsibility (Short Form)

Use this form when you are communicating with someone and sense your self-talk in the background is sabotaging you, or you need to stop the negative reaction in a conversation.

"You are not responsible for how I feel. Nothing you can say will change that. I know I am accepted, loved and all right, no matter how you react or feel about me. I accept you as you are. I love and forgive you unconditionally. I would like you to do the same for me but, if you are unable, that is all right."

The conceptual pattern of both affirmations states how we want to live our lives as spiritual beings. We want other people to understand that they have no control over us. The long form specifies what you say to yourself to affirm your new direction in life. If you write out the affirmation to change your programming, use the long form. Say the short form, either to the person with whom you're involved or to your-self (as appropriate) whenever a feeling of rejection comes up or your self-talk starts to say, "I am not all right," "I am not accepted" "I feel guilty," "They are or he/she is rejecting me," etc. You may not be able to say this out loud verbally because the person you are talking with may not understand what you're trying to accomplish. If so, repeat it internally.

You may need to write out the affirmation in long-hand to get it to work for you, typically 21 times a day for 21 days. This transfers it kinesthetically to your mind. (It must be hand-written, for a typing on a keyboard will not achieve results.) If it's not locked after 21 days, keep going, even up to 40 days.

Finally, remember that you must have installed Ego (file manager) before doing any affirmations.

15

A Nine-Step Process for Mastering Emotions

It may seem that emotions happen to you as a result of the actions or attitudes of others, but they don't *happen* to you. They are a goal-oriented activity, something you *do*, expecting to elicit a particular response from another person, or produce a certain result in a given situation. Emotions seek to achieve something.

There are no positive emotions; love, joy, and happiness are not emotions but *feelings*. Feelings can and do precipitate into emotions. Love, joy and happiness do not trigger negative emotional responses.

Only when you accept this concept of emotions can you reclaim your lost personal power. You see the actions, reactions, and emotions of other people for what they are, instead of as personal attacks on you. Imagine how much better you would feel every second of your life if other people could no longer trigger strong, negative emotional reactions in you.

At workshops with Paul Solomon, I learned an invaluable nine-step process. (I don't know whether he developed it or relayed it from another source, but whatever the source, I extend my gratitude to the Universe and Paul for providing this information.)

The intent of this process is to reprogram those feelings that activate emotions. If you follow this process and commit to using the steps, they will walk you through emotions so that you can understand why you engage in the particular behavior pattern. It is better if you can find the cause for each emotional pattern and trace it back to the root cause but, even if you can't, the process will still work. A certain person or incident may be the *catalyst* that causes the emotion to surface, but that is not the *cause*. The cause is always within you. It's got your name on it, and you cannot blame it on someone else.

I have interpreted and named the steps, and can attest to their power. Before using the process, first you must commit to becoming a *master* (see Part 1). This process is about making your Subconscious Mind become conscious. (Remember to install the file manager program so Ego can retrieve the files for you.) Please do not assume that, just because you have learned the process, it's automatically working in your life. Just like everything else, *you must make it work!*

The 9-step process is not about *suppressing* emotion. If an emotion is appropriate and serves you, go ahead and express it, taking full responsibility for the outcome. The process is for understanding your emotions and for ensuring that they are appropriate in a given situation. (For best results, use the Validation of Worth section in your journal. See Journal Process in the exercise section of part 6.)

The Nine Steps are:
1. Recognize your moment of decision.
2. Describe the emotion honestly, accurately and *negatively!*
3. Accept responsibility for your action.
4. Objectively identify the catalyst of the emotional response.
5. Identify the real cause of your response.
6. Identify the validity of the belief.
7. Identify your "carrot," or payoff.
8. Determine the cause/effect relationship between action and carrot.
9. Select and act out a more appropriate action.

Let's look at each one of these nine steps in detail, and please remember that for a real working wisdom of the process, you must apply it in your life. If it doesn't work at first, keep trying, for *the process does work.* Maybe seek some help, so that you can add this incredible tool to your toolbox. As with everything, the more you use it, the better it will work for you.

Step 1: Recognize your moment of decision

There is a particular moment in a situation when you decide to respond emotionally. It is important that you recognize and own that you're doing this, for denial is far more common than we realize. Try to catch the moment of the emotion's onset, and do not deny with, "I'm not mad," "I'm not irritable," "I'm not jealous," or, "I'm not upset."

Step 2: Describe the emotion honestly, accurately and *negatively!*

Suppose you hear that a group of acquaintances has been laughing at you behind your back. Instead of saying, "I am angry," speak the truth. For example, say, "I don't like the way they are acting towards me and feel belittled, so I want to manipulate them into acting differently in order for me to feel better." It is not anyone's responsibility to make you feel better. This must be an inside job. You have to do that.

In other words, examine what you're *really* feeling. Don't use socially acceptable labels such as anger, jealousy, or depression. Describe your emotions in socially unacceptable terms, so you see them as they really are. Most people do not own up to how they really feel and try to suppress the feeling. You must recognize in negative format how you *really* feel in order to change the behavior.

This process teaches you that, when you see others expressing emotions, you see those emotions as actions they choose. When others see you expressing emotion, they know it's something you're doing by choice. No longer can you claim that an emotion is something that just *happens* to you, as if you were its victim.

Step 3: Accept responsibility for your action

Instead of saying, "You hurt my feelings," notice that what's *really* happening is that you're choosing to feel hurt in response to the other's words or actions. You could interpret them differently, or you could choose any number of other feelings. *But your choice is to feel hurt.* So be honest and accept responsibility for what your choice. Say, for example, "I assume total responsibility for what I choose to feel and express. What they did may be wrong, but it does not obligate me to any particular response. I engaged in this action because I wanted a payoff. I wanted them to recognize what they did was not right."

Step 4: Objectively identify the catalyst of the emotional response

Ascertain exactly what caused you to decide to react with an emotional reaction. Describe as objectively as possible what triggered your action. The catalyst—a group laughing at you, say—may be what you *think* caused your emotion, but it's not necessarily the *real* cause of your response. It is just a catalyst. Your Middle Self went into the files and asked Ego to bring up the program from the past that applied to the situation. Every emotion has a catalyst attached to it. It will be activated first.

Step 5: Identify the real cause of your response

The real cause of your emotional action is a belief you hold about the catalyst. Because of your belief about the catalyst, you feel you must respond in a certain way to get a particular result or to rectify the situation. The beliefs that trigger strong emotional responses are usually *irrational* and are the result of the programming in your Subconscious Mind, for example, laid down, say, when the other kids would laugh at you in the schoolyard. When consciously examined, your beliefs may well change. For example, you may uncover the belief that, whenever any group of people laugh together, they're laughing at you. Many times it comes down to inaccurate interpretations that were made by your Middle Self when you were a child.

Step 6: Identify the validity of the belief

To identify your belief about the catalyst may very well be the most difficult step in this process. You have usually hidden these irrational beliefs in denial or denial-of-denial in order to avoid responsibility for acting in a more mature manner; i.e., to avoid growing into a responsible adult. Now you must examine the validity of the belief. Is your belief about the catalyst rational and is the emotion a valid response? Usually the answer to both questions is a resounding, "No!"

Step 7: Identify your "carrot," or payoff

Your carrot (often called your payoff, reward, etc.) is the result you hope to get from your emotional action. For example, a wife expresses anger in order to elicit her husband's appreciation for her hard work in preparing a meal. When he doesn't notice, she becomes sullen and angry. What's her carrot? At first, she just wanted a simple compliment. Now, however, she wants an apology and contrition. She wants more now for the extra trouble of expressing an emotional reaction.

Identifying your particular carrot may be easy or difficult. You may want to feel better than someone else, want control of a person or situation (anger), want power from someone, maintain the status quo (no change in your life), avoid responsibility, hide from someone or something, make someone feel guilty, transfer responsibility to someone else, live in a fantasy world, or be taken care of by someone else; the list is endless. For example, your carrot may be that if you let the group know that you feel hurt, they will invite you to join them, and you can obtain their approval of you.

In general, a carrot is something that allows you to stay in your present situation and avoid growing up. If you cannot find your carrot, it's because you don't want to get rid of it yet. If you cannot find your carrot after honestly searching for it, check to see if you're still in victim mode. Odds are, you will be.

Step 8: Determine the cause/effect relationship between action and carrot

Is the action likely to produce the result you want? If not, what's the likely result of your action? Do you want to produce that result? Is your emotion working positively and constructively for you? Does the emotion get your carrot? Do you still want that particular carrot?

For example, you feeling hurt may just provoke the group to more laughter. Laughing back in return may be more positive for your growth.

Oftentimes, your response will get a carrot that you no longer desire, but you have acted out that particular response so many times that you keep doing it, even after the old carrot is no longer attractive, so now your response to the situation must change.

Step 9: Select and act out a more appropriate action

If the emotion/action you have taken doesn't work for you, or if it makes you suffer and even then fails to produce the desired result, you may now want to be aware of that cause/effect relationship in the future. You may want to select a more appropriate response to such a catalyst. This would involve a change in beliefs, a change of behavior in the same situation, and a change of behavior patterns in general. It becomes your responsibility to locate that time line and bring it up so we can delete the program and script a new one.

As we saw in the example in the previous chapter, Bob selected a new appropriate action by not entering into the attack or defending himself to Jim. It created a win-win situation for both people.

By using the process regularly, you will see that you have a standard set of carrots you try to get from everyone around you. Love, acceptance, validation, recognition, peace, happiness, harmony and joy come not from other people, but from within. By trying to get from others what they don't yet have and couldn't give you anyway, you only compromise yourself. You decide to give your personal power away to others (who are willing to use their power, usually against you). You will not sense love, acceptance, peace and harmony from others unless they already have those qualities in their lives. People who feel that they are not being given acceptance, validation and recognition cannot give it to someone else.

When you exhibit the qualities of acceptance, validation, recognition, love, joy, happiness and harmony in *your* life, the people who can give you those responses back will do so since they see them in you. It is unfortunate that most people so not feel strong enough to reach out to those people who need it most.

Using emotions to try to elicit these desirable qualities leads only to frustration and more acting out of negative emotions. Remember, if an emotion serves you in a given situation, continue to express it until its time is done, then drop it cleanly and clearly, and move on. Dare to live an emotional life, but recognize that *emotions are goal-oriented behavior* designed to draw a reaction. Change those emotions that don't serve you and continue to progress. Remember, emotions are all negative in their reaction. There are no positive emotions. Feelings are positive unless they proceed to emotions where they become negative. Feelings of peace, happiness, joy, harmony and love are not emotions but positive feelings.

Some Suggested Definitions of Major Emotions*

- *Fear*: Entertaining a fantasy of a danger that has not occurred; false evidence appearing real.
- *Anger*: Loss of control over others or the situation and an attempt to regain it.
- *Hate*: Protection of self when not feeling safe with a loved one; misplaced expression of love, loving against.
- *Worry/Anxiety*: Incapacitating self to avoid preparing for a situation; avoidance of responsibility.
- *Guilt*: Indulging in concern over a past event to avoid taking action now; unexpressed anger.
- *Hurt*: Denial of responsibility for own feelings; feeling another isn't acting as you want.
- *Rejection*: An unsuccessful attempt to gain approval, love and acceptance.
- *Self-pity*: Indulging in helplessness to get attention; substitute for self-love.

- *Jealousy*: Misidentification and feelings of inadequacy and insecurity towards a competitor; fear of loss, which may or may not be true; wanting to control or have possession.
- *Resentment*: Anger or fear about a situation over which you have no control.
- *Grief*: Loss of control over a source of attention or love; inability to let go in loss.
- *Self-righteousness, indignation, contempt, disdain*: Feeling superior in order to feel secure, in control; "better than" to satisfy need for acceptability.
- *Shyness*: Waiting for someone else to give you attention and approval.
- *Regret*: Feeling inferior because of perceived inadequacy.
- *Confusion, Indecision:* Laziness of mind to avoid dealing with situation; avoidance of responsibility.
- *Boredom*: Not taking responsibility for your own happiness or entertainment; autopilot.
- *Loneliness*: Placing responsibility for your happiness on someone else; lack of self-esteem.
- *Homesickness*: Placing responsibility for your happiness on *someplace else* as your security.
- *Embarrassment*: Worry about others' opinion of you; lack of self-worth and self-esteem.
- *Hopelessness*: Usually associated with self-pity; refusal to take responsibility for self.
- *Arrogance*: Feelings of separateness and superiority to enhance self-worth and self-esteem.
- *Judgment*: Observing a situation in negative manner (many times attached to self-righteousness).
- *Abandonment*: Feeling left out or rejected by a loved one.
- *Indifference*: Not an emotion but the most incapacitating form of rejection one can feel.

Parts excerpted from information and material developed by the Paul Solomon Foundation, Virginia Beach, VA.

Sensory/Thought Communication Processing Patterns

NEW SENSORY INPUT
(Visual, auditory, touch)
NEW THOUGHT FORMS
(Creative/inventive theory)

PROCESSING DIALOGUE
(Negative/positive thought forms.
Flashback memories.
Misinterpretations)

2. INTERPRETATION

Processing through the
Subconscious Minds computer
records and programs for past
reactions or responses.

⑩

3. ASSIGNMENT OF FEELING

Determination of action to take
based on your belief of what the
perceived effect will be on you.
You make an instant decision,
following it to a final result.

4. CATALYST

Fear/anger rises, giving away
your personal power. Loss of
control pushes you into the
emotional reaction, into denial
of self, and into illusion.

5. NO CHOICE/NO DECISION

You review how you handled
reactions to similar situations
acting out this victim feeling
with no control. The feeling is
based in fear of threat, rejection
abandonment, loss, jealousy,
anger, loss of control, etc.

6. EMOTIONAL REACTION

1. Flight=fear, run from feeling
2. Fight=anger, defense/blowup
3. Justification/defensiveness,
   stuffing feelings & emotions
4. No reaction, repress feelings

7. DENIAL/JUSTIFICATION

Falling back into the illusion of
past denial, assuming/justifying
that your behavior is an accurate
truthful way to handle situations.
The lesson will return.

8. RECYCLE LESSON

Do I want to feel/react this
way now and in the future?

⑨

10. CHOICE/DECISION

I choose to snap out of denial, illusion & justification. I will not act out, repress, react or control. I have 30 seconds to recognize the anger/fear, detach from the emotion or go into recycle.

③

12. DENIAL REACTION

Inability to maintain control of responses. Loss of control pushes you into emotion. You recycle lesson again.

11. RESPONSE

You review the possible avenues and responses to handle the situation with acceptance, love, and forgiveness. You detach from potential emotion immediately.

9. RECOGNITION OF DENIAL

1. Review ineffective behavior.
2. Recognize lesson's effect.
3. Move to recovery and write new program for Subconscious Mind.
4. Change the negative justifying reactions to positive responses.
5. Loving and forgiving yourself.
6. Shift from victim to cause.
7. Recognize you create lessons.

13. DETACHMENT

1. I don't have or need to have authority or control over anyone.
2. I am not threatened. I don't need to attack, be attacked, or defend myself in any way.
3. I can respond in a positive way to every feeling &person.
4. I always respond with love, kindness, and foregiveness.
5. I am all right under in all situations. My self-esteem, self-worth are not affected by this.

14. TRANSFORMATION

Unconditional love, peace, harmony, happiness and joy. Release of fear, control judgement, and justification.

Self-Empowerment

Assertiveness vs. Aggressiveness

When we begin to master emotions, we are ready to take our power back. The next challenge is self-empowerment. We all have a right to be heard and understood, expressing ourselves and feeling good about doing so. How we achieve this depends on our ability to communicate effectively and discern between assertive and aggressive behavior, yet very few people know the difference.

Nonassertive Behavior

The dictionary defines an *assertive* person as one who expresses boldly, positively and confidently. Now, *nonassertive* people will perceive assertive behavior as *aggressive* because they are afraid to stand up for themselves and are self-denying. The goals of a nonassertive person are to always be accepted and validated, and to avoid rejection at any cost. The result of this behavior pattern is to be a *human doing*. They feel they have to do something to get acceptance, and will appease and placate, anything to make other people happy so they will give them acceptance and approval. They are codependent, feel powerless and guilty, and get hurt easily when they perceive another as rejecting them, even though the other's behavior is not aimed at them. They tend to tell people what they want to hear rather than say what they want to say so that they will not put themselves in the vulnerable position of being rejected.

The common ailment of non-assertive people is shoulder pain—bursitis, rotator cup and even muscle pain in the arms just below the shoulder. Most do not question authority and, as a result, are followers rather than leaders. Many people go to the grave in this state, but others wake up when they realize they have been living their life through other people.

Parents will live their life through their children, trying to please them so the children will give them acceptance. Quite often they feel guilty because their children strayed off the path into drugs or alcohol, or the children did not achieve the level education the parents felt they should. As a parent myself, I realized that, when children reach the age of 18, we have done all we can. If we have made mistakes in raising them, we must forgive ourselves and move on.

Many of my clients spend their lives trying to prove to their parents they are acceptable, even long after the parents are dead and gone. This is a vicious circle, however, because we will treat our children as our parents treated us, unless we can wake up and realize that we do not need to prove anything to anyone, and nor do we need the validation of other people. Instead, we must learn to validate and empower ourselves. Nobody can do it for us.

Assertive Behavior

The opposite of the nonassertive "human doings" are the *human beings* who know that all they need do is to *be*, and that they can have in their lives what they choose. They are bold and decisive leaders. They know they are entitled to be accepted, acknowledged and supported and, deep down, they accept *themselves* unconditionally. And because of the self-image that these people radiate, other people naturally respond in like manner through the law of resonance.

Of course, many people try to "fake" it by *willing* themselves through life to *appear* as if they know what they're doing. Eventually, however, the thin veneer cracks on them because you cannot force yourself through life in a way that is counter to your true personality without the stress eventually causing a breakdown—mental, emotional or physical, and often all three.

Many people look down on assertive behavior, seeing it as bullying just to get your way. These people cannot see the difference between aggressiveness and assertiveness. Assertive people will not in any way try to take advantage or put another person in a compromising position. They always try to create a win-win situation so every one is treated evenly.

On the other hand, aggressive people are only looking out for number one, have to be right and get their way in any given situation, and strive for win-lose outcomes. Who you are is irrelevant to them, and they will step over you to reach their goals. In fact, *aggression* is defined as "hostile, invasive, attacking, or quarrelsome behavior that is injurious and distressing to its targets."

They are usually counter-dependents, which makes their behavior a front to protect themselves and their pitifully fragile reality. If a strong, assertive person confronts them, after an initial show of bravado, they usually crash and run. Some will fight to the end but they are few and far between.

The exception to this are people who are being aggressive to protect themselves. Most aggressive people are also compulsive/obsessive and often react without thinking. They are operating out of fear, feeling everyone is trying to take advantage of them, so they "do unto others before others can do unto them." Most of the time they do not know they are reacting this way, because it is an autopilot survival tactic.

Few aggressive people will tell the truth about how they feel because they do not really know themselves how they feel about a situation. Most of the time, their feelings are stuffed so deeply in denial-of-denial they do not understand why they are acting out to protect themselves. But their behavior clearly reveals their self-image and how they really feel.

A case in point is one my clients whom we'll call Jenny. Her marriage to husband James ran perfectly smoothly as long as it adhered to traditional husband and wife roles. When the children left home to begin their adult lives, Jenny wanted to begin a career, so she went back to college. James was supportive of this endeavor until she graduated and took a job that meant she was not home as much. James' resistance grew, and he began constantly complaining that dinner was not ready when he arrived home, that the housework was suffering, and she was not helping him anymore. He began to ask her to run extra time-consuming errands in order to furnish himself with additional complaint ammunition.

Jenny tried to appease him, but when that failed to work, she finally confronted him about her working but he denied that he had any resistance. Jenny asked me, "How do I handle this because his complaining is getting worse, but he refuses to own up to his behavior?"

What we discovered was that James was all right with her as a "mousy homemaker" but felt threatened when Jenny became assertive, empowered herself, and stood up to reclaim her personal power.

We began by releasing all the programs about a women's role according to her parents' viewpoint that she had accepted from childhood. However, the more she asserted herself and took on the role she wanted to pursue, the more threatened James felt. He was afraid of her becoming equal to him and usurping his role as the "authority" in the family. Also, as her financial independence grew, he began to worry that she would leave him. None of this was true, of course, but fears were making the marriage unmanageable.

Jenny tried to get him to go to counseling to deal with his fear but he refused. Over time, however, she was able to become strong enough to let him fret about in his fear without letting it bother her. When he realized that the imagined threats were not manifesting, he let go of some of his fear, which made the marriage sufficiently workable for them to get along. She did whatever errands and housework she had time for but let James know that she was not just his gofer whom he could control.

Reclaiming Your Personal Power

To get to empowerment, you must reclaim your personal power. Once you get there, then you can be assertive. The process involves letting go of the past programs you accepted from your parents and society's viewpoint about how you should act in a given role. Everything is being turned upside down now. I support the intentions of the National Organization of Women (NOW) but disagree with some of the methods they use.

It seems as if about 85 percent of the population is on autopilot, and assumes that everything is just perfect the way it is. For example, a man came to my lecture out of curiosity. He had seen my flyer about reclaiming personal power and after the lecture he asked me, "Do you know many people who go through life feeling empty, as if each day was the same as the last? After listening to your presentation, I feel as if my life is hollow. It has all the right outer indicators but inside I feel empty. I didn't realize that there could be so much more to life than this competition to win all the outside status symbols of power and position. I have all the things one could want in life, such as the million-dollar home, cars, yachts, memberships to the golf club, the tennis club, and the yacht club. But that doesn't give me a sense of accomplishment anymore. I feel as if I'm just the workaholic 'moneybags' who exists simply to support my family, and they expect it. How do I get off this merry-go-round?"

In his first session, we began to unwind the programs that were driving his behavior. We found a childhood of rejection and non-acceptance. In one way, his was a functional family as his parents treated him properly, but they did not know what love was, or how to validate a child. So he excelled in school, becoming a super-student trying to prove to his parents that he was all right. However, they never seemed to approve of all his achievements in school. He got into a good university, which his parents paid for. But once he was out of the family home, he was on his own emotionally because all his parents did was write the checks. What saved him was that he was a survivor. When he made his mind up that he could do something, he invariably did it, which is how he arrived in his present situation. He has built his company into a successful enterprise but now feels that, in continually winning the battles of business and money, he's lost something along the way but has no idea what.

We found that, as in childhood, no one in his family appreciated him. The point here is you will never escape the lessons put before you. They will dog you in every endeavor until you face them. I suggested, "Go home and have a conference with your wife and children. Ask them what they want out of the future."

At our next session, he reported, "All my kids want is for me to continue paying for their education so they don't have to take on a part-time job when they attend college. My wife can't see anything wrong with her life the way it is. I asked her to read those books you suggested and she refused, saying she didn't have enough time. I told her, 'All you do is run around with your friends and go to the clubs. Everything is provided for you around the house. You don't have to do a thing, and yet you tell me you don't have the time. Why don't you just say you don't *want* to read them?' "

When he came to our next session, he was frustrated because none of his family wanted to talk about his newfound interest in spirituality. His children thought he was weird and his wife wanted nothing to do with it. He asked me, "Where do I go now?"

I replied, "Are you happy with all the people you associate with at your clubs?"

"No, they're all hollow, just like I used to be."

"Then why do you continue to attend their functions?

"I'm not, and that's creating considerable friction with my wife because they are her life. Where do I go from here?"

"Well, there are activities you could attend, such as a spiritual church, study groups and various workshops and other activities."

He began to attend them, meet more spiritual people, work on changing his outlook on life and creating new awareness of how he could be assertive and stand up for what he wanted in life. This caused a major directional change. He came to the next session with a pronouncement. "I decided to take your advice and become proactive in my life. I decided it was time to empower myself and become assertive. I told my wife, 'If you feel that our life is acceptable the way it is, then I'm leaving because it's not acceptable to me. I don't want anything to do with all the shallow, hollow people you associate with. There is more to life than money and status."

"How did she react?" I asked.

"She couldn't understand me at all. It was as if she hadn't listened to a thing I'd said over the past months. It shook her up, of course, but she wasn't willing to change, so I'm out of there. I asked her give me a figure of how much she wanted to settle and we would get a divorce. She could keep the house and the cars and all her clubs, but I'm not going to pay the dues after this year."

"So where are you going from here?"

"I am not sure at this point. I've moved on to the boat and will keep the yacht club membership as I have common interests with some of the other members."

"How about your children? How are they reacting?"

"I called them to tell them that since they thought I was weird and didn't want anything to do with my new life, I was going to continue to be weird. When my youngest graduates with his B.A., his financial support for college ends. My other two are in graduate school and their support ends with this school year. If they want to finish, they'll have to get jobs or grants to support themselves. 'Daddy deep-pockets' is stepping out of their lives. Is that empowerment or what?"

"Where are you going from here?" I asked again.

"I'm setting my company up so I can work part-time and begin to enjoy my life. I don't need to be a workaholic. I'll let that go. I no longer have to prove anything to anyone."

"How is your wife dealing with this new turn in her life?"

"Not very well. She now knows that I won't be there to handle everything so that she can run around with her friends. You know, Art, I really don't care how she deals with her life. But she'll have be careful with money from now on because we made a lump-sum settlement in lieu of alimony."

This case is interesting because here is a person who was nonassertive in his personal life, yet was highly successful in business because he was willing himself through life as a workaholic. Then he made a 180-degree turn and restructured his life totally, working part-time and living on his boat in a marina. He is now happy with where he is. Self-empowerment is the key, but you must let go of all the programs that are driving the dysfunctional behavior before you can become assertive.

The courage to change is tough to muster up for many people because it puts them in jeopardy of being rejected by others if they stand up for themselves. Vulnerability is a state most people do not want to get into, yet it is where we *must* go if we are to become liberated from fear. Getting to the point where you can trust that you will make the right decision is also hard. I know this one well because, in the past, I would start a project but never finish it because if I did, I believed that I would be held responsible for executing it perfectly. For example, once I removed a wall in order to open up the kitchen in our house, and it sat unfinished for three years. That way, no one could pass judgment on me about the finished quality.

Ironically, the person whose opinion I most feared was that of my father who had died years before. He was a perfectionist and, according to him, I never did anything right. Sometimes I would sabotage myself in a job so that I could get put down for not doing it right. I knew I could do the job right because I did do so quite often, yet I would do things that I knew were not perfect in an effort to set myself up for rejection. We will do whatever it takes to get us validated according to our self-image. Regardless of what we would *like* to do, we will sabotage ourselves until we get the lesson.

Your mind will set you up to get the lesson no matter how hard you try to avoid it. However, now that I have empowered myself to know that there is not a judge and jury out there just waiting to criticize me, this no longer happens. If someone doesn't approve of what I do, it makes no difference anymore. You must achieve your all-rightness before you can reclaim your self-esteem and empower yourself. Once you do that, you put a firewall between you and the emotions that criticism brings up. Once we get through this lesson, we no longer set ourselves up to fail.

One of the big steps is creating boundaries for yourself. People who are codependent let others walk all over them because they have no boundaries. They want to be accepted so much that they allow people to do things that an assertive person would not tolerate. Another aspect of boundaries is the ability to stop people from projecting their feelings or interpretations on you. When you are in your own power, you can stand within your boundaries and tell yourself, "This is not my issue, and it does not affect me because I have no need to defend myself." When you do not feel vulnerable, you are not subject to attack.

Those without personal courage do not own their reactions to things and try to pin them on others. For example, a client once told me, "I'm afraid to say what I want to my partner because I know what his reaction will be."

My response was, "Are you really sure, or are you projecting this from a prior relationship where it did happen? Why not check it out by asking and see what his response is. You have empowered yourself enough to stand up for yourself so, if the reaction is as you feel it might be, it won't affect you. But you will have to see if you can make this a win-win situation for yourself before you can get through this lesson."

As it turned out, her interpretation was wrong, and her partner responded positively and listened to her without any criticism. In fact, he told her, "Your interpretation has often been off-base because many times I couldn't understand why you would cut a discussion short and change the subject with no reason."

Creative listening

One of the most important parts of empowerment is to empower other people by listening to them creatively. We all have the ability to think as we talk, yet most people are thinking about what they are going to say next even while the other person is still speaking. Even though our mind is taking in what the other is saying, another part of it is rehearsing what we're going to say next. As a result, we're not giving the other our full attention or consciously listening to what's being said. To those who are observant and recognize that you're not really listening, this can be disconcerting and they may drop the conversation. I often do this when I know I don't have the other person's attention.

Conversely those who monopolize conversations view the situation quite differently. Their motivation is the need for validation and acceptance, so they interpret other people letting them control the discussion as acceptance.

A case in point was a friend who had participated in many of my workshops and often facilitated events for me. However, she usually dominated any discussion of which she was a part. Because of her training, I assumed that she would be able to handle a gentle comment on her controlling conversations. One day, she had talked nonstop for over 45 minutes. I felt she might need the catharsis so I just let it go but, when she started repeating herself, I finally asked her if she would allow me to continue the class as she'd had the floor for almost an hour. This triggered a violent eruption because she was charged up with what she was telling us and felt that my comment was an affront to her. She jumped all over me because I had interrupted her. As she stormed out of the room, she announced that she would no longer facilitate my events, do any kind of work for me, or even be in my life. Two weeks later, she wrote me a letter telling me how arrogant I was and how I took advantage of people in conversations.

Her life has gone downhill continually since then, and she is currently on disability, living with her mother. The trouble with dealing with disempowered people is that you never know when you'll hit their weak point or how they'll react. Five years later, she still hasn't cleared this lesson, and I doubt that she will deal with it in this lifetime. According to a mutual friend, she has reached a plateau of denial now, so at least she is not sinking any further, but she's now living in a state of pure survival.

With the levels of anger prevalent today, we must be very aware of possible outcomes before we take an assertive stance. In the above example, I had no clue that the woman would react so explosively. She took the flight option of "fight-or-flight" but she could have gone the other way, which can result in rage.

With increasing road traffic levels, road rage is a relatively new but growing phenomenon in which drivers act out their stress in a physical manner. In Pennsylvania, road signs proclaim: BE CAREFUL OF ROAD RAGE. This warns both those with it and other drivers.

Before being assertive in a particular situation, we should observe the situation to see if it is appropriate, or whether we could trigger a fight-or-flight response. People can act out in ways that nobody would have thought possible 25 years ago. With the stress levels extremely high now, particularly after the recent terrorist attacks in New York City, people can go completely out of their rational mind, and even kill people in rage following say, being reprimanded or fired from their job.

There are no easy answers or quick fixes to these dilemmas in today's violence-prone society, so we just must be very observant of people's behavior and try to read them correctly before we respond. We must use appropriate caution, assess the situation, and take time to consider the possible consequences to our action. We must ask, "What do I expect to achieve from being assertive, and will it be received without overt reaction?"

But neither should we take the opposite reaction in order to avoid taking risks. Everything we do entails risk. We must just observe carefully and act appropriately. But, to avoid risks and conflict is to avoid living fully.

What Does Assertive Behavior Look Like?

The main quality of self-assertive people is they are not controllers. They do not need to have authority over anyone, or be the kingpin or the self-righteous know-it-all. Here are some qualities of assertive people:

- Self-expressive without commands
- Respectful of others rights
- Honest, direct and firm
- Ethical and in integrity
- Socially responsible
- Responds positively, but can be negative to make a point, but not demanding
- Behavior is appropriate for the situation or the person
- Able to listen without confronting
- Can be non-verbal, but very effective
- Non-judgmental
- No need to have authority over situation
- Always supports other people's right to self-expression

I find if you have no axes to grind and no attachment to a particular outcome, you can respond in an assertive manner. The catch is *detachment from the outcome*. Being attached to an outcome and having an expectation of what you want to happen will quite often backfire on you.

Also, your mind can deceive you if you do not believe in the action you are taking. We pick up other people's attitude from the meta-communication before they say anything, so we must be clear with ourselves about our intent, or that lack of clarity may backfire on us. Strength lies in the alignment between our outer behavior and our inner response, strength that we do not have if we are unclear about who we are.

A good example of this is seen in our interaction with animals. If you do not exhibit any fear of animals, they will respond in a friendly manner. If you exhibit fear, they pick up your fear, run it through their bodies, and may attack. (Exceptions to this are often found with animals who have been mistreated.)

We live in a rural setting and many people bicycle and jog along a path near our home. It is interesting to watch how our dogs react to the people who go by. With some, they growl and look as if they would attack but for the sturdy fence: with others, they just bark a greeting.

One of the best examples of this was a client who was a respected computer scientist whom we'll Jim. He was highly esteemed at his company and had good relationships with fellow workers but, in personal relationships, his score was very low. He always felt that he was "out of the loop." People would talk over him and around him but not involve him in the conversation. Normally when he went out socially with his colleagues, he felt left out so, to avoid the feelings of rejection, he would end up getting intoxicated.

In his first session, Jim told me, "I'm fed up with my behavior and want to make a major shift in my life. I'm willing to do anything you suggest if it will bring about change."

We spent several sessions clearing his childhood experiences so that we could level the playing field and tackle his major problem of feeling as if people reject him all the time. I suggested, "Keep track of your experiences with a journal. When an emotional experience comes up, document it and evaluate how you feel so that we can work it out in the next session."

Jim threw himself into the journaling project with abandon, and brought the following situation into a session. "I went to a local watering hole with my colleagues as I had done in the past. The same feelings came up as my buddies had a great time with women who were present but, as usual, everyone talked over me or around me even though I was right in the middle of the group. But, instead of getting drunk, I sat back and monitored my emotions and feelings to see if I could get a handle on the situation. I just can't figure out how I could be in the middle of the group but still be excluded."

So we began a search for the cause. What we found was that he was the younger of two children. His sister was six years older and she resented him intensely because, after he was born, he took all the attention from her. Their father gravitated to the boy, so she received little attention from him. She would fight with Jim and mistreat him all the time. When he complained to his mother, she did nothing to stop the turmoil. This led to an erroneous interpretation about girls and women. His mind set up a program to reject them so they would not be able to hurt him or reject him in the future. Over time, this program became established as an operation program in the Subconscious Mind.

We erased and deleted the program and installed a new one. The following week, he returned to the same bar and the whole scene had made a 180-degree shift. He was now in the middle of the group and all of the women were talking with him. He was now able to be assertive and join in the group where, only one week earlier, he'd been nonassertive and felt totally rejected from the group. Based on our subconscious programming, we project out to the world how we feel about ourselves, and people respond as we project to them how we want to be treated.

In addition, how we feel about ourselves controls our behavior. In a business setting involving computers, Jim could be very assertive because he knew the field and was secure in his knowledge and expertise. He could trust his ability and be very effective in discussions. In personal relationships, however, and especially those with women, he had no self-worth, self-esteem or self-confidence since the programs were of a different nature.

In the past, many times Jim's group supervisor would come to work and pick fights just to unload on people. In the past, Jim would take the bait, try to defend himself and get into an argument that he could never win. So we worked on detachment and non-reactive behavior to prime him. Jim's non-reaction called for him to sit and listen to his boss until he was done with his monologue. By not reacting, Jim's boss had no backboard to bounce off and couldn't figure out why he was not getting the usual reaction. After he was done, Jim asked him, "Are you done with your monologue now?"

There was no response from the boss as he couldn't understand, so Jim asked, "Can you answer the question. Yes or no?"

"I guess I'm done. Why do you ask?" the befuddled boss asked.

"Did saying what you said to me make you happy?"

"No, not really"

"Then why did you unload on me like you did? I'm not just a chicken in your pecking order."

"Look, I'm sorry, Jim. I guess I was out of line," the boss apologized, feeling uncomfortable.

At this point Jim was in the driver's seat and was now ready to find out why this happened. His next question was, "Since you were not comfortable with what you said to me, would you like to understand why it happened?"

The boss became even more insecure and vulnerable. "I guess, if you could figure it out."

Jim continued, "What I'm going to do is use the same form of questioning that my therapist would use since I assume you wouldn't go see him."

"Why would I want to go to a therapist? There's nothing wrong with me," the boss objected.

"I'm not saying there *is* something wrong with you. We need to understand why you often come to work and unload on someone. It upsets the whole office when you do. Are you willing to take a look at the cause so it won't happen anymore?"

"Well, I guess we could."

"Okay, so what happened this morning to set you off?"

"My wife just seems to chew me out over some trivial thing, and if I say anything back, it erupts into a real battle, so I walk out on her. I have to let go of that anger somehow, so I pick a fight with one of you."

Jim spent some time with him working out a possible plan to avoid the morning go-arounds with his wife. Since Jim had considerable experience with this process working with me, he was quite good at it. He uncovered that his boss had the same syndrome he had. His wife was a controller and ran roughshod over him all the time, so Jim trained him in how to be detached and non-reactive, and to counter with questions rather than a defense. After that, Jim had a totally different boss.

A few weeks later, Jim asked his boss, "I notice that you seem to be happier now since we haven't seen your old behavior around here lately. How do you feel?"

"Well, let's say it's caused some major changes in my wife's behavior. Now that I'm non-reactive and assertive, she's going through some major changes in her life. She can't control me anymore and is pretty flustered."

This had a ripple effect, as his supervisor's behavior affected everyone in the office, triggering new respect for others' right to self-expression. Communication also measurably improved in Jim's office with the change in the supervisor's new attitude. All it took was one person's new empowerment to start the entire shift.

Different cultures have different attitudes and beliefs about how self-assertion is applied in their society. Many cultures do not share the western view of direct expression and self-assertion, and have a system whereby the male has control and women are subjugated, not allowed any self-assertion at all. Asian cultures value the concept of *face*, in which how one is seen by others is more important than the concept of self. *Politeness* is the pattern and quite often indirect to avoid confrontation or offending another person. *Tradition* is important in India and the Middle East. In Latin and Hispanic cultures, *machismo* is prevalent for males, whose aggressive behavior is the accepted norm.

An example of this was when my wife, Susie, was the quality control chemist and the bottling line supervisor for the Calistoga mineral water company. She had total control over how the bottling line was operated. Most of the employees working under her were male Latinos, who resented having a woman boss. To them it was an affront to have female as a supervisor. (A man had previously held the position and had had no problems.) Making peace with them took her a long time but eventually they would work in an acceptable way under her direction. She had to be assertive yet try to work with their cultural differences.

As the world shrinks due to communication and air travel, the western behavior pattern is spreading all over the world, yet many people who have integrated into the U.S. culture are not ready for this new assertive pattern of behavior. It is not just those people who have traditionally not associated with self-assertion or place value on it either. Self-assertion is not a norm in the multicultural society of the U.S., as it is not taught in most family systems as a general rule.

Isn't Aggression Just Human Nature?

Yes and no. In some cultures over the centuries it seems that aggression has been programmed into people's DNA, such as in the Bosnia/Serbia situation. One of my friends lives in the U.S. but is from Serbia. He called his brother back in Serbia after the crisis in the area to find out how he was doing. He asked his brother, "When is this conflict going to stop?"

His brother's reply floored him. "It will not stop until the last Muslim is dead."

In reply, my friend said, "I do not want to associate myself with that behavior. As far I am concerned, you are out of my family and no longer my brother. This will be our last contact."

He later received a letter from his brother who could not understand his remark.

The terrorist attack in New York on September 11, 2001 provides a good example of the Middle Eastern aggressive cultural view. To them, this is a religious war and they will be rewarded in the afterlife for their suicide death.

Over the last 3,000 years, more people have been killed in religious wars than in all the political wars. When you feel you have God behind your aggression, it is validated and accepted since you are fighting the noble cause of stopping imperialism. The players in the war have changed, as have the tactics, but the central view is the same. Everything comes down to whose god is providing the validation and direction for your action.

As my book, *Opening Communication with GOD Source* points out, there is only one GOD Source, no matter what our delusions may be. The same species that creates war can stop it and create peace. An attack is always a call for love and forgiveness. If enough people can create a massive flow of love, it will trigger a critical mass and make a major shift on the planet. I feel this will happen in the future, as the energy began to build rapidly in the aftermath of New York City.

Aggressive behavior is not acceptable under any terms. Its intent is to have authority over, manipulate and control others. It is an attempt to force your way on others and deny them free choice. Quite often you can try to be courteous, yet be rebuffed by an aggressive person. There are no absolutes in this area, however, as we must consider cultural differences and interpretations. Many people in the psychology field feel that we must consider *intent* and the *effect* of the intent.

Based on their orientation, people may interpret an assertive message as aggressive. For example, I do not like people smoking in my house so I tactfully ask visitors to not smoke indoors. When my father-in-law visited and began smoking, I asked him to smoke outside. He took offense to my request and continued to smoke, saying, "Who do you think you are? I have a right to smoke anywhere I want."

How would you handle his aggressive reaction? The non-assertive person would just give up, drop the subject and suffer the smoke. Also, a culture that honors one's elders would see *my* behavior as aggressive. Conversely, the assertive western view would be, "This my house and I have a right to ask you not to smoke. So please either go outside or leave. And I will not invite you back again unless you agree to follow my rules."

When I said this, my father-in-law got mad, but his wife insisted he not make a scene and go outside. She was also asserting herself because she wanted to avoid a conflict with her daughter.

Creating a Model for Personal Growth and Assertiveness

One of the best improvement tools is tracking your growth in a journal using the process described in Chapter 22 of Part Six. You can evaluate your reactions and responses to track how you handle the situations in your daily life. Becoming aware of the times when you are aggressive, assertive or non-assertive will direct you to a point where you can handle all situations assertively.

It is important to set goals and ideals of how you want to achieve the level of assertiveness you desire. Each day, set up a priority list of tasks you want to take care of that day. The next morning, rewrite the list with the items you did not accomplish the day before. Add new ones to the list, giving them their appropriate priority amongst those that got carried forward.

Monthly, reevaluate where you are with your goals and intentions. Do not berate yourself if you're not where you want to be. Just increase your desire and discipline to accomplish your goals with intention. Intention controls 80 percent of the success in getting to your goals, but be flexible and make only feasible demands on yourself. If you know you are a slow starter, only put demands on yourself you know you can meet. Otherwise, you will feel that you're failing because you cannot meet your goals.

Make sure you set up goals with timeframes so your mind cannot sabotage you by justifying that it's not important to finish something or set you up to avoid doing something. Again, it is 80 percent *intention* and the only one who can keep the intention is you.

You also need to work on clearing all the negative sub-personalities that are driven by the personality self and work to defeat you or negate your ability to set goals and keep intentions. (See *Your Body Is Talking; Are You Listening?* for the list of sub-personalities and the process to clear them.) You may have to create a list of positive self-statements and affirmations that you write down 21 times a day in long hand so they get to your mind though your kinesthetic senses (see Chapter 14 for details).

You may think everyone is unequal as some are more talented, some more intelligent, and others get better breaks in life because they are "just lucky." At one time, I used to believe that I was plagued with bad luck but, over the years, I have modified my view of that interpretation, having cleared my life of the obstacles that cause "bad luck." I feel now that we must all level the playing field ourselves. This book gives you the tools to do so.

There is no such thing as bad luck. It is all controlled by our flight plan, and our karma and lessons attached to it. You may look at the tragedy of September 11, 2001 in New York and see that as lucky for some, unlucky for others. Now many fireman were killed, but why did one fireman ride the building down from the 82nd floor when it crashed to the ground and came away unscathed yet many others who were with him on the same floor became trapped in the rubble? The answer is simple. His flight plan was in order, and he had no karma where the lessons were not taken care of. The flight plans of all the others led to a different outcome (see Chapter 20).

Applying Your Assertiveness

Standing up for yourself does not mean being aggressive! It means that you do not let people run over you or use you for a doormat. It means that you insist on your free choice and take control over your life.

For example, a friend of mine always used to ask me out to dinner because he enjoyed my conversation. Being someone who would not accept anything from others, I always insisted on paying my way. After I cleared all the programs about accepting help, we went out to dinner one night and I discovered that I'd forgotten my wallet. When the time to pay the bill came, he expected me to chip in my share. I had told him recently that I was now willing accept from others as I had finally come to a place in my life that I was not afraid to let people give me help and gifts. He had apparently forgotten that discussion as he was surprised when I said, "You asked me to come to dinner with you, remember. Do not ask me to do things you don't want follow through with."

He reluctantly paid the bill, and I later paid him back, but I made it clear that I was expecting *him* to take me to dinner. He never asked me to go to dinner again.

In being assertive, you must make sure you are clear about your intentions. In a management magazine article, I read about the owner of a company who told his employees that they could not bring food from the break room back to their desks because it made a mess. He noticed after this that productivity fell because the employees were taking longer breaks. He also noticed that they were bringing their own drinks to work and taking longer to get to and back from the break room. He tried to figure out what he could do to be assertive yet not alienate his workers. He decided that, rather than say anything negative about their habits, he would provide free soda pop, coffee and tea, and allow them to bring their drinks back to their desks. He installed a free soda pop machine, a coffeemaker and put teas in the break room. Productivity immediately went up 25 percent. In this way, he built better relationships with his employees without putting any negative statement out.

Other People and the New Assertive You

The first thing you must ask yourself is, "Does it really make any difference what other people think about me?" You will find that, when people recognize this new you, they will respond positively. People like to have boundaries and know where they stand with you. They will pick this up from you via meta-communication before you even say one word. Some, of course, will erroneously interpret your assertiveness as aggression, if they feel they cannot express themselves properly. Projection is one the tools that non-assertive people use to block feelings of being rejected and invalidated.

It is not the intent of an assertive person to create a feeling of not being accepted but you cannot enable a person who needs to learn a lesson about assertiveness. You may get the opposite reaction and other people become overly apologetic or humble, because they feel they have done something wrong. Explain to them that putting themselves down and rejecting themselves is not acceptable or desirable to you, and that you were just making a point assertively so it would be understood.

Committing to Assertiveness

These statements should be written out in longhand so that your Subconscious Mind 'gets" it. Handwriting brings the concepts in through kinesthetic awareness and locks them in. Write them out as many times as it takes to bring them to reality in your conscious mind so you make them an operational habit in your life.

My goals:

1. I alone am responsible for how I feel; I recognize that and will no longer blame you for my feelings.

2. I have begun a new life. I will no longer be passive, non-assertive or allow people to take advantage of me. I will be different and I know people will notice the change.

3. I do care how others feel and will be compassionate and detached. I no longer need others' validation or acceptance. Do not expect me to be a savior or rescuer as I will no longer enable anyone's negative behavior. I will not think less of you or pay you less attention if you do not accept my views.

4. My intention is to love everyone more and express it better. My goal is accept everyone as they are, not judging their behavior or who they are.

5. I am committed to open relationships with people, accepting them without the need to control or manipulate.

6. I am also committed to myself, to loving myself, forgiving myself, to establishing and recognizing my own self-worth. To require others to recognize and respect my self-worth and who I am. I will not require anyone to accept or validate who I am because I am the only one who can do that.

7. I will respect the feelings of others but will not accept guilt if others choose not to accept me as I am.

8. I will not allow others to invalidate or attack my self-esteem or self-confidence.

9. I will keep my commitments and agreements. If I do not, I expect you to bring that to my attention and will correct it immediately.

10. If you find my behavior or any of my actions unacceptable, please bring this to my attention as soon as possible and I will listen without judgment.

There are many resources available to help you in your process of enlightenment and becoming more effective and assertive in your life. I found the new tape set by Wayne Dyer, *There is a spiritual solution to every problem*, exciting and helpful. I thought it was better than the book by the same title. The best book I have read over the years on assertiveness is *Your Perfect Right* by Robert Alberti and Michael Emmons. First published in 1970, it has continued to be a best seller.

Your Attitudes in Life*

Controller/Victim Attitude	*Spiritual Attitude*
Attack...Fear	Love
Selfish	Selfish/selfless balance
Holds Grudge	Forgiveness
Top-Dog/Underdog	Equality
Competition	Cooperation
Judgment	Spiritual Discernment
Guilt	Innocence
Self-righteousness	Personal opinion
Life as War	Life as School
Fights Universe	Lessons, challenges
Bummers, problems	State of Grace
Pessimistic	Opportunity to grow, optimistic
Insecurity, self doubt	Self-confidence
Powerless, out of control	Personal power, self-mastery
Anger and depression	Emotional invulnerability
Attack—defensive or hurt	Love
Neediness, dependency	Preference, want
Victim, effect	Master, cause, chooser, creator
Self-pity	Takes responsibility
Impatience	Patience
Suffering	Joyous and happy
Reacts	Responds
Vulnerable	Invulnerable emotionally
Sees sin	Sees mistakes
Attachment	Involved detachment
Laziness, procrastination	Discipline
Jealous	Whole, complete, nonattached
Law of the jungle	What you sow, you reap
Demands	Asks
Moody, bad moods	Good mood all the time
Self-punishment	Self love and forgiveness
Mistakes, negative	Mistakes, positive
Ego Sensitivity	Unchanging self worth
"Giving is Losing"	"Giving is Winning"
"Stealing is gaining"	"Stealing is Losing"
Rejection	Remaining centered, whole

Self-centered	One team
Intimidation	Uses power appropriately
Autopilot	Consciously creating life
Over or under-indulgent	Balance, integration, moderation
Past thoughts, future fears	Now—present centered
Lonely	Finds wholeness in self
Stranger	Brothers and Sisters
Embarrassment	No judgment of others or self
Martyr	Selfish/Selfless balance

*Excerpted from material developed by Joshua Stone

Your Activities in Life

Controller/Victim Attitude	*Spiritual Attitude*
Gossip	Remain quiet if you have a judgment
What will others think?	Inner-directed, nonconformist
Worry, anxiety	Faith, Trust in self, higher power
Indecisive	Decisive
Envy	Happiness in another's abundance
Attached to other's lessons	Responsible only for own lessons
Comparisons	Not insecure, inner directed
Undeserving	Deserving
Sickness	Can handle dis-ease and let it go
Sexuality (no love)	Sexuality with intimacy and love
Poverty consciousness	Prosperity consciousness
Arrogant and insecurity	Humble and self-confident
Sullen, serious	Humor, objectivity, perspective
Fault finder	Builder and lifter of others
Rebellious or conformist	Inner-directed
Curses	Blesses
Scattered	Focused, purposeful
Fear of failure or success	Successful
Aggressive	Assertive
Harsh	Gentle
Emotional roller coaster	Emotional stability
Disorganized	Organized
Bored	Not enough time in the day
Abandonment	Whole, complete within self
Sadness and grief	Involved detachment

Disappointment	Involved detachment
Rationalizes and excuses	Self-honest, tough love
Immature honesty	Spiritual honesty
Needs center stage/hides	Flexibility suits occasion
Conditional love	Unconditional love
Inappropriate response	Appropriate response
Rejecting	Accepting
Lessons as punishment	Lessons as gifts
War zone, dog eat dog	School for spiritual evolution
Total power/no surrender or total surrender/no power	Power plus surrender
Limited	Unlimited or limitless
Intolerant	Tolerant
Conflict	Peace
Illusions	Truth
Hypocritical	Honest, consistent
Despair	Hope
Closed-minded	Open-minded
Distrustful	Trust and faith in self and others
Defensive	Defenseless, nothing to defend

Excerpted from material developed by Joshua Stone in 1984

Forms of Communication*

Communication takes many forms:

A. Physical plane forms:

    1. Spoken language is a tiny part of communication.

    2. Meta-communication: radar-like nonverbal projection.

    3. Nonverbal body language.

B. Spiritual plane Forms:

    1. Meditation

    2. Dreams

    3. Extra-sensory-ESP

    4. Direct voice contact with a teacher

    5. Deja vu

    6. Revelation

    7. Psychic

* Our mind is in operation 24 hours a day, continually recording and interpreting everything that happens or comes to us in any communication. If we allow it to take control, it will also censor communication coming to us.

Forms of verbal communication:

1. Active speaking.
2. Active or creative listening.

Forms of nonverbal communication:

1. Positive sends out supportive messages about self and others.
2. Negative sends out, "I am not all right" message about self and negates others.
3. Body language indicates how a person feels about self and situation.
4. Body odor will sometimes indicate a person's mental/emotional state.
5. Eye movement or blinking can indicate stress.

I. Effective Communications

1. The Tao of Communication
   a. Perfect balance
   b. Separate parts
2. Yin - receptive, feminine and passive
   a. Listening
   b. Drawing Out
   c. Incubating the message
3. Yang - dynamic, masculine, active
   a. Making a point
   b. "Putting out" a message
   c. Sending

II. The Effective Communicator

1. Notices facial expression and body language
2. Knows Yang is not a space of listening
3. Becomes Yin in the presence of "Yang"
4. Is charismatic
5. The principles of effective communication:
   a. Yang cannot hear; Yin cannot be clear.
   b. Two Yang's create argument.
   c. Two Yin's create stagnation.

III. Effective Yin

1. Listens attentively.
2. Draws out partner.
3. Works on understanding.
4. Has advantage of knowing partner's thoughts and opinions.

IV. Effective Yang

1. Expresses own point of view.
2. Asserts self.
3. Expert at inducing Yin in partner.
4. Responds; is also effective Yin.

V. Application in Family and Parenting

1. Members care what others think or feel.
2. Parents "draw out" children with Yin listening.
3. Parents demonstrate both Yin and Yang.
4. Children learn to be effective without arguing.
5. Children learn to learn.

VI. Five Steps in Communication

1. Body
2. Mind
3. Emotions
4. Beliefs
5. Action

VII. The Aspects of a Communication

1. Self
2. Other
3. Feeling
4. Situation

VIII. Aspects of the Four Elements in Communication

1. Earth
   a. Positive: de-emphasizes feeling.
   b. Negative: eliminates self, other, and feeling.
2. Water
   a. Positive: de-emphasizes self.
   b. Negative: eliminates self.
3. Fire
   a. Positive: de-emphasizes other.
   b. Negative: eliminates other.
4. Air
   a. Positive: de-emphasizes situation.
   b. Negative: eliminates self, other feeling and situation.

IX. The Five Freedoms

1. Freedom to see and hear what is there.
2. Freedom to say what you feel and think.
3. Freedom to feel what you feel.
4. Freedom to ask for what you want.
5. Freedom to take risks in your own behalf.

Conversing with Your Child or the Child Within

Effective communication depends upon the total attention of *all of you*:
1. Body: "When I notice, see, hear ..."
2. Mind: "I think that means ..."
3. Emotions: "I feel ..."
4. Beliefs: "I believe ..."
5. Action: "I want you to respond by ..." or, "I would like you to..."

This may be especially helpful when your child (either the child in you, or the other child) is feeling unheard or misunderstood. Ask the child to state clearly what happened (insist on objectivity):
   a. What does that mean?
   b. What are you feeling?
   c. What do you believe about that?
   d. What do you want to do now? What should be done?
   e. What would you like to do, feel, right now?

You're Gonna Need God

A. Help needed in parenting:
    1. Job is complex
    2. Laws and rules are ill-defined
    3. Many uncontrollable factors
    4. Guidance and wisdom needed
B. Help is available:
    1. Assume:
        a. There is a Source
        b. Lift lid off limitation
        c. Discover it works
    2. Ask:
        a. Prayer
            (1) Warm conversation
            (2) Expectancy and anticipation
        b. Accept response
    3. Listen
        a. Greatest challenge
            (1) Listen instead of think
            (2) Hold regular intimate conversation
        b.   Communicate with the Source of life - God

The Aspects of Every Communication

Any communication, whether verbal or nonverbal, has four parts:
1. The Self
2. The Other (the person spoken, responded, or reacted to)
3. The Feeling (the emotional content or dramatic effect of the communication)
4. The Situation (the "here and now" with which participants are engaged)

Positive communication includes all four aspects, although some may be de-emphasized. Negative or dysfunctional communication lacks one or more of the aspects.

The Four Elements in Communication

Astrologers often use the four elements (earth, fire, air, water) to classify personality types. These four qualities are used in communication as follows:

Earth:

- *Positive earth* is practical, reasonable, sensible, dependable, and analytical. Communication is natural, sure, steadfast and confident. The body is grounded, centered and strong. Gestures are steady, firm and clear. Voice is resonant with heart. Content says, "I care about your experience. This is my experience. Let's hear from others. Let's understand and share."

- *Negative earth* communication is opinionated, stiff, computer-like, uncaring. It is void of feeling and negates the importance of self and other in favor of the situation. The body is stiff, rigid, unmoving. Gestures are few, stiff, and jerky. Content is rational, logical, cold and uncaring.

Water:

- *Positive water* communication is caring, yielding. The body posture is yielding, welcoming, receptive and non-threatening. The gestures are giving and reaching out. The voice is from the heart, soft, supportive and gentle. The content is an offer to help and understand, to care and to listen.

- *Negative water* communication is wishy-washy, placating, self-deprecating, denies the importance of self, and recognizes only others' feelings and the situation. Posture is hunched, head hanging, eyes pleading or apologizing. Gestures are weak, perhaps despairing. Content is placating and self-blaming, over-pleasing, sticky, insincere.

Fire:

- *Positive fire* in communication is enthusiastic, assertive, dramatic, strong, determined. Body posture is alive and moving, dynamic. Gestures are enthusiastic, illustrative. Voice is excited, full of feeling and spirit. Content is encouraging, reinforcing.

- *Negative fire* in communication is blaming, demanding, hot under the collar. Body is tight and agitated. Gestures are pointed and threatening, and jabbing. Voice is harsh, shrill, and loud. Content is accusing, finding fault, placing blame, establishing guilt.

Air:

- Positive air in communication is light, free, joyous, bright, positive, filled with a sense of humor, supportive, flexible. The body is flexible, light, comfortable; gestures are graceful, open and free. Voice is bright, musical and fun-filled. Content is optimistic, affirmative and finds fun even in difficulty.

- Negative air in communication refuses to deal with reality or even to be relevant. It dismisses the importance of self, others, and the situation. The body posture isn't centered, moving. Gestures are unfocused and do not communicate meaning. Voice is flippant, artificial and perhaps insincere. Content is "airy-fairy," unrealistic, non-serious, non-supportive, and irrelevant.

Spiritual Psychology: Part I Contents

Questions from a workshop program:
    I. Did you think of two things you wanted to work on?
        1.   A trait you act out _____
        2.   A blockage to progress you hold on to: _____

    II. Where did you come from and why does it matter?
    III. What are you doing here and why does it matter?
    IV. How can Spiritual Psychology help you right now?
    V. The basic principles of spiritual psychology
    VI. Choosing Mastery
        a.   Responsibility.
        b.   Reclaiming personal power.
        c.   About emotions.
        d.   About beliefs.
        e.   Assumed limitations and faulty assumptions.
        f.   Blaming and victims.
        g.   Negative payoffs.
        h.   Masks or acts.
        i.   Incongruities in goals and values.
        j.   Resistance to what is.
        k.   Mirroring.
        l.   Fear.
        m.   Need to be right.
        n.   Expectations.
        o.   Clarity of intent and the three D's.
        p.   Lack of aliveness or motivations.
    VII. Processing problems
        a.   Discussions

For more information about this course, the topics taught herein, and other activities of the Institute, please write to us at the address in the front of the book.

Spiritual Psychology: Part II Contents

I. Two things to work on in this workshop:
   a. An emotion you express frequently, that you don't like anymore.
   b. What triggers that emotion most often?

II. Goals of this part of Spiritual Psychology:
   a. To help you to understand your false self.
   b. To learn to be honest about your emotions.
   c. Tools to work with your emotional responses effectively and responsibly.

III. About the False Self:
   a. What is it?
   b. How did it come about?
   c. What must you do about it?

IV. The four qualities and how they relate to emotions:
   a. Alrightness.
   b. Non-judgment.
   c. Detachment.
   d. Creating your own reality/responsibility.

V. The observer space:
   a. Detachment again.
   b. How do you view your life?
   c. What is the most productive way to view your life?
   d. About you, your body, your mind, and your soul.
   e. You and your higher self.
   f. Everyone else's higher selves and God.
   g. Reaching the observer space: asking the question.

VI. The nine-step process for mastering emotions:
   a. What is the process?
   b. Why does it work?
   c. How do you apply it in your life?

VII. Discussions using your emotions as examples.

For more information about this course, the topics taught herein, and other activities of the Institute, please write to us at the address in the front of the book.

Part Four

The Third Step
in Transformation

16

Healing the Physical Body

The first two sections of this book described how to understand why we ended up where we have on our spiritual path in life, and how to make friends with our inner selves and create inner peace to stop the internal battle in our mind. Our beliefs control us to the point where we give our power away to authority figures and, if we are running on autopilot, we will accept whatever is placed before us as sensory input.

It is not what you eat that will heal you; it is what is eating *you* that will destroy you. You can eat the most effective vegetarian raw food diet and still get cancer or any other life-threatening disease. One of my clients is a woman who was a raw food vegetarian. She rode her bicycle thirty miles a week, participated in aerobics three time a week and jogged three miles a day, yet she ended up with breast cancer.

It is the *programs* in our mind that destroy us, not the food we eat. Of course, we hear of people who go on a strict diet and it heals their cancer, etc. However, it's not the diet that healed the cancer at all, but what they believed about what the diet would do for them. This is called "the placebo effect" and is one of the most effective tools we have available for use in healing. The only problem is that we have no control over clients' direction in this. All we can do is to impress them with the ability of the process to heal them, and leave it up to them whether or not to believe in the process.

The next two cases reveal the power of our mind to heal or destroy us. Mr. Wright had tried all the available forms of treatment for his cancer condition, yet it continued to deteriorate. When it metastasized into an advanced malignancy, Dr. Bruno Klopfer conferred with other doctors and they agreed that since he had only days to live, they would let him try any form of treatment that might give him relief. Wright had heard about an experimental drug, Krebiozen, that was being tested and asked to be included in the testing. Feeling they had nothing to lose, his doctors agreed that the compassionate thing to do was to give him the experimental drug. To their amazement, his tumors began to shrink and he recovered and was discharged from the hospital. They assumed that the cancer was cleared so they closed the case.

Two month later, Wright read the news accounts of questions about the drug's effectiveness, since a research team had doubts about it. Within a matter of days, his cancer returned, threatening his life again. His doctor was clever enough to recognize that the placebo effect had caused his remission and called him to tell him he had received a new shipment of Krebiozen that was much more potent than the original drug. He asked Wright to go to his office so he could inject him with the new formulation.

The doctor injected him with only saline water, but his tumors disappeared and he went into remission again. He remained healthy and in good spirits for the next year, until the next report came out about the drug being ineffective against cancer. Apparently, FDA and the AMA tests had shown that Krebiozen was worthless as a treatment for cancer. Wright died within two days from the cancer that had not existed one week earlier. That is the power of the mind.

In June 2000, I met a doctor at Book Expo America, the yearly exposition of new books for the book trade. He had written a book about Placebo Medicine, in which he described many of his experiences with giving sugar pills and injecting saline water. He said, "I no longer prescribe drugs or give any drugs by injection, and my success rate is greater now than when I was practicing allopathic medicine. I feel that the placebo effect is the main form of healing now. Even when I did prescribe drugs, I don't think it was the drug that caused the healing to take place so much as the patient's belief in the drug or doctor."

So again in healing, it is not the food or drugs that heal you. It is *you* that heals you. The only catch is that you must know that the food, drug or supplement will work for you. I have clients who follow a very poor diet in my estimation, but they are healthy. I also have clients who eat a rigid, strict diet and are not healthy until we clear all the dysfunctional programs.

The third part of this book lays out the process for erasing and deleting the malfunctioning files and programs. When we end the separation with our selves, we can begin to detach from anger, fear, judgment, control, manipulation, authority, codependency and victim consciousness, and empower ourselves to take responsibility for our life. We can delete and erase the self-defeating scripts and tapes in the files and rewrite new programs so we can live in unconditional love, peace, happiness, harmony and joy. As we have seen, our body is controlled by our mind.

All disease and illness, and all mental, emotional and behavioral dysfunction are modulated or controlled by neuropeptides, cytokinins, seratonins and interlukins to name a few but, if we do not give them the proper tools and food to nourish our cellular structure, their effectiveness breaks down. With all the negative influences we have to fend off each day, just keeping our balance and center in our life path is hard enough to do. But if we do not give our body good building blocks to help support our physical structure, even though we might have a positive mental attitude and image to support our mind function, our body will break down eventually due to physical overload of toxins.

Granted, negative sensory input can create more toxins than a poor diet, but we can't assume that, since we have achieved mind over matter, we can eat anything we want. We can transmute an occasional detour in our eating habits, but we need to stay on a good diet. I am aware there are exceptions, such as people who smoke, drink and eat a junk food diet, yet live to 80 or more. Statistically, how many of these exceptions with strong constitutions and a genetic background are there as a given percent of the population? Very few and they are not on the spiritual journey either. When you are on the path, you are required to be more disciplined.

Quite often, it is hard to realize we created it all. As we have stated before, everything that happens to us is our responsibility even if we don't want to accept it. Being the repository for all our emotional trauma, the physical body is the database for our Subconscious Mind. The cellular structure of our body is akin to a "network computer" that holds all the cellular memory of past negative sensory input. We can run it down if we do not recognize that we are programming it with negative thoughts and emotions. The same goes for our body's health. We have free choice to run it into the ground or create perfect health. Body/mind/spirit are unified; there is no separation. We are the one who disconnects the body from the mind and/or the spirit. This again is taking control and disciplining ourselves to take responsibility for what we eat and how we treat our body.

What this means is that you do not put anything into your body that causes a toxic reaction. This covers a wide range items we have to consider. The first are the poisonous substances. Smoking, alcohol and food preservatives create free radicals in your body. Tobacco contains nicotine, a poisonous substance. When I was young, my father used a nicotine-based spray on plants and he told not me to touch the plants after he had sprayed them. Prominent on the label were a skull and cross bones and the words EXTREMELY POISONOUS in large letters. This spray was so toxic that it was taken off the market. It was made from only tobacco. Does that tell you something?

Alcohol disrupts brain function when you take more than an ounce. The addictive qualities are well known and need not be discussed. Preservatives such as nitrates and nitrites will convert to nitrosameens which are free radicals and very toxic. Hydrogenated oils are not digestible at all, yet we find it in many foods as it stops the oil from going rancid quickly. It's also what keeps margarine solid at room temperature.

Most people eat too many foods with saturated fats in them. I stopped eating beef, pork and lamb in 1976. I also cut back on dairy and fried foods because my cholesterol was at 325—almost triple what it should be. With exercise and a proper diet, it dropped to 124 in two years and has stayed at that level ever since.

To keep your health on proper basis, try to eat as many alkaline foods as possible. Most people eat too much high acid-producing foods, such as meat (except fish and poultry). Digesting red meat takes a pH stronger than battery acid. The pH factor is a measure of acid/alkaline, and is determined by litmus paper, which comes in strips of paper that can be dipped in liquid. It indicates the pH of the liquid, showing acid or alkaline, by changing color. Most people are running an acid level of 4.5 pH, and the ideal is between 6.5 to 7.0. It also indicates toxicity level. The average person has a toxic level between 40% to 80%.

Most people carry 10 to 50 pounds of dead fecal matter in their intestines, which causes poor assimilation of nutrients. Few people digest their food properly, which results in lack of energy and breakdown of the physical structure, even if they eat a proper diet.

Carrying excess weight is caused by programming that triggers the body to revert to a subsistence program that allows the body to assimilate only simple sugars. The program pevents all the protein building blocks and any other nutrients from being assimilated.

Some of my clients who have been on high protein-no carbohydrate diets are outrageously hungry all the time and, when they eat some fruit, the hunger goes away. This is because the digestive system is trying to find the sugar in the protein but there is very little, so it puts out demands for sugar to satisfy its needs. When the person consumes some form of sugar-containing food, the demand is satisfied. This is why overweight people pile on the carbohydrate-saturated foods. The same can happen to thin people, too, except they have a high metabolism that uses up the sugar faster so they do not put on visible fat. We can rewrite the digestive program but the body will revert to the original program until we locate the base cause that caused the malfunctioning digestive program to be installed in the first place.

Excess weight can have other implications, too. Unresolved past life programs can have a major influence on this life if, say, one died of starvation. The stories people tell of starvation or lack of food can have a major effect on children when they reach the same age as the storyteller. My forthcoming book *Mind/Body Medicine Connection* (to be published in June 2001) will offer a complete coverage of this subject, with charts and descriptions.

After diet, the next requirement is exercise. Statistics have shown that only 15% of the population has a regular exercise program. Most of us know that we should exercise, but we find all kinds of reasons not to, such as we don't have the time or can't get motivated. The lymph system in the body carries out all the waste material, but it does not have a pump, so we must exercise to pump out the waste materials and the toxins. Our legs are the pump and we must practice some leg movement to achieve the result. In addition to emptying the lymph system, exercise such as running, brisk walking, bicycling or stationary rebounding also activates cellular metabolism.

Most people retain too much water, which can be used up and released by exercise if you do not have a potassium deficiency. From my experience over the last twenty years, I have found the average person has a sodium-potassium imbalance. The common misperception is that we only lose salt when we perspire but, in fact, we lose more potassium than sodium. Potassium is also a salt and we release more of it than sodium with exercise. When we have a potassium deficiency, we retain water because our body is trying to maintain a balance of electrolytes. Excess sodium penetrates the cell walls, which causes the cells to increase their water content. I have discovered in my work that most people carry from 5 to 50 pounds of excess water in their body. Further, if the water is emulsified with white fat, it is harder to release.

How do we clear this up and get on the path? It takes a three-pronged approach. We must:

1. Take responsibility for where we are in our path

2. Set up a program with priorities

3. Discipline ourselves in what we eat, think and get our act together so we can be in integrity with ourselves.

I have had dinner with many people who say, "It's all right for me to eat this way when I go out to dinner occasionally," yet when I visit their home, I find them eating the same garbage food they ate at the restaurant.

The average person's life runs on autopilot with very little direction. Are you one of those people? If you run into boulders, logjams and crashes in your life, you may very well be. We must step out of the illusion and be honest with ourselves in every avenue of our life. Granted, sometimes we do not know the rules in some situations, but it is our responsibility to learn the universal laws and spiritual principles of the spiritual journey. Ignorance may be bliss for the uninformed, but we must become aware that integrity, honesty and ethics govern the spiritual path. There are no excuses or justifications that will allow you to avoid responsibility.

Many times, parents bring their teenagers or young adults to me with the plea, "Can you help them to make a decision to eat right and do something with their lives? They are driving themselves into the ground."

I can clear all the problems and challenges that face them from childhood, past lives, their false interpretations and beliefs, but I cannot force them to make decisions or take responsibility. Many times I have been able to clear all the sub-personalities, the childhood trauma programs, get all the mind's operating systems to network together and clear any "I want to die" programs, yet they still refuse to make a decision to step out of their confusion and denial. It is usually tied into a conscious decision to hold themselves in confusion and avoidance, so they do not have to take control and responsibility for their lives. Quite often, they will say to me, "I don't understand what you're trying tell me. I don't think you can help me because you do not understand my problem. Everyone tells me that I'm the only one who can make the decision but I don't know how to."

Most of them end up in a doctor's office taking drugs that dull their consciousness, but they can survive in confusion.

If the parents hold themselves in guilt because they think they are not taking care of their children properly, they will usually end up taking care of their adult children for many years or for the rest of their life. It is not the parents' responsibility to take care of a physically and mentally able adult child. (Of course, it's a different story if the child is physically or mentally disabled from birth or an accident.) Most of the adult children I have seen have succeeded in making it through high school and/or college and usually are above average intelligence, and their behavior is usually seated in anger, resentment and rebellion against the parents or someone close to them at whom they have undefined anger but refuse to recognize it. It is totally a conscious decision even though they will not own it.

Healing and recovery requires us to get out of denial and begin to take inventory of our childhood experiences. As described before, we must forgive and accept what has happened in the past to release all the programs. The first step in the spiritual journey is healing our body on the physical level. This is an integrated approach because, to heal the body, we must begin with the mind since it controls the body. As we have said before, all illness and disease, and mental, emotional and behavioral dysfunction are caused by the mind. This being the case, we must go back to the mind's files and locate the causes. The main theme we must remember is that transformation can be immediate. It can happen in an instant, or it may take ten hours, ten days, ten months, ten years or ten lifetimes. It is your choice. It simply requires that you to let the old self die and be reborn by taking responsibility and becoming the master of your life.

At a conference on Adult Children Of Alcoholics, I attended a workshop by Wayne Gertzburg on recovery for therapists. He asked all attendees to complete a questionnaire on their effectiveness as therapists. He said, "Please answer all the questions honestly because if you try to bag, avoid or give the proper answers, it shows up in the profile, and the ones that are out of context will be thrown out."

While Wayne gave his presentation, his assistant went through the questionnaires. About half way through the workshop, he presented the results of the survey, and said, "Just as I suspected, about 85 percent of those here are not in recovery. If you expect to help others, you must first heal your life. You must be in recovery yourself or you are going to sidestep your clients' issues when your issues come up with them. If we are going to be effective in helping others, we must first heal our own life."

Over the last twenty years, I have found that we cannot avoid our own issues in Neuro/Cellular Repatterning and, if you try to do so, they will slap you in the face. My issues often came up while I was working with a client, and I had no choice but to deal with and clear them on the spot. Many therapists find this to be uncomfortable and that is destroys their credibility, so they will go back to a less confrontational therapy process so that they can avoid dealing with their own issues. This explains why we do not have more practitioners in this field. I am also finding now that more people are going to step to the forefront in healing and reclaim their personal power so that they can become more effective facilitators.

See Appendices A and B for more information on Neuro/Cellular Repatterning. For a yet more detailed description, see my book *Your Body Is Talking; Are You Listening?*

Part Five

Universal Laws and Spiritual Principles that Guide Us on Our Spiritual Journey

17

Universal Laws of
Spiritual Development

The following Universal Laws were developed by Paul Solomon, of the Inner Light Consciousness Institute and are reprinted here with permission.

1. *Everything in GOD's Universe operates according to GOD's Universal Laws, including GOD.* Whatever any man has accomplished on this earth or in this universe, any other man can accomplish, given the same conditions and applying the energy in the same way. The GOD Source is not whimsical and They honor their own laws.

2. *The laws of the subtler plane are the same as the laws of this plane, except more subtle.* In order to know the laws of the subtler planes, look for a law on this plane that corresponds, for the laws never contradict each other.

3. *That which is born of flesh is flesh; that which is born of spirit is spirit. (John 3:6)* We spend most of our lives attending to the physical body and developing the physical senses. The spiritual senses, however, are not found in the physical body, but in the spiritual body. As we redirect our energy and give attention and recognition to the spiritual body, we give birth to the spirit. To do so, you must have cleared the physical plane lessons and handled the lessons that you came into a physical body to tackle.

4. *Deprivation of any one sense enhances the other senses.* We close our eyes to hear something better. Applying it spiritually, we must turn off the physical senses to enhance spiritual perception. To do this, you must learn how to turn off the internal self-talk created by the mind.

5. *The inner voice is a still, small voice (1 Kings 19:21); the voices of the senses and appetites are screaming things.* It is the nature of GOD Source to be heard only by those who wish to hear Them. The chatter of the mind must be stilled to hear that quiet voice. GOD Source cannot lower their vibration to come to our level. We must raise ours to meet them, and step out of the physical world to make contact.

6. *Familiarity breeds recognition.* Every mother recognizes her child's voice on a crowded playground; her child's voice is familiar. You will know for certain when you have heard it, and it will bring you joy. "The sheep follow him for they know his voice." (John 10:4) When you contact the GOD Source, you will instantly know that contact. It is not that of a spirit guide.

7. *Practice makes perfect.* By putting these concepts and exercises into practice over time, we build consciousness of our inner light. Developing this inner connection takes discipline, commitment and practice. One cannot expect to develop a pattern with out setting down a priority and following it. The mind does not like procrastination and confusion.

8. *Like attracts like.* Confused thoughts and habits attract people and teachers of equal quality. To attract a Master Teacher, we must align ourselves with the standards, the ideals, the goals and the purposes of the Master of Masters. Even if we feel we are ready to make that step to become an earth master, the only mark by which we can know your level of enlightenment on the path is whom you attract to you in your life.

9. *Direction of aim, plus steady release guides a projectile to a selected destination. (The Law of Zen Archery)* If we expect to attain perfection, we must set an ideal, and state a purpose. "Direction of aim" must be toward nothing less than union with the highest. "Steady release" does not allow distractions along the way. A tiny slip of a finger sends an arrow far from the target. It is necessary to continue to focus the consciousness on the bull's eye. Your progress is quite visible to those who are above you watching your journey on the path.

10. *All bodies require food and exercise.* Spiritual food and exercise are just as necessary for the health of the spiritual body as physical food and exercise are for the physical body. Spiritual food consists of meditation, prayer, and devotion. Spiritual exercise includes resisting temptation, meeting the daily challenges of the highest places on our path, and service. The only person you can fool is yourself. Justification of mistakes and avoidance of discipline hurt only you.

11. *You have as many lifetimes as you want to traverse the spiritual journey on the path to enlightenment.* Nobody hinders or stops you but you.

18

The Quest For True Self: Enlightenment And Evolvement On The Path To Soul Consciousness

Enlightenment is a waking up process. It is the knowingness that we are becoming aware of who we are so we can begin our spiritual journey. The mistake most people make in the waking up process is thinking that enlightenment is a spiritual process only. We are triune beings so must address all aspects of ourselves: body mind and spirit. In growing up to adulthood, most people lose their true identity along the way. In the quest for true self, we must recover our lost self. Some people mistakenly describe this as "soul retrieval." Our soul is not lost; it knows exactly where it is, where we are, and what we should be doing. However, we have lost contact with it; our soul did not lose contact with us.

Almost all people operate from the personality self, which is run by sub-personalities and autopilot (as described in previous chapters and my other books). It is the personality self that gets lost in the scuffle to survive in daily life. The main reason that most people do not advance very far along on their spiritual journey is that they skip the main reason we even incarnate in this earthly body.

Our soul and spirit reviewed the Akashic Record and laid out all the lessons for us in the flight plan before we incarnated. Since we are the spirit of self, we approved the flight plan but, on entering the physical world, we promptly lost the flight plan. Basically, we lost our true self before we even took our first step. We had no choice but to develop the personality self since that is all we knew. Our real true self is the spiritual self, but we cannot develop it until we begin to work on the lessons that we came to the physical world to address. In almost all my research, I find that very few teachers address the need to deal with physical world lessons. Most enter into deep philosophical dialogues about what spiritual paths and disciplines we must study and practice, and ignore the basics of recovering the lost self.

We need to address the situations of everyday life and get the lessons of self-esteem, self-worth, self-confidence, relationships, communication, self-validation, self-acceptance, and letting go of judgment, control, manipulation and authority. The most important lessons are unconditional self-love, receiving love, and forgiveness. The list is quite long as was described in prior chapters.

Enlightenment is only the first step in the spiritual journey. The evolving process requires that we let go of the personality self so that we can be reborn and take on the qualities of the spiritual self. This also involves becoming free of emotion so that you can view all situations from a nonattached perspective where anger, fear or the need for control are no longer an issue. This is not reserved for a few evolved gurus or teachers, however; this quality of life is available to everyone.

The Christian Bible tells us, "Some are called; few are chosen." This misinterpretation has effectively controlled the masses for centuries so that a few leaders could declare themselves intermediaries between God and the people. This sentiment is also duplicated in many other cultures so that their spiritual leaders can maintain control. The passage *should* read "All are chosen, few chose to listen." The major lesson here is empowerment. We must reclaim our personal power so we can empower ourselves and take control our life. When we can rise above the need to control or allow others to control us, we can take the next step in our evolution.

I find, too, that most teachers are missing this in their own life. If you do not have the basics in your own life handled, how are you going to impart this to your students? Enlightenment is about recovering your lost self so that you can make the transition to a spiritual being. You can have all the awakening *déjà vu* experiences you want, but true enlightenment causes a spiritual awakening where you go through a transfiguration that results in becoming a spiritual being in a physical body. The spiritual journey has specific steps, or initiations, that you must go through, as detailed in my book *Journey Into The Light*.

How can you be in the world but not of it? This is an age-old question that has been asked since ancient times. If you are living in the world, you do not have a choice about being in it. Our major lesson is detaching from personality self. If you are locked into the world of emotions, control and competition, striving to make your life function in a fearful, angry world, you are mired down where it is hard to see the illusion and denial. Rising above illusion takes detachment. Now detachment is not forsaking the world, transcending it, and running away from responsibility. The illusion that you can achieve spiritual enlightenment by escaping the world and retreating to a monastic lifestyle, meditating eight hours a day, is false. Transcending the world is a cop out. To be a rounded individual, you must deal with and experience *all* facets of life.

At the risk of being redundant, let's look at why you're here in the first place. Surely not to escape the world. You've done that each time you crossed over with unfinished lessons left hanging. You can sit on the spiritual plane out-of-body and contemplate what you're going to do next time around. Since you've gone to all the trouble of filing a flight plan to guide yourself through this life, why not get on with it and begin to practice the lessons that you planned to work with? Enlightenment is only one step on the spiritual journey. Avoiding dealing with the flight plan does not get you anywhere. You must demonstrate your ability to detach from the emotions of the world, yet be able to interact in the world. It *is* possible to be in the daily function of the world and succeed at all levels of our life. There are downturns and high-reaching times on your journey, and it takes commitment, consistent effort and discipline to succeed in a many-faceted life. Every time I think about this concept, I am reminded of Eric Hoffer's *The True Believer*, a great book on the way people allow themselves to be controlled and follow people because they do not want to take responsibility.

I do not see my past of being married and bringing up two children and working in the world as a sacrifice of my spiritual pursuits in any way. In fact, I see it as *part* of my spiritual journey since each experience gave me more awareness of the spiritual path. The challenge of raising two children to have high self-esteem, self-worth and self-confidence was part of my own enlightenment. I do not have to look back and fault myself or feel guilty that my sons did not succeed as *I* wanted them to because I detached from the need to control them. As it turned out, they *did* succeed very well. Sure there were ups and downs in our lives over the past 36 years. Susie and I could have ended up in divorce three times but we knew that in our spiritual journey we would encounter closed doors and boulders as in the past. It was our challenge to work through the bumpy spots and continue on the path. We could have taken detours and avoided many lessons but we would not be at the point we are now.

When I discuss this with my two now-adult sons, they can't even remember it being a struggle, as we always had enough and were able to support each other. Even though we lost everything when our business went under in 1987, we found ways to survive. We recognized that it was just part of the enlightenment process. Everything worked out because we worked together and knew that, one day, we would see the light from this lesson.

The lesson was an opening for me because it pushed me to higher levels. Previously, I had worked out of one location, and therefore had only a local influence. Today, I have an ever-expanding audience all over the world. We recovered all our financial losses and have succeeded way beyond where we were in the downturn in our lives.

Many people do not want to risk making their life work so they run away from it. There are many ways to do this, such as the routine job that pays a guaranteed salary every month. I was never looking for security, however, so was never threatened by creating my own income.

So where does that leave us at this time? A very tight family unit that lives *in* the world and in the present moment, ready to deal with whatever challenge comes up in real time. We are not *of* the world because the problems of the world are not our problems. We did not create them. We can be compassionate and detached, and help to change the challenges facing the people of the world but we do not have rescue or save anyone. We can show people the way out of their mire if they are willing to listen, but we are not attached to the outcome or whether they take on the challenge or not. When you become unattached to the outcome and are above emotions, then you can live in the world but not affected by it. Other chapters echo this, but it needs to be said again. Feelings are not emotions; they are interpretations that we make when we observe something. Love, joy and happiness are not emotions. Emotions are feelings that have a payoff with an outcome attached.

In my work, I have found that few people on the spiritual path feel they are entitled to money or even that they deserve it. Some feel that accumulating money is not spiritual. This is a program that can easily be rewritten. When I cleared all my past life lessons around money and rewrote the program, we got back on track financially and have now passed where we were in 1987. I contend that if we were to level the playing field and pool all the money on this planet, and then redistribute it equally to every person, then each person would have the same amount of money to begin a new life. The unfortunate story is that, after ten years, those who have the wealth today would have it all back. We have proven that in our own lives.

Soul vs. Spirit

To understand all different philosophies in researching this topic, I read widely on many theories and concepts and held many in-depth discussions about what soul is in relation to High Self, Spirit, Presence of God, Holy Spirit and the GOD Source. According to what we received in our conversation with the GOD Source, it seems that many people have a misconception as to what spirit and soul are.

Quite often people will say that "spirit" guided them to do this, take this action or they were told to move to a certain location. Those who use a pendulum will ask a question, and then ask "spirit" to do a clearing, remove a program, etc. I did not believe this was the proper way to handle situations but I felt that, if it worked for them, fine. Many times, however, I observed that the action taken did not reap the results the person asked for. I have many friends who claimed that spirit guided them to move to a certain city or area but, when they had been there for some time, their life or financial picture had not changed. I often wondered why, if they had the proper guidance, did they miss Shangri-La.

When I recently put these questions to Source, I was told that *we* are spirit. It is spirit that activates and enlivens our body. Without spirit, our body would die. It travels with us and has been with us since our original incarnation. Therefore, when we ask spirit to do something, we are really asking ourselves to do it. If we do not specify who we want to accomplish the task, then it defaults to our spirit to perform the task. If we are working with other people, we are asking their spirit to accomplish the task. On the assumption that spirit is a force outside of ourselves, most people give much more power to spirit than themselves.

Spirit is really not a force that accomplishes tasks, however, but a power that controls the life in our body. It is related to High Self and the Presence of God within us, as it operates and functions with them. It is not the soul, but functions with it to activate our life in the body when we decide to take on a body and be born into the physical world. Spirit cannot operate separately from the soul or High Self because it is part of High Self's makeup.

The *Presence of God* within is just that. It is our source of knowing who we are. It contains all the spiritual principles and God-like qualities that embody who we were in the beginning before we fell from grace. We know what these principles are, but we do not live by them until we wake up.

The *Holy Spirit* is synonymous with the GOD Source, although many people are more comfortable with the term "Holy Spirit." Throughout history, many different names have been given to God, such as Elohim. "Elohim" is a powerful word to use in chants or mantras, as it's a power word for God that was used in the ancient mystery schools.

Soul and its role in our life are perhaps the most misunderstood concepts. Some people believe that the soul can lose its direction and become fragmented or splintered, which is why we can get lost in our direction in life. Many people relate the soul to our physical world, believing that it controls our behavior in some way. Others believe that a soul having a hard time living within the body will leave to rejuvenate and refuel in some way.

Over the years, I have had many discussions with GOD Source about the soul, and this is what I have learned:

The soul exists in, of and around us. It is not locked into our body at any point. It is a vitalizing force when spirit enters and activates the body. Without soul and spirit, a baby would be stillborn, as there would be no energy to activate the body once independent of the mother's energy and sustenance. The soul/spirit enters the body up to four hours before or after birth, and Holographic Mind downloads the flight plan to the mind. (Holographic Mind is our connection to the soul that will provide the basic information for the body/mind to begin life.)

~ ~ ~

Some small children are actually in touch with their mission until adults get them to block it out and no longer recognize it. My mother would not believe most of what I tried to explain to her, so the information was blocked in my life, too. My wife and I tried to keep it alive in our children but it was dulled and eventually blocked when they went to school. The events happening in our younger son's life reveal that it is now starting to reawaken in him. Many people would say, "Oh, it's just luck," but we know that he is reclaiming his lost self and beginning to understand who he is. For example, a friend of his called to tell him, "I'm booked on a one-week cruise to Acapulco, Mexico, but can't go. The ticket cost over $450, but I'll just give it to you."

Most children lose their flight plans and end up bogged down in the mire of a dysfunctional family, which may explain the odd notion held by some people that souls get fragmented or splintered. The soul is not lost or fragmented in any way, even though we may become dysfunctional in our life. The still small voice within is there but drowned out by the dysfunctional self-talk and invalidation by the mind's interpretations of the outside world. I have found that most people take 40 or more years to wake up to the fact that something wants to get through to them and provide direction in their life. Unfortunately, less than ten percent of the population wakes up at *any* time in their life. So they must return just where they left off on the downward spiral.

A striking example of this is a client who lived a literal traumatic hell for 47 years, not knowing she was playing out karma. At the soul level, she had chosen to clear past life karmic contracts by taking on the challenge in this lifetime of being born into a family where she knew she would be rejected at birth. She not only played out *her* karma but she played into her mother's karma by causing her to have a near death experience while giving birth.

This woman's life was one long series of traumatic incidents and experiences as she unknowingly played out her subconscious beginnings, plus complex past life issues, too. Fortunately, her Higher Self's teachers and guides got her to attend my lecture so she could learn that she could clear these flight plan lessons. After the lecture, she made an appointment. In just one session, we cleared the karma and, in three more, we cleared the results of 47 years of built-up trauma. We claimed Grace, and with self-love and forgiveness, we cleared the past life lessons and the karma, and put it all in the archives.

In the first session, when I touched the acupuncture point on her left shoulder blade, the following information replayed as vividly as a movie. I saw her father, furious with her mother for getting pregnant. Even as a three-day-old baby, she faithfully recorded his anger at her and filed it in her Subconscious Mind. The father was screaming that not only had the mother had another child that they couldn't afford, but also that medical complications required an expensive week's hospital stay, and he'd also had to hire in-home help for the other children at considerable expense. The mother, being a powerless codependent, did not resist this verbal assault, and reacted with great fear. The baby felt rejected by her angry father for simply existing and putting her mother's life in danger. Worse, she even felt rejected by her own mother. "I almost killed my mother and my father rejects me because of it."

Even though this record was right on the surface, she was unable to access it because she was disconnected from all the sources that could have informed her about the forgotten hospital-room incident that had basically destroyed her life. For years, she'd been in psychotherapy and hypnotherapy trying to locate the root of the problem, but had failed. Why? Because the experience was locked into denial-of-denial, and neither hypnosis nor psychic reading could access it; it was simply karma playing itself out.

If she had been in contact with her Holographic Mind, her soul could have fed the information back to her through her Higher Self so that it could be located and cleared. (Holographic Mind is our main source of guidance and direction, as it is the Soul-Mind connection. It has access to all the files and can provide us with the information we need to clear and rewrite files and programs.)

As with many of my clients, this woman's soul was unable to get any information to her because of her separation from her spiritual self. She was identifying with her actual life experiences as real, and living in illusion because none of the sources of information within her had a voice.

Clearing a lifetime of trauma allowed her to put her life on a whole new path. Six months later, she called to tell me that she'd got a really great job and was engaged to one of the partners in the company. Her life was finally filled with the peace, happiness, harmony, joy, financial abundance and unconditional love that she'd sought so desperately.

~ ~ ~

The soul is not fragmented or splintered in any way; we lost contact and separated from Spirit Self in childhood. When this happens, we cannot hear the dialogue with our soul and lose contact with Source. Our soul would like to support and give us guidance, and help us recover our flight plan, but many are not listening or cannot listen, which is the most common problem of the time. Our Holographic Mind is our direct line to the High Self and our soul. It is ready to communicate for us; all we need do is address it with the right words.

Some people also contend that our soul is so frustrated with us that it often leaves for periods, which is why people sleep so much. People do go on journeys when they sleep, but it is the astral body that leaves, and not the soul. Sometimes our soul tries to get messages to us in dreams but our mind may overlay it with such symbology that it's almost indecipherable.

Our soul has no agenda to force us to learn any lesson or to make any progress in our life, but it does get frustrated when we do not listen. However, it is willing to stand by and wait for us to check in and listen. If we did, and began to listen, we would find that we'd have more energy and sleep less. Why? Sleeping long hours is an escape from responsibility and my experience suggests that when people begin to take responsibility and reclaim their personal power, they begin to stay in tune with their lives. People who sleep long hours and have a hard time getting up in the morning are procrastinators, indecisive, confused, unwilling to take responsibility, and undisciplined in their life. This has nothing to do with their soul because the person has little interaction with it.

Once you find your lost self, your spiritual journey can begin. It does not start in spiritual work as such, even though all self-healing could be considered "spiritual" work. I continually stress that too many people get caught up in looking to start their spiritual journey without first building the foundation that will support that journey. We must first clear our childhood experiences and recover our flight plan so that we know why we came here in the first place—work that requires committed discipline. When we finally realize what it's all about, everything begins to fall in place.

I have observed this in my clients over the years. For example, in a recent case, the client felt locked into a dead-end job with no opportunity to move up either in salary or position. For the last ten years, every time a job was advertised in her area of expertise, she applied for it but was always turned down. Because her funds were limited, she saw me only monthly for nine months but, in the last session, we made what turned out to be a major breakthrough in her life. A friend told her about a supervisory job opening, but she felt it was over her head. However, she mustered up the courage to apply, and the interviewer called her in immediately. This shocked her as it had never happened before. The following day, she was called back for a final interview with a manager. She and I worked on her blocks against getting the position and cleared them so that she could go to the interview without any sabotaging programs. After the session, she felt that she would get the position. She later called me with the news that she got the job, a great opportunity that almost doubled her salary.

The client's 16-year-old daughter was also a client, and had many programs about peer group rejection. On one occasion, she ran into a peer pressure situation with her high school basketball team members. The team was collecting money and asked her to buy a gym bag to present to the coach as a gift at a sports night dinner. They all wanted to sign their names on, something she disagreed with. So she bought a more expensive bag using some of her own money but would not let the team members write on it. She came under intense pressure but would not go along with the plan. Eventually the team sided with her when the members saw the bag but the conflict had taken its toll on her body. Her eyes went out of focus and she had pains all over her body plus a sore dry throat. Even though she had empowered herself and stood up for her belief, she reacted as if she had given her power away. This story reveals that, no matter how strong you are, you are tested if you have any programs that conflict with the action you take. This reaction will not recur, however, as we released all the programs that created the double-bind.

In another test, she decided she would run for the student body vice-presidency. Nobody felt she could win because they all viewed her as she had been a year before—a passive, non-assertive average student. Since she had been working with me, she had become a top athlete with excellent grades. She turned the situation into a win-win lesson for herself in empowerment and taking responsibility under pressure. She won the election for vice-president yet, just a year earlier, her fellow students had put her down and not recognized her at all. People will honor and recognize who you are when you become the true empowered assertive person, as she did.

Both clients told me at their last session that not only did they feel better about themselves but also that they had cut their heath care costs by two-thirds. They attributed some of their success to the journal process to track their lives and to meditation, which made connection with the soul's directions and with the GOD Source.

With yet another client whom we'l call Jill, she came to one of my lectures in her town over 15 years ago. She lived in a small town about 175 miles northeast of San Francisco. She felt locked into a job as an alcoholic rehab counselor in a small town. She was a former alcoholic herself, so she had considerable background and understanding for her position, but there was no future. She liked the field but felt she was over-qualified for the job category in the position she was in. She was committed to move to the San Francisco area but was turned down each time she applied for a job. We cleared her limitations and the cause for her alcoholism so that she could move forward in her life. She followed all my directions to use a journal to track her life and meditated to make connection with her soul's directions so she could get back on track with her flight plan and get in contact with the GOD Source.

Jill's confidence became so strong that she decided to put her house up for sale and move to the San Francisco area. She was physically fit so she found a job as fitness counselor at a health club. It paid enough to pay the rent and the payment on her house but little else and she was undaunted in her search for her dream position. Once she lived near my office, we were able to work more often and clear more of the programs that were blocking her.

She went to many interviews and finally found her dream job as an assistant supervisor for alcoholic rehab program in hospital. Her friends and co-workers had criticized her for quitting a secure $14,000 a year job for a subsistence job at a heath club. It took three months to find this new position at a salary of $25,000. We continued to work with her limitations and she focused more on her spiritual journey now that she had more funds to work with me.

She was not satisfied to stop there, though. Jill was focused on the success in her personal, spiritual and financial life. Three months later she called me with a request. "Is there some way we can work this out ASAP. I have an opportunity to get my real dream position—Director of Alcoholic Rehab. It's a new program that I would have full control of and put together the way I want to, but I cannot get in contact with the doctor who holds the key."

I looked at the situation and told her, "The doctor is in town and the nurse will be able to give you his home number."

She replied, "The desk nurse knows that I'm the ideal person for the position, but balks at giving me the doctor's home number."

I told her, "This is lesson in empowerment, assertiveness , patience and persistence, so call the nurse back."

When she did and explained her situation, the nurse gave her the doctor's home number. He was little miffed that she'd called him at home but softened up when she explained to him her credentials and experience. He was going out of town so he could not interview her and asked her to make an appointment with his nurse, saying he would go along with her judgment.

The only time the nurse could see her was the following afternoon, which conflicted with Jill's obligation to teach a class. When her supervisor threatened her with dismissal for not teaching the class, my client said, "I'll have to take that chance."

She went to the interview and the nurse recommended her, but Jill had to return the next Monday to interview with doctor for the final decision. She got the position.

My case files are full of success stories such as this that reveal that the keys to success are discipline, commitment and empowerment. I hear countless "miracle" stories from people who are committed to following through, who drop attachments and fear, and trust they can empower themselves to make the right decision. As we get on-line with our soul mission, the universe seems to set up a phone line with the soul to provide all the connections we need to succeed in our spiritual journey.

Countless times, I have needed funds for a task but couldn't see how I would accomplish it. For example, my son was graduating from a vocational college 900 miles away but my wife and I simply did not have the money for airfares and accommodation. We had resigned ourselves to the lengthy drive, but the day before were going to leave, a check for $1,000 arrived unexpectedly in the mail. In the envelope was a note that read, "This is to demonstrate to you my gratitude for your help in the past. I cannot thank you enough."

When I needed $5,000 in 1991 to buy a new computer to begin writing my books, I had idea where I would get the money. I was telling a client about my desire to write books about my work, and he asked, "So when are you going to begin?"

"When I've saved up enough money to buy the computer. My old Apple Two won't do the job."

At his next appointment, he handed me a check for $5,000!

Again, as I was close to finishing this book and looking at the cost of printing it, two of my other books needed a second print run in order to keep up the pace in getting the word of my work out. And again the universe came through with the funds I needed.

How do these things happen? It's not luck or even prayer, although we have used the prayers in Part Six of this book to manifest situations and items in our lives. When you are engaged with your soul's mission, the universe will provide for you. The only catch is that you must release all the limiting programs and replace them with positive supportive programs. This is described in Part Four, in the appendix of this book and in my book *Your Body Is Talking; Are You Listening?*

The diagrams on the following pages show how we deal with decisions that are presented to us as lessons each day. There are only two methods to deal with conflicts in our lives (see over):

- Defensive and closed, which causes flight or fight syndrome.

- Non-defensive and open, with no judgment, manipulation or control.

Defensive, closed reaction

This causes flight or fight syndrome, which leads to the intent to protect, control or shut down and survival against anticipated fear or pain. This will also suppress the immune and endocrine systems, causing a breakdown in the physical body resulting in depression and/or illness.

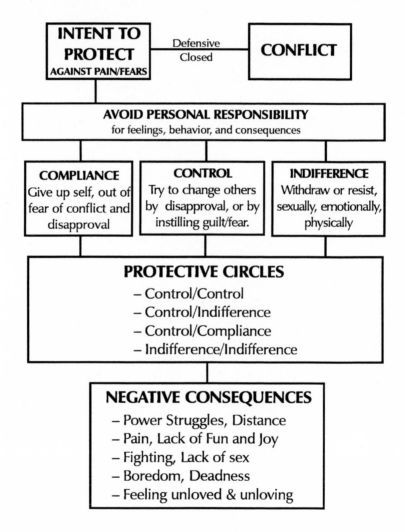

Non-defensive and open

Typified by lack of judgment, manipulation or control, plus the intent to learn from the conflict, and understand the lesson being presented. With this approach, we go into exploration of the causes, with resolution and transformation as the result.

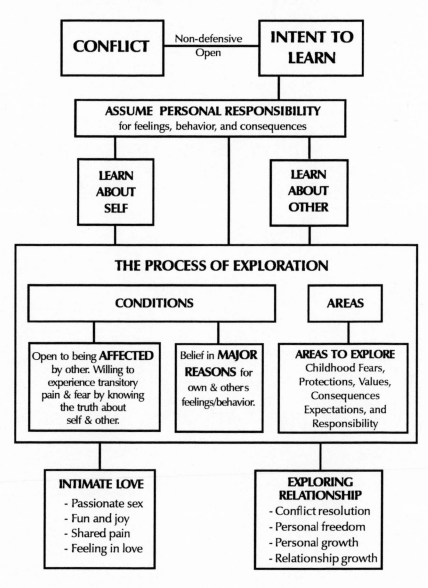

19

The Great Mystery School of Life

Esoteric mystery schools have always interested me since I was first introduced to them by Paul Solomon in 1978. He also warned me, "You must be extremely careful, however, because many people who claim to be mystery school teachers have not been trained at an actual mystery school. Many people set up mystery schools and advertise in magazines, newspapers and flyers for students, but this is not the way it should be conducted. You are chosen to attend a school after careful scrutiny of your credentials."

Historically, these schools would subject potential initiates to rigorous testing before they were admitted. Today most of us could not meet the strict requirements. In today's world, the White Brotherhood selects initiates and sets up their training once they have passed the fifth initiation in their journey to the light. I have recently discovered that all the experiences that I have gone through since 1986 were actually mystery school training, even though I was not formally attending a mystery school. Everything has been orchestrated for my benefit but I would not have chosen many of the teachers I have encountered in the last 15 years. Paul Solomon had also warned me, "I have not had an easy road, and it will not be easy for you either."

When you commit to entering the Mystery School Path, you are assigned a teacher who oversees your work and progress. You are not enrolled in an actual school; your life becomes the school. You choose some of the teachers, and others come into your life to teach you specific lessons. You set up some of the lessons and others are set up for you. The curriculum is given to you in daily lessons that are put before you, such as lessons on temptation and attachment, to see if you are listening to the guidance from your teacher and the Source.

I have found the reasons for most failures are lack of discipline and commitment. Daily discipline is required to complete the lessons, but most people do not want to devote the time it takes, so they drop the ball and their teacher drops them. Most people do not even recognize that lessons are before them or they will claim to have mastered the lesson. They may get away with this until a conflict or confrontation arises that must be dealt with on the spot.

A common trait is to blame the conflicts in our life on other people or situations rather than look within and try to see what the lesson is offering to teach us. But if we can evaluate the content of a lesson and respond effectively, we can learn from the situation rather go into a downward spiral of fear, anger and emotional reactions. If you do not get the point of the lesson, it will keep coming back, each time more intensely.

My feeling is that eastern philosophies have no connection with the concept of the mystery schools and that is why they debate being in the world or renouncing it. This will be thoroughly explored and researched in another book

For more information, see my books *Journey Into The Light* and *Opening Communication With GOD Source.*

20

The Final Step on the Path to Enlightenment and Transformation: Past Lives and Clearing Karma

Most people are unaware of the effect of karma in life. In fact, most people do not understand or believe in reincarnation. If reincarnation and karma were common knowledge, there might be a lot less crime. If people knew that their lives were being assiduously recorded in the Akashic Record and that they would be held accountable in their life review on crossing over, they would be more responsible for their behavior and actions while alive. This is not like a credit report that clears itself every seven years or a police record that can be sealed. The Akashic Record is never deleted or erased because we have no control over it. As long as people do not feel that they will be held accountable for their misdeeds, they will continue to commit them.

Karma is a common word in the jargon of those on the spiritual journey but, to the average person, it is a foreign concept. The Sanskrit word has many definitions, but we are going to discuss here two basic forms: karmic contracts and karmic agreements.

Karmic contracts arise during interactions that result in a negative outcome, and one or more parties have no intention of clearing the conflict. *Karmic agreements* are situations where one party has a pre-arranged agreement to kill another person. There are other categories, but I find that almost all karma falls under these two headings. In questioning the Source, Universal Law does not condone the taking of human life under any circumstances, including state-sanctioned executions, regardless of the crime. In today's world, value for life has become so degraded that we see striking consequences that create karmic agreements. If you take any part whatsoever in killing someone, you are creating karma. It makes no difference if it's war, or a mandated criminal sentence in which you're "just doing your job."

Most criminals are driven by mental imbalances in their mind. None of the deterrents that society comes up with have any effect on the thinking or feelings of those intent on seeking revenge or taking out their resentment. They are operating out of anger or fear, and do not weigh the consequences at the time.

Recently, the news media interviewed a boy who killed two and wounded twelve students at his high school. His response was that he had been teased, put down and beaten up all his life. He felt that his parents didn't care, nor did they even know how he felt. He could see no change in the future and felt that most people did not like him. He had thought about suicide but decided to take out his anger before he killed himself. During his rampage, he had no thoughts about the death penalty. Society is actually responsible for his behavior since he was given no guidance or support.

In the NYC terrorist attack, the perpetrators were so misguided they did not realize that many, many future lifetimes will be spent paying off the karma they created. They will have to experience the same terror they caused, many times over.

What about the people who died in this disaster? This was only one of the disasters that will take people off this planet in this manner. Every person who died had unfinished karma that was completed in that disaster. One may say that looking at this tragedy in this way is callous, but it's no different than any war. The players are different but the end result is the same. The terrorists are no different than Hitler as they played out their role in the big picture. In 1979, I predicted that there would be 40 percent fewer people on this planet by the year 2015. Will that come to pass? If we keep on the downward spiral we have been on in the last 2,000 years, it will. When we view the overall picture, we see that one lifetime is but a fleeting instant in universal time.

The struggle for control over this planet has almost destroyed it many times in history. Will we do it again? I feel that we *will* pull out at the last minute with a critical mass move in consciousness that will cause this planet to make a quantum leap.

Must we stoop down to the level of lowly animals that kill the weak so the strong may live? Are we resorting to survival of fittest, claiming that the willful destruction of human beings is a justifiable act? We must train parents to teach their children to respect all life, but can they teach something that they do not understand themselves? The statistics reveal that few parents have created a functional family. Three out of five children are rejected before they're born and grow up feeling as if they do not fit in, are not all right and are "rejects." When new mothers return to work immediately after giving birth, who takes care of the child? Preschools and nannies do not work. One of my clients is a nanny who takes care of the children of executives, and confided, "The boys I take care like me better than their parents, who are so busy that they have two shifts of caretakers."

The media, movies, video games and television are full of violence, and children take their values from what they see as accepted. Adults may say, "It's only a game. Kids know the difference," but a child's mind is like a computer that takes everything it experiences at face value and does not interpret it as, "This is good; this is bad." Everything simply goes into their database and is stored.

Children who feel that there is no future and cannot see their life getting any better act out in resentment and anger. Do we have the right to judge people who see no future for themselves when the other side of society is rolling in money and material possessions? In a way many Third World countries have the same viewpoint. To them, the U.S. is the big bully that wants to run the world. We can point to many incidents where the U.S. has gone in and killed innocent people on false information. All wars are fought for control of some form.

Karma is a complicated process. I once had a client with pains in his neck so intense that he could not move his head without agony. A review of his past life file revealed that he had operated a guillotine in a past life. Once we cleared the programs and had him forgive himself, the pain went away. How many doctors are going to suffer from administering the fatal shot during an execution? Or prison guards who pull the switch during electrocutions or in the gas chamber?

Karma is created whenever one person participates in any activity that harms another person or even limits that other person's self-expression. It can be as simple as putting other people down, which damages their self-esteem, or taking something that does not belong to you. The Golden Rule urges us to treat other people as we would want to be treated, and to be sure that we always function from ethics, honesty and integrity. Acting in any other manner is inexcusable.

For example, in a discussion about ethics I had with a man at my health club, he said, "My father was a very successful businessman and extolled to me that I must be honest, ethical and integrity at all times. I remember when I was a young boy and stole some candy from a candy store. This bothered me so much that I went back and paid for it. I later told my dad, and he rewarded me for acting honestly. From that time on, almost everything I want just falls into my life as if I'd prayed for it."

I replied, "In the past ten years, I have become so aware of karma that I wouldn't take anything even it were going to be thrown away. Ten years ago, if I saw the same towel hanging on a rack at the health club for a few days, I might have taken it, but I wouldn't do so now."

"The thought of taking something that wasn't mine wouldn't even enter my mind," he replied.

As we talked further, I began to see how he values honesty, but how people who try to take advantage of him learn some heavy lessons about integrity. His life runs easily. There are no boulders in his path or any pitfalls, as he has nothing to justify. Everything is upfront and honest. Since our conversation, he has found his dream career as a movie writer and director. A major studio gave him $45 million to produce his first film. Judging by the way his life works, he has cleared all the karma that could affect him.

In the past, karmic completion could wait until some later lifetime but, because the quickening is speeding everything in our lives up, including karma, completion comes swiftly, if not immediately. When you run into a troublesome situation in your life, do you look for someone to blame? Or do you ask, "Now what is this supposed to teach me?" If you shift blame to someone else and do not take responsibility for your own behavior, you have just created karma that is entered into the Akashic Record.

The Akashic Record also stores the lessons we came here to learn. We cannot sidestep or avoid them, although we can postpone them for many lifetimes, but we have only so many time-outs. When we have used up all the time-outs, the lesson will be presented to us to be dealt with. This is why some people have crashes in their life.

Christians do not believe in past lives or the concept of karma because Jesus Christ died for our sins. I find it hard to believe that someone who died 2,000 years ago could atone for mistakes that weren't even made back then. To me, it's a cop-out to avoid taking responsibility. Christianity also maintains that we live only once and will be taken to heaven for judgment. This begs the question of personal responsibility. Of course, you have been forgiven by GOD, because you never stood accused, but how can we go through life acting irresponsibly and not owning our own behavior? Other people believe that clearing karma is no longer necessary since some magical event will automatically clear all karma as we proceed into the new millennium? None of this makes any sense to me.

Past lives can have a string of events that tie together many past lives. Quite often in my sessions, when following the string of a client's past lives, I see something that explains a current challenge in this lifetime. If you fall into a rut, say, you can continue in this rut from one life to next. You enter the next life at the same juncture you left the past one. If you are killed in a past life, your death will connect to another lifetime where you killed someone. That way, you get to experience both sides of the coin. Karma is inexorable and inescapable.

One exception to the "eye for an eye" nature of karma occurs when you understand the lesson, forgive yourself, and ask for forgiveness. Then you can release the lesson without having to go through pain, death, chaos, anguish or whatever to release the lesson. All we need to do is acknowledge the mistake we made and claim Grace. The Lords of Karma accord Grace to us for understanding a lesson and asking for forgiveness. Once we do this, the Akashic Record notes the lesson as learned and we do not have go through the pain of karma. However, if we repeat the same misdeed, the karma will recur, only more intensely, so do not claim Grace as a routine way of clearing of karma and forget the lesson.

Here are some instances in which I have invoked the Law of Grace with my clients. One client dropped out of college because she could not focus or handle the work. She could not hold a job or finish anything she started. In her earlier years, she'd had a chip on her shoulder and blamed everyone for treating her badly. Quite often, she would draw that behavior out of people, even when they had no intention of doing so. She saw everyone as a potential adversary and would react accordingly. We found that she had been doing this for eight past lives. It began in a lifetime when she was constantly criticized by her family. She entered into another lifetime with the same type of family and received the same treatment. She went further into denial and confusion, which led to more procrastination and avoidance in future lives. Now she is breaking free of this pattern and beginning to empower herself to take responsibility. She is pulling out of her downward spiral and moving forward in her life.

Another client had a friend whose practice was failing due his chronic stuttering, and he asked me if I could cure stuttering. Speech therapists and neurologists could find nothing that would help him. I saw the friend and we cleared the stuttering in twenty minutes. He had been stuttering for fifteen years since his house had burned down. I connected it with a past life, and we found that he had burned a farmer's barn down in anger. The stuttering was a message to get in contact with the lesson. Simply understanding the lesson and claiming Grace cleared his karma and he stopped stuttering. His problems didn't end there, however, because he was caught up in the medical model and had 86 doubter sub-personalities and 36 skeptical sub-personalities so they kicked the stuttering program in again. Once we cleared all the programs five years ago, he has not stuttered at all.

Quite often we come face-to-face with a situation that causes extreme fear and pain yet we do not get the lesson. One of my clients was fearful of becoming pregnant, yet she was committed to have a baby. She was unaware of the lesson that would bring overwhelming fear on the day of the birth of her son. When she went to the hospital during labor, the doctor explained, "We will need to perform a caesarian section as the baby isn't turning and is crossways in the uterus. You can't have a normal birth without an extremely high possibility that the baby won't make it through the birth canal alive."

The fear became so intense that she asked the doctor, "Could you make a horizontal incision rather than a vertical one?"

The doctor agreed, but had to delay the procedure because the anesthesiologist was late. As she left the operating room, her mounting panic diminished to almost nothing. When she had to return, the fear was more intense. When the doctor told her, "We need to strap your arms down," she refused to let them do it, but she couldn't understand why. She was afraid to have another child due to the fear that came up during the first delivery.

Her past life files revealed that she had been pregnant during the Spanish Inquisition, and the Inquisitors had strapped her to a rack and slit her open vertically. After they had removed the baby, they tortured her to death. We found three other lifetimes with similar instances of being tortured and killed.

In a session with another client, she said, "I am very overweight and have tried all the weight loss programs but none of them have worked."

When we investigated her past lives, we found one in which she had slipped off a trail in a deep canyon and starved to death before she could be rescued, because she'd been very skinny and had no fatty reserves. She was also held captive during a lifetime in the 1400s and had died of starvation. In her current lifetime, at the age of eight, she'd overheard her father and grandfather discussing World War 1. The grandfather said, "I survived the prisoner-of-war camp because I was fat. Only the fat people survived."

This had all made such an impression on her mind that she decided she would be overweight. Once we cleared all the programs, she began to lose weight for the first time in her life.

In my own life, I had problems keeping money. I could make it easily but could not keep it. I always managed to lose it on bad investments, dishonest people and expensive legal battles. We found that in two past lives, I had been a tax collector who would use any means to force people to pay their taxes. In many others, I had been a dishonest business person. Once we cleared all these past lives, my money problems began to disappear. There was one more catch to this, however. Most people in the spiritual field do not feel they are entitled to money. When we cleared all of these programs, my money woes stopped. For more information about this, see my book *Your Body Is Talking; Are You Listening?*

In our conversations with the GOD Source, they have consistently maintained that we must learn the lesson from our past mistakes. They also contend that we are all forgiven for every mistake no matter how grievous *on condition that we atone for it*. Nobody, including GOD Source or our teacher, will force us to clear our karma. We have as many lifetimes as we choose and we are the only ones who can clear our karma. The "Catch-22" is that we can do it *only* on the third dimension. When we are in spirit between lifetimes, we have access to all our files but we cannot clear anything. We must come back into the body to work out our karma and deal with our lessons. The challenge, therefore, is to remember our mission when we get back into a new body. We have the flight plan all laid out when we get ready to incarnate but lose it in the shift from spirit to physical.

I see the spiritual journey as a process of reclaiming our power and getting back on the track we laid out in our original flight plan. When we recover our lost self, we can get on with our mission and carry out our life plan.

We are the producer, director and lead player in our personal play. We write the script, produce, direct, and play the leading role. How many plays we put on and how many acts we take to complete each one is up to us. Getting in touch with our personal page in the Akashic Record serves as a coach or teleprompter to show us our progress in the play and give us clues that would make faster progress. It is all there for us to view and look at it right now. All we need is discipline to use the tools, and follow the directions that are laid out.

This book gives you the keys, and all you need do is to use them. Have a wonderful flight. Your High Self and your soul are in your cheering section. They are waiting for you to pick up the controls and get into the pilot seat. When you do, they are ready to assist you on your flight to being a spiritual being.

For more information on this process, see my book *Journey Into The Light*.

Part Six

Exercises
and Processes

21

Tools for the Spiritual Journey

S etting up a framework that you can use to get on a spiritual path will take diligence, dedication and concentration. I have found certain tools useful to guide us on the spiritual journey, the most important of which are meditation and the Mystery School Journal. I have also found that *A Course In Miracles* can help shape the path, too.

We must tap into the Akashic Record to get the information we need to guide us in our journey. This requires that we follow a very specific protocol, which does not involve using your psychic abilities. As we said before, the psychic process works through the third chakra and can be colored by your beliefs and interpretations. Instead, we must use clairvoyance and clairaudiance, similar to remote viewing. (Remote viewers will tell you their process has more restrictive protocol, but the only way you can make contact with other dimensions, the Hall of Records, Collective Mind or Source Consciousness is through the Akashic Record.)

There is still a catch in this process. Clarity is vital, and you must be clear of all outside influences that could misdirect your channel to their frequency or information source. You may think you have a clear connection but astral beings are subtle in their methods of controlling people. They can slip in if you are not using the proper protocol to get past their influence. Many alien beings have joined with the astral beings to offer their technology to them, such as the rebel Andromedans who can project programs and beliefs into Middle Self, which will accept them and try to control you. If you have not made peace with Middle Self, so that it works with you, it is open to subtle covert mind control.

I have heard people say, "I don't believe in dark forces, negative entities or alien beings, so I don't attract them. You only attract them if you focus on them."

I didn't believe in the dark forces twenty years ago either, but when you begin the spiritual journey, you seem to put up a red flag that attracts them. It may be that "ignorance is bliss," so you feel you negotiate through life without being controlled. That may be so if you do not take responsibility but function on autopilot. The dark forces may see you as no threat and leave you alone but, once you begin making the shift, all that can change. In my practice, I rarely work on anyone who does not have some form of astral being attachment.

Paul Solomon taught a specific technique to achieve our goal, which involved discipline and consistent follow-through. To begin the program, one had to have the desire and determination to take responsibility. Commitment was important because you're dealing with a "computer" in your mind and a Middle Self that will step in and take over if you go on autopilot.

I have worked with people who have tried to get on the path only to give up due to lack of discipline and follow-through with the practice. And if you're not consistent in your pursuit, your mind will assume that you really don't mean business. If your Middle Self and your Conscious Mind's autopilot have to take over, they will not be as willing to work with you the next time you attempt to step on the path. (Which spiritual path you embark on is irrelevant but, once on one, you must stay on it, or your Middle Self will take over and be reluctant to relinquish control next time.)

Take, for example, a client who had been to many seminars and workshops over the last fifteen years, and who'd had a short run at therapy. When we tried to get her Middle Self to work with her so that she could reclaim her personal power, she became upset, heaved her insides out, suffered chills and couldn't focus on anything. She left and returned later wrapped up in a blanket and with a hot water bottle. She said she'd been so sick that there was nothing left to throw up, and had diarrhea until everything was evacuated. Her chills had been so bad that she'd gone to bed, buried under a pile of blankets to get warm. Just getting her body functioning again and having her Middle Self to work with her took a full session. I told her, "If you go off the path, you will go through a dark night of the soul," and she vowed never to do it again. Many sessions later, she has gotten her life in order, is still on the path, and is following the directions. Everything is now moving fine with her.

In a battle of "the dark night of the soul," you may feel that you are alone in a vast wasteland, with no one to help you. This is because your teachers from the White Brotherhood have set up lessons for you, and will bring people into your life to work those lessons out with.

One would assume you have free choice to take the path you want to at anytime. That's true up to a point but, when you embark on a spiritual journey, there's no turning back. You can take detours, but you will have to return to the path, and it can get harder and more intense as the above example indicates. Once you commit to following the spiritual path, there is no free will. I want to emphasize that you still have free choice to follow the detours for lifetimes. Your teachers are not concerned with time. They are looking at the big picture, not just this lifetime. They are willing to help you make the transition from third-dimensional reality to the fifth dimension, but you must do the work. Contrary to some metaphysical teachers' illusion, there is no quick fix that will rescue you from your need to follow the discipline.

There is a specific course in the Mystery School of Spiritual Discipline that involves a certain diet for transfiguration. You must also attune yourself to the Presence of GOD within through meditation and prayer. But the hardest part of this path is letting go of controller, manipulator, justifier, provoker, and authority sub-personalities that operate out of fear and anger. They cause disorganization, procrastination, and allow your autopilot to take control of your life. You must also heal your body and release the denials that control your life before you can make this transition.

The more disciplined and committed to the path of transmutation and transfiguration you become, the lighter your body becomes as you move to higher frequencies. Then, making contact with the Akashic Record becomes immediate and accurate. It has been made very clear to me that Source Consciousness cannot lower its vibration to come down to us. We must become lighter so that we can move up to a higher vibration to contact them.

I discovered that I could live in duality and move between dimensions to make contact easier but it threw me out of sync at times. I found that, as I released most of my third dimensional habit patterns, I was able live in a higher dimension yet still exist in the third dimension. When I took all the anger and fear programs that were controlling my behavior out of the internal files, it became much easier to move between dimensions.

Building a Separate Reality

Many cultures, societies and organizations teach meditation. Some describe it as "the be all and end all," the only thing you must do to reach enlightenment. In my experience, however, that is not true. Yes, meditation is an important part of the process, but I know people who meditate up to three to five hours a day, claiming that the *length* of the meditation is what will raise their vibratory level, thereby allowing enlightenment to happen. In my opinion, that time could be put to better use serving the planetary enlightenment.

According to my Source, sitting on a mountain or in silence by yourself contemplating what you could do does little to change the planetary energy and consciousness. To actively participate with groups who are working together is more powerful and seems to me to be more valuable.

I agree that one should meditate daily, but feel it should be limited to 30 to 45 minutes, even shorter if you meditate two to three times a day. I also believe it should be active, say, a dialogue with your Source, because my training and experience has shown that passive meditation separates you from you from your body. *On the other hand, it is very important to be able to leave your body in the process of meditation so that you can have a clear channel. Getting a clear channel is a real challenge.*

The following is a way to attune yourself to your Source. Begin with stretching and breathing exercises to relax the body. Then, let go of physical reality by building a separate reality, maybe a meadow, as a jumping off place for beginning to separate from the known reality. As we involve ourselves in the visual process, we will let go of the past and enter into this separate reality. The separate reality is not a "no space," but a place that is so real that it becomes somewhere you go when you want to communicate with your Source or teacher.

As we explore this new reality and become comfortable with it, we will become aware that we have other senses that parallel the physical senses. Our physical senses have limited perception, in that they are limited to our immediate location, but our more subtle senses are less limited.

There is more to reality than we experience with our five physical senses. Physical reality was built from something, but what, and where did it come from? As we develop the subtler senses, we will find a new world that is much larger than the physical world. We will be able to see, hear and feel in the limitless alternate reality and, the more we practice, the more familiar it becomes.

We will also discover a greater creative mind that has more wisdom and knowledge than we do, and this mind can impart knowledge to us that can help us live our lives more effectively. Our own mind is part of this creative mind since the presence of God is within us. We need to turn it on and become more familiar with it. Through the use of our five subtle senses, we can become more connected with the Highest Source of Our Being. Our inner teacher can impart information to us by entering a separate reality in which we are open to new material because physical reality is not blocking perception. There are no limitations in this reality.

Once you separate from the physical and move to the alternate reality, you are ready to shift into true meditation. Of course, all input from physical reality must stop, or it will prevent you from making the shift. You can play soft music if you wish, but nothing should distract you, such as voices.

Many teachers present what they call "guided meditation," but it is really guided *visualization*. Meditation involves total silence so we can step out of the conventional third dimension and immerse ourselves totally in our alternate reality.

You must also realize that you can only communicate with an ascended master if you are nearing that level of enlightenment yourself, which may cause many people to believe that they are highly enlightened because they believe they are communicating with an ascended master. However, Paul Solomon said many years ago, "In my experience, less than two percent of those claiming to communicate with ascended masters are actually in touch with them. If you are going to contact an ascended master, you are close to mastership yourself."

Many people convince themselves that they're communicating with an ascended master and conclude that they must attaining mastership. This is, of course, basing an invalid conclusion on a false assumption. Both are denials of the illusion. My book *Journey into the Light* describes how you can evaluate where you are in your enlightenment process.

Used properly, meditation is a wonderful tool but, to use it properly, you must understand that simply closing your eyes and quieting the body is not meditation. It is *relaxation* and often does not stop the incessant self-talk that goes on in your mind.

Being able to master the self-talk is key, and only then can you begin the task of contacting your Higher Self and on to your Source. To develop an intimate relationship with your Source Self, with which you will eventually be in contact at all times, requires using visual imagery to build a separate reality outside of yourself that can become so real that you may want to stay in that other dimension. The challenge is live in both worlds at the same time.

Meditation is a beginning, not an end, because it allows you to communicate at any level you choose. My goal was to access the Akashic Record and I had to meditate for a few years to get to the place where my communication lines were open. I found that when we unify our High Self with the Middle and Lower Self, we can begin to communicate at will with the Sources of Light. Meditation is a process of attuning to, and communicating in, a clear place. The closer you align with Source and listen to its wisdom each day, the more you will become anchored in your body.

Ronald Beesley, a teacher with whom I studied in the 1970s said, "Meditation is not to remove you from your body but to connect you more solidly to your body. You came to this planet to work on lessons in enlightenment because you cannot get them on the spiritual plane. Life is a workshop and you came here to work, play and have fun. It's only a drudge if you choose to view it that way. You must live with your feet on the ground and your head in the clouds."

Beesley is saying is that we must be aware of where we are at all times. We are the programmers who must direct the course of our life.

I have found that meditation is a direct phone line to GOD, a process for getting information on where we are and how to direct our life. Also, it seems to work best when coupled with the journal process (see the next chapter).

My book *Opening Communication With the GOD Source* presents an exhaustive discussion of the meditation process.

22

The Journal Process

The Mystery School Journal is a most useful tool to use in tracking your life cycles. There are as many authors who say their process is the way as there are derivations of journal work. If you have a process that works, use it. The main intent is to use some formal process to track your life cycles and keep a record of the lessons that come to you each day. In this way you can record your progress with those lessons, and I have found that knowing where you are in your path is extremely important. This section offers some guidelines to follow.

Few people allow or give themselves the time to focus on personal growth and transformation but, as this and many other books stress, the spiritual journey is a path of commitment and discipline. The journal is one of the most important transformation tools because it is a running record of your lessons and, if you review it regularly, you will recognize how many times a particular lesson has been presented to you. They may have different formats and situations but, when you go over the situations in your life and begin to recognize a pattern, you can deal with the lesson so you do not have to repeat it.

Dealing with lessons may not be easy at times, and there will always be detours that lead us off the path if we let them, such as, "I do not have enough time now," "It's not important right now," "Other people need my help," "Other things are more pressing," and "It's late and I'm too tired." However, there is no time other than *right now*, but the more you try to find the discipline, the more your mind is going to find excuses to avoid the journal exercises. It realizes that if it can get you to lose control, your Inner Middle Self and Inner Conscious Mind will install autopilot control sub-personalities to control your life.

If your avoider, confuser or procrastinator sub-personalities take over, you have lost the battle. Your mind will also install justifiers or any sub-personalities that are in line with your behavior, which further cause you to falter in your discipline. If you recognize the lack of control and can reclaim your personal power, you will need to delete, erase and destroy the sub-personalities that were created during your lapse in self-discipline.

After a few weeks, you will recognize the value and benefits of the journal process, and how, when used with other transformational tools, they all complement each other. If you focus on just one tool, such as meditation, you miss many of the lessons that are presented to you. In my case, I was unwilling to slog through life, continuing on the same path, believing that I had no choice. I attended many workshops and seminars, and picked up many tools. I also met many people who were moving through their pain and limitations, and got a clear picture of the time and commitment needed to break through the barriers and limitations with which we self-sabotage ourselves. I found out the hard way that to stay on track in my path, I had to focus on the *all* the tools I had picked up.

I had the desire and the commitment to follow through, so that was not the problem. Establishing the discipline to keep the journal, however, took some time but, once I had the routine down, follow-through came easily. I used this journal process almost every day for about six years, and it's now automatic, though since I now immediately recognize the lessons in situations, I no longer use the journal. However, getting to this point took 20 years because I did not know how the mind processed information. Please see my other books that describe how the mind works. Understanding how the mind processes sensory input will make your transformation easier.

For the journal process, carry a small notebook with you to record each incident in your daily life that feels as if it may have an impact on you. Impact situations might be ones in which you're irritated over something, you get into an argument, feel you're being attacked, find yourself defending yourself, want to run away from a conversation, back out of a situation, make a judgment, or see yourself as better/worse than someone else. All these situations have a lesson buried somewhere in them. Make brief notes about the situation and outcome and, at night, enter the information in the Daily Entry section of your journal.

Expect each day to bring new lessons and, when you can recognize the lesson as soon as it comes up, you will be able to work through it. A vital part of mastery is the ability to recognize lessons and the potential initiations that they may signal, and also not allow your Middle Self and/or Conscious Mind to create enough fear to make you back you away. You can become victimized by a situation if you do not recognize and understand the lesson embedded in it. Whether or not you enjoy the situation is not important. What *is* important is that you're aware of the situation and have no judgment about it. If you resort to justification, or go into fight or flight, you fail the lesson.

The main function of the journal process is to remind you that have already been through this before, so that you will recognize the lesson the next time it comes up. It will also allow you to see the value of what comes to you to each day. Because you're evaluating the situation and processing the lesson immediately, you won't internalize, stuff or repress any associated emotion. But even if you don't get the lesson right away, at least you're setting yourself up so that it won't happen again.

Recognizing a lesson after the fact is better than not recognizing it at all because, unfortunately, when you don't catch it the first time, it comes back more intensely each time, seemingly in multiples of two. The fourth time will be sixteen times more intense than the first time.

The journal process allows you to get the lesson by knowing what to look for next time, but it's only as effective and useful as your commitment to being alert to the interactions that happen to you.

The concept is to grow into 24-hour consciousness, becoming constantly aware of everything that happens. Then, you can rewrite your life script, including dreams, and can change the outcomes and probabilities that are projected for the future. Contrary to some people's interpretations, the future is not locked in. If you know it, you can change it. There are no limitations for the possible human. Also, as you begin your journey through the various initiations, or gateways, in life, you will find that miracles do happen in your life, so keep track of them; they are win/win situations.

Your life is a spiritual journey and, the closer attention you pay to each disruption, procrastination, and refusal to take responsibility, the more quickly you will recognize the lessons you are trying to avoid. The more you discipline yourself to deal with each lesson as it comes up, the sooner you will arrive at the destination and your goal.

Setting up your journal will prove time well spent. Place seven 3-ring binder dividers in a binder and label them with the following seven headings. Then add blank paper in each section.

The journal is divided up into the following sections:
1. Daily Entry
2. Dialogue
3. Dream Log
4. Inner Wisdom (listening)
5. Stepping Stones (minor initiations)
6. Discovery (history of your life)
7. Turning Points (major initiations).

The Dream Log is to record your dreams and the direction you are getting from them; the Inner Wisdom section records the revelations you receive, twilight imagery, intuitive feedback, dialogue in meditation, and direct contact with your Source.

Stepping Stones are the minor initiations that you're working on between the Turning Points, such as the temptations you experience, and how you are dealing with them. The Discovery section is your past history, the raw material of your life, lifecycles up this point in your life, turning points in the past; the crossroads and the forks in the road.

The Turning Points are the doors to ascension, your experience at the time you open the door and how you handled the temptations in your progress.

1. Daily Log Section

The Journal section is made up of two subsections:
(a) *Captain's Log*, a daily entry for all the interactions during the day that records only the actual interaction, with no evaluation.
(b) *Validation of Self-Worth*, or how you reacted or responded to the temptations and lessons presented to you each day, an evaluation of your understanding of the lesson, the value you gave the experience, and whether you appreciate and validate yourself.

1(a) Captain's Log

For this journal section, carry a small notepad with you at all times. Life is never dull when you're alert, for nothing happens by accident and no one ever enters your sphere of existence without purpose. The

"Captain's Log" is the opportunity to make *brief* notations of the day's experiences to be used with the journal work and the evening's meditation.

The name clues you to how it works. It helps to view your life as a journey on "space ship Earth" and note the occurrences in your life that would be reported in a Captain's Log. The routine occurrences are only recorded by mention. For example, a captain might enter:
"*Jan. 6*: We had just completed our meeting with the crew when ..."

The "when" actually constitutes the entry. The ordinary events provide the setting, but the unexpected or meaningful occurrences are the recorded events. Do not wait for an outstanding event to make an entry in the Captain's Log; neither should you waste time and energy filling journal pages about mundane events. Keep your entries brief: just the "who, what, when and how." This section is a running account of the setting in which the incidents of your life occur. These incidents must be examined for meaning and purpose, for accurate and misdirected reactions and, most of all, for lessons contained in your reaction/response to the situation.

Examples

Jan 6, 7:09 am: Was on my way to the airport, traffic was heavy and I was in a hurry. A traffic light was flashing red—took 15 minutes extra to get through the intersection. Because it was later in the day, the freeway was jammed and I missed my flight. I experienced great anxiety because I had to reschedule my meetings. I recognized fear and frustration, a loss of control and feeling of being a victim. My stomach and nerves suffered from the anxiety. My whole day was affected.

Jan 7, 9:00 am: Due to freeway accident, arrived at work 30 minutes late. I hoped no one would notice. I tried to look unruffled. I was sure my anxiety showed. No one said anything. Took all morning to relax.

4:05 pm: Uneventful day at work, so I meditated for 5 minutes before driving home. It is pleasant to feel high and start home feeling good. I was able to resist getting angry with other drivers.

Jan 8, 7:00 am: Woke up feeling really good, yet everyone was upset, which threw me off.

12:30 pm: Tried to set up lunch with my girlfriend. She said I was not considerate of her time and needs, and turned me down. I felt rejected and alone.

3:30 pm: Got to my appointment but Jim no-showed. I'd prepared and was angry but chose not to give my power away to him. It's Jim's problem, not mine. Readjusted my plans and went on my way. Noticed that I was able to detach from the anger. Got the lesson this time.

Jan 9, 2:30 pm: Was enjoying the day with my girl friend. I had to start my motorcycle with the kick starter because the battery was dead. My girl friend did not get off while I was trying to start the engine. I was trying to hold the bike up with her on it and because I was off balance, my foot slipped off the pedal and I burned my leg on the exhaust pipe. I wanted to blame my girl friend for not being considerate and getting off. I realized this was a lesson. I could have asked her to get off. I resisted the temptation to blame her and took responsibility and did not get angry at her or myself.

Some days may contain more entries than this but some may not. It is vitally important to make an entry every day. What doesn't seem important right now may be meaningful later. Every time a feeling, sensation, fear, anger, or any other emotion surfaces, or something catches your attention, write it down. Keep track of everything, and you will be amazed how quickly the lessons come.

You will not repeat many lessons when you stay up with each incident that happens in your life. It's important to list the wins and times when you feel good about what happens. This will validate your progress. Each day before you go to bed, transfer your notes from your notebook to your journal in the appropriate section. As you get into the format, you will notice that you become aware of the lessons as they arise. When you can spot or recognize the lesson immediately, it will be defused and will not affect your body.

1(b) Validation of Self-Worth

If you are searching for greater meaning in relationships and communication, this section is one of the most important of your journal. Understanding cause-and-effect in your interactions with other people can change your entire life path.

You must recognize the meta-communication that you send out, for people will react to your subconscious projection of who you are, even before you say anything. If you can change the unspoken communication, people will respond to you completely differently. If you can understand how you project yourself, you can release the need for facades, fronts, masks, games and covers. We are living in illusion and denial if we think they work, for many people can recognize the facade or mask you are putting up. For example, you may wonder why you were dismissed by someone when you felt you made a good impression. If you will be honest with yourself, this process will reveal to you exactly how you sabotage your efforts.

No one "accidentally" comes into your life, so everything is there by design and your invitation *at some level*. Suppose you notice a person and make an observation. Does that observation trigger judgment, jealousy, surprise, or embarrassment, or does it motivate you in some way or teach you something?

Depending on your mind's programming, every observation will cause either a negative reaction or positive response. This is a way to recognize autopilot reactions. It will also help you realize how you validate or invalidate yourself. If you are honest with yourself and evaluate each situation without denial, you can break through all the illusions in your life. If you do not recognize the illusion, the denial continues. If a person points something out to you, you need to evaluate rather than justify, for the latter always indicates denial.

All rightness is a quality you learn when you detach from the need for outside validation. You cannot find self-esteem, self-worth, self-confidence, and self-love until you self-validate that you are all right under all situations.

If you can recognize that everything is in your life for a purpose, you can change your life path into happiness, joy, inner peace, and harmony. When you begin to recognize the value of others, you will be appreciated more than you ever dreamed possible. You are never a victim unless you choose to be. If you so choose, then everyone will seem to discount or put you down. The challenge is to recognize your all rightness and people will respond supportively. Nobody can reject you except you. You have to buy into their game and give away your power to become victimized.

Start by observing the people close to you in your life and honestly evaluating how you respond to them. For each one, note how this person affects you. Look at the situations and incidents in which you have engaged with them. As you get more familiar with this section, you will able to make instant evaluations. Try to find key words that describe the situation, then make a short entry.

This section is designed to instill a new appreciation for the cast of characters in your life. If you do not like the actors and actresses in your play, you can change them. But, you must first recognize the lessons they bring you. You and your inner plane teacher, who knows what you need to learn, carefully chose them. *Do not put "shoulds" on yourself.* Evaluate the situation as it happened, with as little emotion as possible. As you work with this section, you will able to evaluate from an objective observer's standpoint.

Here are some guidelines to make this section work for you:

1. Validate the person and not the incident.
2. Appreciate the value of the person and do not enter the negative.
3. Do not consider what you think you *should* feel or how you *should* have responded. Do not put *shoulds* on yourself. Work from your feelings.
4. Always appreciate your value in the situation. Even if your response is negative, find something positive and meaningful about yourself.
5. To change your reaction and correct your faults, you must see some value in yourself. You will make more progress when you are aware of your own value.
6. Do not leave yourself with feelings of guilt or lack of self-worth.
7. If you can recognize the lesson and the temptation next time, you may not fall into the trap.
8. You must be able to evaluate the incident honestly and without denial. It may be a challenge to enter a description of your value in each situation. Was I of value? Did I help those I have validated? Did I do what I could do to help the situation? Did I validate myself? Did I show appreciation for myself in understanding the lesson presented?

The only way this section will work is by being totally honest with yourself and recognizing any denials and illusions.

Examples

Person: Boss/Challenger, motivating, demanding, controlling
Spouse: Clings, codependent
Friend: Seems to put me down all the time
Mentor: One-ups me all the time, acts superior.

- *Incident:* Boss challenged me by snapping at me. Embarrassed me in front of others.
- *Worth:* Made me deal with my victim/self-pity. He seems to be unfeeling in his criticism. I guess I have missed this lesson numerous times.
- *Self-validation:* I now see that I can present myself more effectively. To be more effective, I must become a self-actualized person in my life.

- *Incident:* Friend put me down because I was complaining. Made me angry.
- *Worth:* Called my attention to the fact I was running on auto-pilot.
- *Self-validation:* The putdown was my interpretation. I needed to hear it but reacted as a victim. I can detach and respond more effectively next time.

- *Incident:* Daughter does not want to communicate with me. Has shut me out her life.
- *Worth:* I recognize I was feeling guilty, rejected and was attached to her.
- *Self-validation:* I am releasing my guilt. I did the best I could at the time in bringing her up; I can't control her. I am all right myself and the situation can be resolved by releasing her. Her inner plane teacher will work, if she listens.

- *Incident:* Driver in car cut me off and almost caused a crash.
- *Worth:* Brought up my anger. I recognized I could not control situation. Autopilot again. Testing my patience.
- *Self-validation:* I automatically get angry when I lose control. Am going to detach myself from situations that I have no control over. I know I can function without getting fired up.

- *Incident:* Mentor tried to one-up me again. He always has a story that's more dramatic than mine.
- *Worth:* Brings up my anger. I was unaware of my complaining and victim attitude.
- *Self-valuation:* I see that I'm trying to get validation from outside. If I describe my situation as a challenge rather than self-pity, people would be more supportive.

- *Incident:* I burned myself on the motorcycle exhaust pipe
- *Worth:* Brought up my anger and the feeling that my girl friend caused the incident. This was a temptation to place blame on someone else and not take responsibility for my actions.
- *Self-validation:* Recognizing that I was ready to blame someone else when I know that I am the creator of all my actions. I stopped the emotion before it took over, learned the lesson and took responsibility.

2. Dialogue Section

You may find you will use this section daily, but it is not required. This section is for your letters and dialogues with various people, sub-personalities, events, etc. It's best to sort issues out in your mind with *dialogues* before you confront or state your opinion publicly. Rehearsing your dialogue may avoid making mistakes. Dialogues may fall into the following categories:

- *Dear Master letter*, to communicate with your teacher and Presence of GOD.
- *Dialogues with other people*, to air your feelings about issues with the people in your life.
- *Dialogues with your job*, to air your feelings or pat yourself on the back.
- *Dialogues with society*, to express your feelings over societal issues.
- *Dialogues with events* help you learn how to clearly communicate about them prior to engaging in debate with other people.
- *Dialogues with your body*, in which you ask it questions. You may be surprised at the answers you get.
- *Dialogues with sub-personalities.* Use your dominant hand (right if you are right-handed) to talk with your Inner Critic or

your Critical Parent, and any sub-personality that is controlled by the Middle Self. Use your other hand to communicate with the selves that come through the right brain, such as Inner Self, Inner Child, Inner Teacher. You can also dialogue verbally.
- *Voice dialogue.* A process developed by Hal Stone to talk to the various sub-personalities. This requires three chairs. You assign a sub-personality to the chairs and move back forth in your dialogue with them. One chair is the positive or power side and the other is the negative or weak side. The center chair is your conscious mind.

Let's take a more detailed look at each type of dialogue.

Dear Master Letter

Since your life is carefully arranged to meet the lessons you need, it is a good idea to assume that a Master Teacher (i.e., the Presence of GOD) is at work in your life, arranging the lessons and people in your daily activities. Nothing and no one comes into your life by happenstance. Your Inner Teacher, Higher Self and Master Teacher have arranged every detail.

With this many beings watching over you, you have considerable help available, and all you need do is ask. However, you must be specific and clear, because they will honor your wishes to the letter. Remember, every word you say or think is a prayer and instruction to them to carry out an action in your life.

This superior intelligence helped you to structure your body and lessons to this point. The presence of GOD is with you at all times when you open the door. They would like to have direct communication with you so they can give you the opportunity to work with them in making your life easier. So, it would be a good idea to get to know the Source of Your Being and learn to communicate meaningfully with the Presence of GOD. Letter-writing is a great way to keep in touch.

You can assume that this Source is able to read your letters; also would like you to write letters to him/her. Until now, it may have been a one-way conversation that you did not understand. You can assume that "I will learn to build a personal relationship with my Source by building my personal relationship with him."

Your letters should reflect your desire to know about specific aspects of real situations in your life. All you need to do is be direct and honest. You can ask any question, the answers are available. There is no specified format for this; just write exactly what you want to say or know. Your questions should be clearly worded, and have basic direction to them. There will be no judgment, for your Source has nothing but love for you.

The purpose of the Dear Master letter is to maintain a constant awareness and dialogue with your Inner Teacher and Presence of GOD. Your teacher is responsible for providing the lessons, but *you* are responsible for taking the lessons through to their end. *You* are the only person who can create your reality.

Examples

Dear Master,

Last night I asked you a question. I held the question in my mind going to sleep. I have not received an answer. I am asking the question again, and await your answer.

With love,

Dear Master,

I know that you are involved in this process of life with me. I feel that I can ask you questions about my direction and situations in life. If my lessons come too fast, I know I can ask you to slow them down. I would really like to believe that you are here all the time. In the past it did not seem that way. But, I am willing to give up my preconceived notions and go with your direction. I may be reluctant at first, but I know that with some demonstration, I will be ready for this new event in my life. I will spend at least twenty minutes each morning listening to you. I know you are capable of giving me direct communication. I will be ready for your communication each day. I will try every way to be ready. You can communicate in any manner you choose. I will be watching for your direction in revelation, dreams, direct communication or meditation, your choice. I will be constantly be aware that you are here. I will write again tomorrow. I am learning to love you.

Dear Master,

Thank you for making me notice the bumper sticker. I am really amazed at the synchronicity by which you bring me the answers.

Dear Master,

A dream from last night answered the question I asked. I know now that I must increase my awareness of the content of "mind chatter" and catch any limiting thoughts. Please help me.

3. Dream Log Section

The dream log is a special part of the journal because this section can give you considerable direction in your life if you use it properly. You may want to use a small tape recorder rather than directly writing the dream down. If you prefer to write it down, always have a small light and a pencil available.

Brain researchers have discovered that we dream three to ten dreams a night while in a REM state (rapid eye movement). Everyone dreams, and those who say they do not dream are not making space to receive dreams. You must declare your state of expectancy to your Subconscious Mind and Higher Self, and open your consciousness for dreaming. In our research, we have discovered that in many of our dreams, we are seeing the mind filing information.

As you become more consciously aware of dreams, your dream state will become more active. Your dreams will also become more meaningful in application. If dreams do not come easily, you may have to change your sleeping habits, or could write a letter to your Subconscious Mind about your intent.

You will notice that your dream symbology will take on the character of your daily events, for the lessons you are going through will be directly associated with your dreams. If your Middle Self is trying to block the information, it may try to cloak your dreams in deep symbology. If you want to avoid an issue in your life, you may find your dreams getting more intense and symbolic.

When you are dreaming, you are in an alpha state, so it is easy to wake up if a dream frightens you. As you pass through the hypnogogic state on waking, most dreams will fade after 30 to 60 seconds, which is why it is important to write them down or record them immediately.

As you become more aware and change your attitude about dreams, they will become easier to recall. If you do not like the dream's outcome, you can go back into the dream and rework it to change the outcome, which will actually change the future.

Here are some pointers to working with dreams:

- Before rising in the morning, make notes on the dreams you can remember. If the dream wakes you in the night, write it down. Move slowly when you are writing because you can shift from alpha to beta very fast and you may lose contact with the dream imprint. You will not lose any sleep once you get into stride. It is important to get down a sketch of every dream. The messengers will give up if you do not commit yourself to recording your dreams.

- Just get the dream down the best you can and worry about analyzing and interpreting it later.

- Write a word or two about how you felt in the dream and how you now feel about the dream. Give it an emotional value. Did you feel apprehensive, scared, confused, scolded or angry? Did it give you a feeling of joy, sadness, nobleness, or happiness? Did the dream seem to be instructive or complementary?

- Look for figures of speech, puns, or clichés. These may give the dream more meaning.

- Look for universal symbols and easily identifiable symbology.

- When you retire at night, write your question down in your dream log. This will usually invoke a dream. If the question is not answered, you may need to write a Dear Master letter about it.

- Remember you are all the people in the dream. Some aspect of you will always show up in the dream. It is possible that an important lesson could be coming to you that you would miss if you thought it was coming from someone else.

- In all of your dreams, it's important to workout and understand your symbols. Everyone has their own set of symbols and the way in which they are displayed. You cannot assume that someone else's symbols are the same as yours and apply them to your dreams.

4. Inner Wisdom Section

In this section, you record your guidance and dialogue with the master teachers in your life. This may be the most pleasant section of your journal. At first you may not get many entries, but as you travel on the path, this will become one of the most important dialogue sections. This section differs from the actual Dialogue section because it is only used for recording meditation, guided imagery, revelations, or knowing that does not come from ordinary consciousness.

When you get to the point of feeling that you have your Higher Self's telephone line permanently connected to the Highest Source of Your Being (Presence of GOD), you will get direction immediately without going into meditation. You can also use this section to write a Dear Student letter from your teacher. It will be dictated to you in any form you want it to come.

This is an opportunity for you to make a close connection with your Higher Self as it is the Presence of GOD within you. When you become attuned to your Higher Self, it will give you the ability to record some of the most beautiful communication that can come as a result of perfect attunement with the GOD within. The Higher Self is the "long distance phone operator" in your universal telephone system, and will connect you to the Highest Source of Your Being. When accessing the Akashic through the Source, you can tap into any person or information in the Universe.

In this process, we are not using psychic senses, as they originate from the Subconscious Mind and the third chakra. The connection in this case is the crown chakra.

The meditation experience is in a space of pure silence. What many people call meditation is, in reality, guided imagery and when you are following a source of communication, you cannot get any inflow from the Higher Selves or your Teacher. They will not interfere in your life, and you must create a space for them to tune in, which in the beginning can only done in absolute silence, unless they have an urgent message for you, in which case, they may break in at any time. (Guided imagery, however, is useful in disconnecting you from physical reality, for you can focus on a process to step out of physical, mental, and emotional plane reality.)

Mantrum meditation is also a form to distract or move you away from your self-talk, as the focus is on a verbal attuning. Chanting is another form that will separate you from your self-talk and bring you to a place of silence. The final step in all meditation experiences is coming to a place of total silence in which all directed imagery and inner self-talk from your Middle Self and Subconscious Mind cease totally.

Meditation experiences may take many forms. If you choose to relax and release stress, it may be a quiet meditation (being careful not to go to sleep). There are two active forms of meditation: moving meditation such as dancing or movement, and writing or dialogue meditation. In the latter, keep your journal and pen handy for, if the dialogue or inspiration is in words, you will want to record it.

Not all your meditations will produce written dialogue while you are sitting in silence, but if they do, you have the opportunity to write it down. These entries may bear no connection with other journal sections, and may stem exclusively from your attunement with the Divine. It is an outpouring of your individual meditation experience.

Before you meditate, you can ask any questions by writing them down in this section and taking them into meditation with you. The Higher Self as messenger will take them to the Master Teachers during your attunement and entry into meditation. The answers may be ready before you get to the place of silence.

Do not feel you must have a dialogue or a message each time. You should be able to enjoy a deeply satisfying meditation without any contact or verbal message. Do not feel disappointed if there are no words. Your teachers know when to give you the guidance you need. If you are "needy," they may withhold dialogue until you release your neediness. Put something in your meditation record each time. It may be just the quality of the meditation or the relaxation you received.

Remember the affirmation over the door of the Hall of Records: "I will bring to your remembrance all things whatsoever you have need of from the foundations of the world."

5. Stepping Stones Section (Minor Initiations)

This is the Mystery School Lesson section of the journal. In this section, you track your progress through each initiation. You will recognize the Mystery School by first being aware that you are enrolled in a school. When you realize your primary reason for being on this earth plane of existence is to attend this school, you have made the first step in initiation. The second step is to view everything with your eyes and ears open. You will start to become discerning in how you handle yourself and the lessons before you. When you understand that life is a workshop and you are in a classroom each day no matter where you are, the lessons become easier. The Teacher provides the lessons but does not say, "This is a lesson; wake up." They are more subtle in their presentation.

The challenge is to recognize your teachers, no matter who they are. They are all orchestrated by your Master Teacher to teach you. They might not be who you would choose as your teachers, but they would not be in your life unless the lesson was before you.

An uncomfortable situation is likely to be a lesson that was presented before but you ignored it for some reason. If you are having a hard time learning the lesson or letting it go, you might want to focus more on what that particular lesson is telling you so that it is not repeated with even greater discomfort.

It is your responsibility to be aware of the lesson, and once you are, write it down in this section. Keep track of the lesson each time it comes up. If you do not recognize the lesson, scan your "Validation of Self-Worth" in the Daily Log. In a short time, you will be able to see the lessons as they come up.

This section may call for a daily entry depending on the level of your commitment to transformation. There may be days when no lesson is discernible; this is perfectly normal for you do not have to have a lesson every day. You could also slide through your life "on vacation," not recognizing *any* lessons; in fact, most people do. However, if you are not constantly on top of the lessons and recognizing them as stepping stones on the path, they are likely to get farther apart, presenting you with ever-widening gaps to jump across or ever taller hurdles.

The path is very clear and discernible when we open our eyes and ears but, just as your Master Teachers are recording your progress in your Akashic Record probably more accurately than you are doing, it behooves you to keep accurate records in your Journal. Your Subconscious Mind is also recording everything that transpires in your life. It is automatic and you have no control over the recording process.

This is an interactive section of your journal, and it will begin to talk back to you when you find how easy it is to recognize the lessons. In fact, your self-talk might talk back to you and say, "This is a lesson;

watch out and take notes." This section interacts with most of the other sections of your journal.

Look at how various lessons are presented to you. The best way to recognize the lessons is by making note of the following:

- Any uncomfortable, agitated, frustrating or emotion-packed incident contains the building blocks of a lesson. This is an opportunity to learn and take a step forward.
- If you become more acutely aware of the elements that make up your day, you will discover the lesson that you have been avoiding or putting off. In fact, the lesson may be right in your face.
- Make sure you are not projecting the lesson onto someone else or justifying it. If you do this, you're not getting it.
- If someone pushes you away or avoids you for no apparent reason, you may want to review dialogue with your self-talk and find the meta-communication that is preceding you.
- Look at how you're setting yourself up for a lesson when no one seems to be involved. For example, you may be having fearful or angry thoughts, or running prejudice against someone or something. Review or dialogue with the thoughts or feelings that come up.
- Go back to the Discovery section and see if you can locate the incidents of the past that have invoked this lesson. If not, work with the Discovery and Dialogue sections to locate it. If it still evades you, work with a practitioner who can help you reveal the lessons.
- Write a Dear Master letter if you are unclear and you may get the answer.
- Ask for an informative dream, or ask your Source in meditation.

Teachers come in every manner of being. You could miss a pleasant friendship by preconceiving how another person will respond to you. Your conception could be false and the encounter could be a joyous happy experience with positive validation. The test is: can you handle your vulnerability effectively without fear?

In processing lessons, you will realize that you cannot make prejudgments about others until you actually meet them. Remember, you are responsible for what you say and how you react. You may say, "I create my own reality so I can say or do anything I want," and to an extent, this is true, but you are also responsible if you use people or shamelessly put them down. In the transformation process, your goal is to end separation, not create more.

There are many minor initiations (i.e., lessons) between each major initiation (i.e., turning point), and you need not master each one in order to move forward. The main lessons are about self-love, receiving love, and projecting love.

Self-validation and self-approval are most important, with the toughest lesson being accepting your own all rightness, and it will recur until this becomes a daily reality in your life. The temptations on all rightness will plague you until you decide that external validation is unnecessary. The qualities that come with all rightness are self-esteem, self-worth, self-confidence, self-validation, and self-love. These are "cluster qualities" in that they are all linked and not attainable separately. People may *appear* to have some of these qualities, but the temptation test will reveal how the person handles the lesson. It is important to keep track of all the lessons that are presented so you can track your progress.

6. Discovery Section

This section documents your history from birth to present age—the raw material of your life. How did you arrive at the present place in your life? Who are the actors and actresses in your play? Have you been the scriptwriter, producer and director in your life, or have others? Who programmed your life and are you the programmer now? Can you track the cycles in your life?

The Discovery section is not a daily entry section; it is a one-time journey of self-discovery and exploration of your past, designed to map out the building blocks and the catalysts in your life experience. It also includes initiations and turning points in the past that you will also want to enter in the Turning Point section when you are able to identify them.

Few people look back at the forks in the road that they could have taken but didn't, and this is an opportunity to look back at what might have happened, but without regret. This section will take you out of the now moment into the past, for we need to understand the past and its programming before we can build a strong foundation.

Most of us are from dysfunctional families and do not have a strong foundation. Most of us hand over our personal power to Middle Self and do not deal very well with the earth plane lessons. At each fork, we took one of two paths: we either avoided the lessons of life and went into emotional/survival existence, or we skipped over all the painful earth plane lessons and jumped into the esoteric, spiritual level without dealing with the earth plane. However, a few decide to hang on and stay grounded as best they can and steer a course that will eventually guide them to the light. If you will be honest with yourself, record in this section which category you fall into, and reveal the illusions and denials in your life.

You will be adding to this section as you discover areas in your life. Take your time to build up the structure. It does not have to be done immediately. Above all, do not create more illusions and denials by building a dream of what you would *like* your childhood to have been. Many times, we put our parents on a pedestal only to have them fall when the truth begins to emerge.

Hiding in the spiritual world doesn't work either. Be as honest as possible as you can, and you may find that you have been hiding traumatic experiences from yourself. False foundations will crumble faster than you can build them. You cannot falsify your records with this system. Many times, people will block out their past because it's too traumatic. If you have a problem with going back to your history, you may need a therapist to help you.

Here are some pointers to completing the Discovery section:

1. Give a short biographical history, with a chronology of your ages.
2. Life Cycles, with the forks and crossroads. Look for the initiations, major and minor, with date, place and players. Give each cycle a title and write a brief overview. Then review your cycles now and notice if you are repeating lessons.
3. Changes within changes. Look for any series of events that brought about new awareness. Use meditation, imagery, free association or regression to locate the source of life changes and explore their lifecycles.
4. Activities. What type of activities and relationships were happening? How did you interact in each cycle?
5. Initiations. (Beginning initiations are not in the 12-door process but occur when you claim your personal power.) Identify your initiations and write down how you recognized that you could be a *cause* in your life rather than a reactive result? When did you decide to step out of victim consciousness? When did you decide to handle situations in your life well? When did you decide to take charge of your life? (It could be only yesterday).

6. Turning Points, i.e., times in your life when an initiation came to fruition and you actually took control of your life. Describe the wrestling matches with whatever teacher was bringing you the lesson? Who was your angel, and your antagonist? Who was the shepherd? Who was the wise man? What gift did each bring you?

7. Review your beliefs. How many of them are copies of your parents' beliefs? Which are karmic-related? Which are your life-driving beliefs. Hint: in analyzing your beliefs, gather at least 50 to 100, involving money, sex, love, power and work. Take a good look at your beliefs about yourself and relationship to others. Separate your beliefs into two groups: those that serve you and those that do not. Then invoke the Law of Grace to discover if the latter beliefs are valid. If not, establish a new set of valid beliefs that you feel will serve you.

7. Turning Points Section

Turning Points are the major initiations in life where you demonstrate you are ready to advance through a door of initiation. In your journey on the path of transformation, you will come to forks in the road, crossroads where you know that you are taking the appropriate path in your new awareness. At these crossroads, you shift gears and begin to take control of some aspect in your life. As a child, it may have been the time you said, "I am not going to let other children bully me anymore." Or the time you decided to get good grades for *yourself* rather than to impress your parents. Of course, this spurt in your independence may not have happened until you were an adult. In fact, for many people, this does not happen until something makes them aware that they have still not claimed their personal power.

Once you decide to take responsibility for yourself and drop the need to have others validate your all rightness, you are at a crossroad and must decide who you are. Your Master Teacher will evaluate your progress, and will not accept illusions and denials.

Evaluate from the Discovery section when you arrived at crossroads or forks in your life where you decided that you would no longer put up with a behavior pattern in yourself or being victimized by others, and vowed to take control.

Turning points where you begin to relate in a different way in your life have the following characteristics:

1. You face your vulnerability and learn how to change your response-ability to emotions.
2. You claim your personal power with the ability to detach from anger, fear, etc., and respond in an effective way to an emotional situation.
3. You detach from the need to react for other people and respond in your own best interest.
4. You get to the point where you can validate yourself without the need for others' approval.
5. Your love is not dependent on another person demonstrating their love for you.
6. You can give unconditional love and forgiveness with no need for love to be returned.
7. You decide to be a human *being* instead of a human *doing*.
8. You let go of poverty consciousness, living in lack and the attachment to money. You take responsibility for your own abundance, and claim your entitlement to wealth, believing that, "God is money in action."
9. You can state the facts with no need to justify. You are all right just the way you are. There is no need to prove yourself to anybody. What is, just is.

When you complete a major initiation and pass through the door, make a note in this section with the date and the incident that you overcame that set you up to go through the door.

Make sure you have passed all the tests before you claim your victory. Many people go through a door and slip back in the testing period because they could not sustain themselves. It can be devastating to find yourself going through the same lesson when you thought you had learned it and passed the test.

Remember, *you* do not make the decision to advance through the door. As you advance through the steps, you will become aware when you are being guided towards a major initiation. You will automatically go through the door when you are ready.

You can test yourself with Kinesiology to check which doors you have gone through (see *Journey Into the Light* for requirements).

Journal binders, separators and instructions are available from Personal Transformation Press for $13.95 (see order form at back).

23

Prayers and Affirmations for Manifestation

We have found in our work that you must have all four of the minds (Middle Self, Ego, Subconscious Mind, and Conscious Mind) networking together to get prayers and affirmations to work. As program manager, Middle Self, must be working with Ego, or file manager, for information to be put in the Subconscious Mind's data base, or Lower Self. The trick is getting all of them to work together, and taking responsibility for every action and behavior, so that Conscious Mind cooperates. When you take your personal power back so that autopilot is no longer running your life, then these prayers and affirmations will work like a charm. But if you're not honest with yourself, or are operating from an illusion, they will not work. (See next page for a synopsis of the various types of mind.)

Kahuna Prayer for Manifestation

Hawaii is home to an ancient religion whose priests are called Kahuna (literally "guardians of the secrets"). They use illuminating knowledge and strict discipline to manifest situations or items that they desire to change or bring into their lives. My research points to them being direct descendents of the Atlanteans. They preserved a repository of clear information when they left Atlantis, trekked across Central America, and set off by boat for the islands of Hawaii, the tops of volcanoes that formed over millions of years. (Archaeologists have found no evidence of human habitation before the Kahunas arrived, so how they knew back then that the islands even existed is still a mystery.)

The Spiritual Mind or God-self

1. Contact is made through:
   a. Meditation
   b. Dreams
   c. Journal writing
   d. Intuition, realization
2. The Inner Teacher:
   a. We must ask for explanations or guidance
   b. Will not interfere with conscious free choice
   c. Can set up lessons that we need to learn but can't see with our physical eyes

Higher Self or Superconscious Mind

The Reasoning Mind

1. Operates only in the waking state
2. Controls the physical body:
   a. "Programmer" for subconscious mind
   b. Decision-maker
3. Uses will-power, discipline, discernment, discrimination, concentration and reasoning to operate and feed in information

12% Conscious Mind or Middle Self

The Non-reasoning Mind

88% Subconscious Mind or LowerSelf

1. Operates in waking or sleep states
2. Operates on impressions, stimulus response
3. Operates physical body (autonomic nervous system and para-sympathetic system)
4. Examines, classifies and stores information:
   a. Thoughts, feelings, emotions, memories, imagination, habit patterns, desires, and instincts
   b. Retrieves this information and feeds back to Conscious Mind without reasoning ability as to the effect on the physical body or mind, creating health or disease
5. Creates most dreams:
   a. Will feed back dreams from Higher Self
6. Operates the inner (sixth) senses:
   a. Psychic abilities
   b. Visualization
   c. Sensing radiation through chakras
   d. Clairsentience
7. Creates energy, which contacts other people and objects through aka cords.

The Types of Mind

Their spiritual and metaphysical information dates back at least ten thousand years, handed down by verbal tradition from one person to another in the family. Since the Kahuna were isolated for thousands of years, their information was less tainted by other cultures. They had direct contact with GOD Source and contacted them quite often. Their contention was that we must follow strict protocol to make contact.

When the Christian missionaries arrived to convert these "savages" to Christianity, they tried to wipe out the Kahuna repository but failed because none of it was written down. The government and the churches could not understand the Kahuna powers, so were afraid of them. The Kahuna were threatened with jail if they practiced their craft which, of course, simply forced them to practice in the back jungles hidden from government sight. Today, much of their history and knowledge are better documented, and their practices do seem to work. Below is a Kahuna prayer for manifestation in your life. Repeat it three times.

Kahuna Prayer for Manifestation

"I am addressing this request to you, the origin of myself, physically, mentally and spiritually. I am aware that you, the Source Of My Being, dwell in me and I am awakening to your power now.

"I ask this request in the service and for the highest good of all concerned. I am aware that whatsoever we shall ask in prayer already exists. We shall receive when we are ready to receive without condition, knowing, accepting, and believing that it exists in your realm.

"I now ask for your help in: _____

"I am not asking from a needy state. This is our desire/choice. We accept your will, knowing that all will be provided, based on our acceptance and readiness.

"I ask that my request for _____ be acceptable and fair to all concerned. I accept the lesson from this request and know that if this request is available to me, you will see me through.

"I ask that this request for _____ be consummated by or during the month or day of _____.

"I know and accept responsibility for taking this action, signed:

_____

"I accept this as done, as is thy will, not my will. I give thanks, loving Father, and now leave this prayer picture in your loving hands to manifest a physical reality in the future. I accept and realize that it is already is a reality on your level of being. I recognize your authority and affirm you have the ability to grant what I ask and I expect fulfillment of my request. Let the rain of blessing fall. I have commanded it. Let it be so and so it is."

Repeat the above three times, and then say the following once only.

"My beloved Lower Self/Subconscious Mind:
I ask you and command you in the name and the service of GOD, the father of the universe, to convey this thoughtform prayer to the Source of My Being through my trustworthy parental High Self. I will provide all the Love, Manna, and Vital Force that is required by you to manifest this thoughtform prayer picture to the Source of My Being. I thank you and accept it as done, and so it is, so be it."

Then meditate on the prayer, giving it to the Higher Source to act on. If you need to support yourself, create an affirmation with this content to say daily. This prayer of manifestation can used for anything. However, be specific and detailed because you will get exactly what you ask for. Make sure you're clear about what you're asking for. The protocol must exactly as written above.

Before we leave the Kahuna, it's illuminating to examine how they divide the human being up. As does this book, they envision three parts (see chart):
- Low Self, or Unihipili
- Middle Self, or Uhane
- High Self, or Aumakua.

	UNIHIPILI = LOW SELF	UHANE = MIDDLE SELF	AUMAKUA = HIGH SELF
The Three Selves	(oo-nee-hee-PEE'-lee) Inner Self, Real Self, Deep Self, "anima," "Subconscious" Self Memory and Emotion Illogical (exact, literal, deductive conclusions) Controls body functions. Controls aka threads and thought-forms. Subject to suggestion. "Conscience." Generates all emotions. Relies on five senses. Telepathy	(oo-HAH'-nag) "Conscious Self," Rational Mind, "Persona," Full reasoning powers. Will power Imagination. No memory. Programs "conscience." Only the Middle Self can "sin" ("the only sin is to do willful hurt to someone"). Rationalization. Ordinary, everyday thinking.	(ah-oo-inah-KOOI-ah) "Utterly Trustworthy Parental Spirit," "Superconscious," "Realization" (mentation by KNOWING), including past, present, and the crystallized part of the future. "Guardian Angel" concept. Symbolized by the Sun (Light, Ra) (Tarot XIX) In contact with higher powers (Poe Aumakua = Great Company of High Selves)
The Three Levels of Mana	**MANA** Vital Force, "Prana," universal life force, low "voltage" energy produced by the body. Can flow over aka threads, flow through to body, or to that of another person.	**MANA-MANA** Double strength Mana. Higher "voltage." Used by Middle Self in all thinking and "willing" activities.	**MANA-LOA** Highest form of Mana. Highest "voltage." A transformed, supercharged Mana used to change the invisible pattern into reality.
The Three Aka Bodies	**KINO-AKA** Physical/etheric body. The energy body of the Low Self. Aka sticks to whatever it touches. Draws out thin, aka thread. Conducts Mana.	**KINO-AKA** The invisible pattern of the Middle Self. Less dense.	**KINO-AKA** Shadowy body of the High Self. Shown as "halo" in art.
THE PHYSICAL BODY: The Vehicle and Instrument of the Three Selves.			

The Ten Elements of Huna Psychology

When Prayer Doesn't Work

We have had people come back and say that the Kahuna prayer did not work for them and, when I asked GOD Source about this, they gave a number of possible reasons:

- Why do you keep repeating the prayer. We heard you the first time. If you need to convince yourself, then rewrite it as an affirmation.
- You are not yet ready to receive, as you are still attached to the past.
- How do expect to receive when you feel unworthy to receive?
- Before you're able to receive something, find a way to be thankful that it is available to you.
- Just because you think you're entitled does not mean you will get what you asked for.
- Take control of your life. Nobody is going to do it for you. Rewrite your prayer.
- If you want something, you're telling us that you do not already have it. You must know that you already have it, and then it will manifest for you.
- If you think you are entitled but do nothing for it, you will not receive it.
- When you have your desire in sight, then work to get it and it will be brought to you.
- Nothing manifests to those who do not take responsibility and expect others to do it for them.
- If you think the world is against you, it will be. What you think, is.
- We are not your servants; we help those who help themselves.

Master's Formula for Effective Prayer

Jesus gave a powerful formula for prayer that is still in use 2,000 after his death.

Formula	Classical Wording	Application
Name	OUR FATHER	I am addressing this request to the origin of myself, physically, mentally and spiritually.
Address	WHICH ART IN HEAVEN	The point deep inside me that is a quiet, peaceful, beautiful place where the Highest dwells.
Description	HALLOWED BE THY NAME	I mean the good part, the God part which always strives for my highest good.
Petition	THY KINGDOM COME	I would like for you to take over just like a ruler.
	THY WILL BE DONE	Make all decisions for me instead of the lower self.
	IN EARTH AS IN HEAVEN	Until my daily life and activities reflect the same peace and order as the Kingdom of Heaven that is within me.
	GIVE US DAILY BREAD	Feed me today on all 3 levels. Remind me to balance my eating habits by feeding all three bodies equally until I am no longer a dominantly physical being
	FORGIVE US EXACTLY AS WE FORGIVE	Cause me to recognize and release any situation or relationahip causing imbalance or blocks between me and you
	LEAD ME NOT INTO TEMPTATION	Give me spiritual exercise by making me strong in temptation so that I learn to overcome evil.
Payment	THINE IS THE KINGDOM	After all, it is your kingdom (I recognize your authority and I really considered that). I affirm that you do have the ability to grant what I have just asked.
	GLORY	I promise to recognize and admit the Source of all that I receive. Especially so that it will increase my ability to expect fulfillment of our requests.
Signature	AMEN	I have commanded it. Let it be so!

Part 1: Name and Address

To initiate the conversation, you must "dial the right number." In the name and address portion of the formula, identify and describe the power and authority you are calling on for any request. That initiates contact between you and that power, and focuses your attention on the issue you are addressing. Make sure you describe the issue clearly, and do not ask for what you don't want. Remember every word is prayer and a request. You will get what you ask for, even if you don't want it. Be careful of your everyday language, because what you say *will* manifest in your life.

Part 2: Petition

Ask your question. If you are using the "half-prayer technique," this is the end of the first half.

Part 3: Payment

The power behind the prayer is belief. The Master said, "Whatsoever ye shall ask in prayer, believing, ye shall receive." (Matthew 21:22) Carefully examine and apply these three elements of belief.

Part 4: Signature

Your signature on a letter states that you take responsibility for what you just ordered. The commandment "let it be so" should never be used unless you are willing to take responsibility, having examined your will in relation to divine will.

Memo To God

Date: _____

Subject: _____ (I am doing these items today)

There is one life, and that life is of GOD.

That life is my life right now. I take responsibility for that fact now.

I will be fully responsible for what happens in my life. I create it all.

I am committed and emphatically know that GOD will give me the answer to the following items today. I will take action today to make sure that these items will be taken care of today.

_____Thank you GOD

_____Thank You GOD

_____Thank You GOD

_____Thank You GOD

_____Thank You GOD

I give thanks for the completion of the above items and so it is. AMEN.

Repeat to yourself, "I am one hundred percent committed to living in peace, happiness, harmony and joy. I am accepting unconditional love in my life now."

(Write it down 21 times a day. You will then get it kinesthetically.)

The Manifestation Process

The manifestation process is a way change to your focus in life. Most people accept the way they are and what they have in their life as "the way it is." This is often caused by a survival fear, or a fear of failure belief and/or program in the mind/body. If you feel you could do better than you are now, then you are a candidate to make this process work for you. However, you must do it with intent and certainty that you're entitled to what you ask for. If you do this just to see what happens, nothing will happen.

Write down on the left side what you have now. Be specific as you can. On the right side write down what you would like to change, the current situation or what you desire to have. Remember, these are not *wants*. As long as you *want* something, you will never get it. You are setting up an *expectancy* not an expectation, and there is a major difference. Also, remember that beliefs are fear-based because you have no knowledge that you will get any end result. In order to manifest your future desire, you must *know* that you can change the present.

The Table for Manifestation

What you have: **What you desire to change:**

_____

_____

_____

_____

_____

_____

_____

24

Personal Evaluation of Self: Creating Your Own Reality Now

ompleting this self-evaluation sheet allows you to be honest and up-front with yourself. It is critical to your receiving the maximum benefit that you be as clear and open as you can.

The more you use this questionnaire as support for discovering who you are, the more you will receive. Please respond to the questions as accurately as possible rather than how you wish things were. Answer from your experience. What is true for you now and how you feel about it is your present reality. Reflection is critical. Skip any questions that do not apply.

1. List at least three attributes that you like about yourself:
    _____, _____, _____

2. List at least three attributes that you dislike about yourself (don't beat yourself up):
    _____, _____, _____

3. If it were not for the following, I would be happier (as many statements as possible):
    _____, _____, _____

4. I would like me better if I was/could/had the following (as many statements as possible):
    _____, _____, _____

5. These qualities have made my life happy and more successful (as many as possible):
    _____, _____, _____

6. I get joy out of these activities:

    _____, _____, _____

7. My biggest challenge in life is: _____.

9. The feeling and emotional reaction I have the most trouble with is: _____.

10. What I fear most is: _____

11. What makes me angry is (as many statements as possible):

    _____, _____, _____

12. My primary problems in life now are:

    _____, _____, _____

13. Things I don't like about my life and life in general are:

    _____, _____, _____

14. What's not working in my relationships with self, men, women and children are:

    _____, _____, _____

15. The following negative potentials continually play back to myself about my life (i.e., my recurring soap operas):

    _____, _____, _____

16. Given unlimited possibility, I would make the following health-related changes:

    _____, _____, _____

17. I would change the following about my body if I could do it now (no limitations):

    _____, _____, _____

18. I am laboring under a fear of lack or a poverty consciousness (yes/no): _____

19. If I had unlimited prosperity, realistically I would:

   _____, _____, _____

20. Given my present state in life, my goals are:

   _____, _____, _____

21. If I had the funds to open up new vistas in my life, my goals would be:

   _____, _____, _____

22. The three goals I think I could accomplish now given my present situation in life are:

   _____, _____, _____

23. If all limitations were lifted, I could accomplish:

   _____, _____, _____

24. Unresolved situations I am avoiding from my past, that are blocking me from progress in my life are (e.g., hostile divorce, children who are disappointments, bad family situations):

   _____, _____, _____

25. My incomplete relationships are (e.g., unhealed relationships with parents, friends or partners who left without completing):

   _____, _____, _____

26. My forgiveness levels in situations or relationships that did not work for me are:

   _____, _____, _____

27. The levels of completion in my relationships with my parents are:

   _____, _____

28. Times I have been physically or verbally violent with anybody are:

   _____, _____, _____

29. My levels of forgiveness for myself for my inappropriate actions and levels of forgiveness from the other party are:

    _____, _____, _____

30. I am an inwardly/outwardly directed person (yes/no): _____

31. Around outgoing and self-assured people, I feel:

    _____, _____, _____

32. Around people who have strong opinions, I am sensitive (yes/no): _____

33. I feel that successful people get all the breaks (yes/no): ____

34. If I were truly successful in life, I would still say that successful people get the breaks (yes/no): ____

25

The Keirsey Temperament Sorter

T he Keirsey Temperament Sorter* is a revealing tool for self-knowledge. Study and reflect on each of the following ques tions and decide whether you identify more with statement (a) or (b). Record your preference in the grid following the questions, by putting a check mark against the question number in either the (a) or (b) column. (If this is a library copy, obviously photocopy the grid first.) Once you've done the exercise, study the interpretation following the grid.

1. At a party, I:
    (a) interact with many, including strangers
    (b) interact with a few, known to me

2. I am more:
    (a) realistic than speculative
    (b) speculative than realistic

3. It is worse to:
    (a) have your "head in the clouds"
    (b) be "in a rut"

4. I am more impressed by:
    (a) principles   (b) emotions

5. I am more drawn toward the:
    (a) convincing   (b) touching

6. I prefer to work:
    (a) to deadlines   (b) just "whenever"
* reproduced with permission

7. I tend to choose:
    (a) rather carefully   (b) somewhat on impulsive

8. At parties, I:
    (a) stay late, with increasing energy
    (b) leave early, with decreased energy

9. I am more attracted to:
    (a) sensible people   (b) imaginative people

10. I am more interested in:
    (a) what is actual   (b) what is possible

11. In judging others, I am more swayed by:
    (a) laws than circumstances   (b) circumstances than law

12. In approaching others, my inclination is to more:
    (a) objective   (b) personal

13. I am more:
    (a) punctual   (b) leisurely

14. It bothers me more having things:
    (a) incomplete   (b) completed

15. I my social groups, I:
    (a) keep abreast of others' happenings
    (b) get behind on the news

16. In doing ordinary things, I am more likely to:
    (a) do it the usual way   (b) do it my own way

17. Writers should:
    (a) "say what they mean and mean what they say"
    (b) express things more by use of analogy

18. I am more attracted to:
    (a) consistency of thought
    (b) harmonious human relationships

19. I am more comfortable in making:
    (a) logical judgments   (b) value judgments

20. I want things:
    (a) settled and decided   (b) unsettled and undecided

21. I am more:
    (a) serious and determined (b) easy-going

22. In phoning, I:
    (a) rarely question that it will all be said
    (b) rehearse what I will say

23. Facts:
    (a) "speak for themselves" (b) illustrate principles

24. To me, visionaries are:
    (a) somewhat annoying   (b) rather fascinating

25. I am more often:
    (a) cool-headed   (b) warm-hearted

26. It is worse to be:
    (a) unjust   (b) merciless

27. One should usually let events occur:
    (a) by careful selection and choice
    (b) randomly and by chance

28. I feel better about:
    (a) having purchased   (b) having the option to buy

29. In company, I:
    (a) initiate conversation   (b) wait to be approached

30. Common sense is:
    (a) rarely questionable   (b) frequently questionable

31. Children often do not:
    (a) make themselves useful enough
    (b) exercise their fantasy enough

32. In making decisions, I feel more comfortable with:
    (a) standards   (b) feelings

33. I am more:
    (a) firm than gentle   (b) gentle than firm

34. I feel it is more admirable to:
    (a) be organized and methodical
    (b) adapt and make do

35. I put more value on the:
    (a) definite   (b) open-ended

36. New and non-routine interaction with others:
    (a) stimulates and energizes me
    (b) taxes my reserves

37. I am more frequently:
    (a) practical   (b) fanciful

38. I am more likely to:
    (a) see how others are useful   (b) see how others see

39. I find it more satisfying to:
    (a) discuss an issue thoroughly
    (b) arrive at agreement on an issue

40. I am more ruled by my:
    (a) head   (b) heart

41. I am more comfortable with work that is:
    (a) contracted   (b) done on a casual basis

42. I tend to look for:
    (a) the orderly   (b) whatever turns up

43. I prefer:
    (a) many friends with brief contact
    (b) a few friends with more lengthy contact

44. I go more by:
    (a) facts   (b) principles

45. I am more interested in:
    (a) production and distribution
    (b) design and research

46. It is a greater compliment to be called:
    (a) logical   (b) sentimental

47. In myself, I value more that I am:
    (a) unwavering   (b) devoted

48. I more often prefer:
    (a) final and unalterable statements
    (b) tentative and preliminary statements

49. I am more comfortable:
    (a) after a decision   (b) before a decision

50. With strangers, I:
    (a) speak easily and at length   (b) find little to say

51. I am more likely to trust my:
    (a) experience   (b) hunch

52. I feel:
    (a) more practical than ingenious
    (b) more ingenious than practical

53. I am more likely to compliment someone who is of:
    (a) clear reason   (b) strong feeling

54. I am inclined more to be:
    (a) fair-minded   (b) sympathetic

55. It is preferable mostly to:
    (a) make sure things are arranged
    (b) just let things happen

56. In relationships, most things should be:
    (a) renegotiable   (b) random and circumstantial

57. When the phone rings, I:
    (a) hasten to get to it first
    (b) hope someone else will answer

58. I put higher value on:
    (a) a strong sense of reality (b) a vivid imagination

59. I am more drawn to:
    (a) fundamentals   (b) overtones

60. The greater error is to be:
    (a) too passionate   (b) too objective

61. I see myself as basically:
    (a) hard-headed   (b) soft-hearted

62. Situations appeal to me more that are:
    (a) structured and scheduled
    (b) unstructured and unscheduled

63. I am more:
    (a) methodical than whimsical
    (b) whimsical than methodical

64. I am more inclined to be:
    (a) easy to approach   (b) somewhat reserved

65. In writings, I prefer:
    (a) the more literal   (b) the more figurative

66. It is harder for me to:
    (a) identify with others   (b) use others

67. For myself, I wish more for:
   (a) clarity of reason   (b) strength of compassion

68. The greater fault is:
   (a) being indiscriminate   (b) being-critical

69. I prefer:
   (a) planned events   (b) unplanned events

70. I tend to be more:
   (a) deliberate than spontaneous
   (b) spontaneous than deliberate

Directions for Scoring

In the following grid, having entered check marks against (a) or (b) as appropriate:

1. Add down and enter the number of checked (a) answers for the column in the box at the bottom of each column. Do the same for the (b) answers. Each of the 14 boxes should then have a number in it.

2. Transfer the numbers in boxes 1 and 2 to the boxes below the grid. For the remaining boxes (3 & 4, 5 & 6, and 7 & 8), you have two numbers in boxes, so copy the left number for each box in the box beneath the right number, as indicated by the arrows. Now add all the pairs of numbers and enter the total in the bottommost row of boxes (3 – 8) so that each box has only one number.

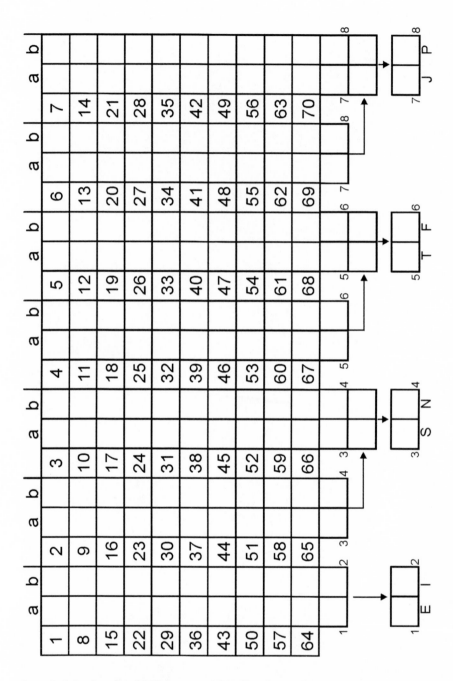

I am indebted to David Keirsey and Marilyn Bates for permission to reproduce this material from their book, *Please Understand Me; Dancing to Different Drummers* (available in bookstores or from the Wellness Institute).

Discovering Your Personality

The Keirsey Temperament Sorter helps you pin down your temperament and guide you to the job, career or relationship that's right for you. Temperament is the set of inclinations hardwired in from your birth, i.e., the "hardware" of your personality. Character, on the other hand, is the disposition or "software" that you develop during your lifetime, shaped by your environment. The combination of temperament (inborn human nature) and character (life experiences) makes up your unique personality.

The Keirsey system arrives at your temperament by examining your scores on the grid. The four pairs of letters—E-I, S-N, T-F, J-P—represent the four Jung-Myers dimensions of personality. Your position in these dimensions suggests stronger or weaker tendencies in your overall makeup, and reveals your temperament.

The Jung-Myers dimensions are:
- *Extraversion (E) vs. Introversion (I)*—a high Extraversion scorer tends to be gregarious and expressive; a high Introversion tends to be private and reserved.
- *Sensation (S) vs. Intuition (N)*—those scoring high in Sensation pay more attention to what is going on outside themselves in the world of concrete things; a high Intuition score suggests one who pays more attention to what's going on inside.
- *Thinking (T) vs. Feeling (F)*—a high Thinking score suggests those who govern themselves and make decisions using their head; a high Feeling score follows the heart.
- *Judgement (J) vs. Perception (P)*—a high Judgment score suggests those who process information and arrange their lives by making their minds up quickly and committing to schedules; those high on Perception take a more *laissez faire* approach and prefer things to be flexible.

Although the eight letters would theoretically yield many combinations, the Keirsey system identifies four combinations that predominate—those who score high in SP, SJ, NT and NF—and names them Artisan, Guardian, Rational and Idealist, respectively. (Each temperament in turn breaks down into sub-categories.) For example, if E=6, I=4, S=18, N=2, T=8, F=12, J=4, and P=16, then S (Sensation) and P (Perception) predominate, so you're an SP, or Artisan. (The E and I scores are used only for subcategories.)

Your score should put you into one these four temperaments:
- *Artisans* (SP), make up 35 – 40 percent of the population. They tend to be playful, optimistic, sensual, unconventional, daring, impulsive, excitable, and adaptable. Because of this, they create much of the beauty, grace, fun, and excitement in the world today.
- *Guardians* (SJ), make up 40 – 45 percent, and are responsible, helpful, hard-working, sociable, loyal, stable, traditional, and law-abiding. Their sterling qualities serve and preserve our social institutions, and are the cornerstone of modern life.
- *Rationals* (NT), make up about 6 percent, and are pragmatic, skeptical, analytical, independent, strong-willed, logical, even-tempered, and curious. This makes them perfect problem-solvers, developers of new technologies, and shapers of our world.
- *Idealists* (NF) are enthusiastic, romantic, intuitive, kind-hearted, intense, authentic, symbolic, and inspiring. As a temperament, they are passionately concerned with personal growth and development. Their quest for self-knowledge and self-improvement drives their imagination ... and the rest of us.

Suggested Occupations

Being concrete in communicating and utilitarian in implementing goals, Artisans are usually found promoting, operating, and creating. Their trust in spontaneity and hunger for impact on others tends to put them "where the action is." They enjoy arts and crafts, working with new techniques, and operations work, from a single machine to an entire nation.

Guardians, also concrete in communications but cooperative in implementing goals, can be skilled in logistics, supervision, and distribution, and are often found in commerce. They could also be judges or other stewards of the social fabric.

Rationals, being abstract in communicating and utilitarian in implementing goals, make good strategic analysts, planners, organizers, and inventors, often in the sciences, technology, and systems work.

Idealists, abstract in communicating and cooperative in implementing goals, can make skilled integrators, diplomats, teachers, counselors, and tutors. They are often found in the fields of the humanities, ethics, and personnel work.

(See Resources for references to Keirsey material sources.)

Part Seven

Afterthoughts

Some of the materials in this book are extracted from my other books, some of which are still unpublished, such as *Recovering Your Lost Self* and *The Doorway to Self-Empowerment*. Some of it came from teachers such as Paul Solomon and the Fellowship of the Inner Light. In truth, there really is no new material because it all has been known for centuries. All we are doing is reforming the information and writing it down to best of our ability. The concepts presented are spiritual principles and universal laws that have been with us for thousands of years from the ancient mystery schools and groups such as the Hawaiian Kahunas.

Many teachers have said, "I cannot do it for you. I can show you the way but you have to do it for yourself." Give a man a fish and you feed him for a day. Give him a fishing pole and you feed him for life.

One of my teachers, Tara Singh, once said to Krishnamurti, "I want to study with you and all that I have known from the past will not affect me."

Krishnamurti replied, "You are a very knowledgeable person. You do not need my help."

Tara said, "It is all gone. I am your student."

Krishnamurti replied, "If you can do that, then you are not my student. You can work beside me."

If I feel a teacher has the way, I will practice what he or she teaches. If it does not produce results, I will evaluate what my blockage to the teaching could be. If I find it, I will try to overcome my block and continue. If I succeed, but the process still does not produce pragmatic results, I will drop it.

If a teaching ever makes me scared or angry, I know I must adjust my perception. When Paul Solomon told us, "This is the way to make contact with the Inner Teacher or Highest Source of my Being," I did it and it worked. He believed that we should meditate three times a day and keep a journal. I did and it worked.

The biggest challenge was starting something and following through. Most people do not have the discipline required, and seek the easy way out. If you try to justify why you didn't do something, then you're clearly in denial. I took the ball and ran with it. I am my own test laboratory; I check out new processes. If they provide results, I adopt them.

A teacher can only point you in the right direction and give you the materials. You must commit to beginning the work, taking responsibility, setting the desire, claiming your personal power, and following through.

On my path to transformation, I encountered many rocks and boulders. When I recognized my need to understand the recovery process, I attended conferences on codependency and Adult Children Of Alcoholic (ACA). I realized that those of us in the spiritual field are avoiding recovery. We must deal with the base causes and core issues in our life that are not working the way we would like them to work. We can channel, do psychic readings, and use all the spiritual tools to uncover our life path, but we must get grounded.

As result, I have become more pragmatic in my interpretation of reality, and have made more progress in my transformation in the last five years than in the last twenty. If we think we are on the path and are fixed, we are in illusion, and the more the illusion is locked in, the more we get locked into not wanting to look.

I do not want to point fingers and judge people who say they are on the path in their spiritual journey but with people in denial, their limitations and resistance stick out like a sore thumb. The adept student or teacher can see the denial clearly, but we make the mistake many times of pointing that out that to a person who is not ready to hear it. When they get the "Aha" message, they will understand and thank the teacher for the guidance. I have seen this happen many times with my clients who can't seem to take control of their life and continue to muddle through. When they understand about reclaiming their personal power, taking control and responsibility, and surge forward in their transformation, they look back and have a tough time understanding why they could not see the truth. Why is it so elusive to us when we are in denial? That was my question for many years. Only recently have I discovered the cause after chasing it for twenty years. Our mind is very committed to keeping us on what it perceives as the track. We may get angry at the situations we get into and what happens to us, but it is all in the flight plan.

Each time a lesson comes up to confront us, we have an opportunity to learn the lesson before we have to go through the pain and consequences of ignoring it, yet we often project it on others or blame them for our situation. When we step back and can view the consequences and learn from it, we will move forward. That is, unless we want to create it all over again!

Most people have a fit if they are told that they are creating their own pain and circumstances. However, once they take control of their life and then look back, they recognize what they have done. Then, it is hard not to get angry and beat yourself up for putting yourself through all the trials and tribulations. Many clients tell me that it is obvious once they are on the other side of the fence to see the mistakes people make, yet you cannot say anything to them as most will get mad at you for pointing it out to them.

Our objective is to get all three selves and all four minds working with you and for you. Ego needs to know that you're willing to work with it and not blame or attack it for working against you. Middle Self must know that you're going to take your power back and who's writing your life script, or it will continue to do it for you. When you can separate the various voices in your play and become the cause in your life, it all smooths out and runs like a well-oiled motor. We all have the same abilities; some people just have more commitment and discipline than others. Commit yourself and resolve to discipline yourself consistently and follow through on each task. You will know when you arrive. As you demonstrate your abilities, your progress will be obvious to anyone who has traveled the path. *Remember, it all begins when you take responsibility for your direction in life.*

Life can be full of inner peace, joy, happiness, love, with a clear understanding of the true meaning of abundance now. Transformation is instantaneous. Change takes time. When you "get it," as they said in est training, you know you have it because it shows in your life. People will see who you are without you saying a word. You cannot fool the true observer.

Someone said to me recently after a presentation, "I could see that you knew and accepted everything you were saying. Not a word was out of place. The people in the audience were right with you." When an audience resonates with me, I have three times the clarity. Dealing with doubters and skeptics is much harder.

May the power be with you. Connect with your Source and your teacher and you will be on the right track. Best wishes on your journey into the light.

With love,

Art Martin, March 2001

Appendix A: Neuro/Cellular Repatterning™

The Practice of Psychoneuroimmunology

Disclaimer

N/CR changes people's lives. Although they recover from illness, disease, and behavioral dysfunction that are inexplicable in medical terms, we are not practicing any form of conventional medical practice nor do we diagnose or prescribe medicines of any kind. We do not claim that N/CR is a substitute for medical care. We are simply asking the body/mind to reveal to us the original cause, core issue, and catalyst that caused the dysfunctional program. When we find it, we delete and erase defective beliefs, programs and habit patterns. Then we rewrite the programs that control illness, diseases and behavioral dysfunction.

You heal your body. You are the only person who can do that by your acceptance of the technique. If you are more comfortable with conventional medicine, then use that avenue. We do not advocate that this is the only way. Although we have seen many miracles in this work, we do not claim that any other process is ineffective.

Psychoneuroimmunology is a process that encompasses all aspects of the body/mind/spirit in healing. Developed by Robert Adler in the early seventies, the technique explores the connection between our psychological aspect and the physical responses that appear in the body. Prior to that, little was known about the mind/body connection.

In 1978, I began my search for a process or a program that would clear my chronic back pain. I attended many workshops and seminars because the leaders said they could heal me, but nothing could permanently clear the pain. In desperation, I began to develop Neuro/Cellular Repatterning (N/CR)™. At the time, I had no idea what I was doing and just experimented with hands on healing processes, energy releasing and other forms of healing. In 1980, I discovered that that all aspects of the body and mind were connected and that you could not treat them separately with any lasting results.

When I first discovered N/CR, defining the process was difficult. For 25 years, I had wandered through all the alternatives to allopathic medicine, looking for a cure for my own physical problems. I could not find a single person who understood my problem or could alleviate my pain.

I tried nutrition, but it was only part of the solution. When I discovered the power of the mind, I realized it was not what you put in your mouth, but what your mind accepts as truth. So I looked for a process that could get to the base cause of dysfunction without having to spend hours on a psychiatrist's couch as he or she tried to dig out the cause out of the client, who was unable to understand it in the first place. Most people don't know what their mind has stored, let alone understand it. Conventional psychiatry seemed bent on pinning blame on someone or something unknown, but I couldn't believe we had to be victims of other people's actions.

Initially, I had no idea that my physical pain was caused by emotional dysfunction within the programs in my mind. Like most people, I thought that physical problems had only physical origins; at least that's what doctors told me. Yet they did not understand why my spine was deteriorating and simply gave me the ultimate prognosis of being confined to a wheelchair.

At the time, I didn't know that my body was continually dialoging with me, and that if only I had listened, it would have revealed the causes. Physical dysfunction reveals *itself* but not its *cause*. Further, since emotional/mental pain is non-tangible, it is difficult to locate and work with. Also, I was not aware that my belief system had suppressed emotional programs that were causing my physical problem.

In my training with Paul Solomon, I approached psychology from a holistic, spiritual aspect; a very different slant from my original training. This opened me up to the dialogue and began helping me understand it, but it didn't heal my body. In a workshop, Ronald Beesley showed me how the body stores the memory and the basics of removing it. With this knowledge, I had the tools to integrate spiritual psychology with body/ mind therapy. This became the basis of my counseling practice, which evolved into Cellular Repatterning™. In this approach, we released the imbedded cellular memory from past experiences.

Each cell retains its perfect blueprint so that it accurately regenerates and replicates itself. In the absence of any pattern of negative or dysfunctional emotional energy, the cell will regenerate perfectly from the blueprint. In 1988, I discovered that the repatterning process was actually erasing these negative patterns from past emotional experiences that kept muscles in trauma, so I added the "Neuro" prefix.

I discovered a holographic, body-based, spiritual psychotherapy process that uses affirmations, with love and forgiveness as the basic modality. We use Neuro-Kinesiology to locate the basic information we need to begin with.

This process works at all levels of the mind/body at the same time. We have four minds that network together. All the information we need is available from the mind/body. The body does not lie; it always tells the truth. It will indicate the original cause, core issue, and the catalyst causing the reaction, disease or illness. If you are living in denial or denial-of-denial, or on autopilot, we first deprogram the denial to get a clear answer. A sub-personality is usually driving the denial-of-denial, and can block any program from recognition if it is frozen in time in autopilot. We must go back to the time when the program was created and release the fear that caused the sub-personality to suppress the incident. Then, we locate the reason that caused the situation to be created.

In the future, N/CR will be a prominent healing process because it can address any dysfunction, emotional/mental problem, illness, and disease without pain, drugs, or surgery. No diagnosis is needed; all that's needed is the recognition and release of the underlying cause. Disease, illness, and emotional or physical breakdown are dysfunctional behavior patterns. Our delusion, denial, and irresponsibility block us from total healing.

In reality, there is no disease or illness. They are symptoms of a breakdown in our ability to understand what we are refusing to observe about ourselves. When we recognize the base cause and are willing to let go of it, healing can take place. There is no need to suffer or die to get away from taking responsibility for the lessons that are placed before us.

The basic concept in N/CR practice is to release the causes and core issues that block us from the truth about ourselves. When we see who we really are and recognize that we are all right as we are, no matter what the past discloses, we can reclaim our personal power and empower ourselves to take responsibility for our lives. Then we can begin to love and forgive ourselves. N/CR is not about paying lip service to make us look good, but about telling the truth about ourselves and accepting ourselves as we are without the need for control, authority or manipulation over anyone.

The miracle of the human mind is actually shared among a number of minds:

- The Subconscious Mind contains a detailed and faithful record of everything that has ever happened to you in your life, real or imagined. When we understand the awesome power of the Subconscious Mind to disable our immune system, we will begin to recognize how disease is created. If the Subconscious Mind holds false beliefs, concepts, attitudes or interpretations, they will create programs that drive our lives automatically, without any conscious thought on our part. Your body is the "hardware" of your Subconscious Mind, and the "software" is any program installed in the mind.

- The Instinctual Mind is just that: if you go into survival mode, it takes over. It has no ability to think, process, or make rational decisions.

- The Conscious Mind is the rational decision-maker but it, too, can also hold false beliefs and concepts you are not aware of. If you do not question these beliefs, they will run your life. Ideally, the conscious mind is on track all the time, but if you "space out" and go on autopilot, the Middle Self and the Subconscious Mind will take over, because somebody has to be at the wheel.

We are finding that, each year, increasing numbers of people are separating from their body, something we call, "a gray out." More seriously, "browning out" can cause memory lapse but you can still function. "Blacking out" happens when a person loses consciousness momentarily. This may be the cause of many single-vehicle wrecks—it's happened to me twice.

In our practice, we have also discovered that most people are running on autopilot more than 85% of the time. Our response to this is to seek ways to empower people to take 100% control over their life. With N/CR, we succeed most of the time, for we get the body to talk to itself so that we can reprogram the mind's various computers.

In all therapy processes, one question often seems to arise in the practitioner's mind: "Am I getting to the actual programs that stop us from attaining the inner peace, happiness, joy, harmony, acceptance, approval and love in the client's life?" Of course, the therapist must be in recovery himself, or the question wouldn't even enter his mind. In my interpretation, effective therapists must be willing to confront their limitations and issues which may block them from becoming compassionate, nonjudgmental, detached and supportive, with no need for controller authority over the outcome of therapy.

The need for control is the most widespread addiction we have today, and both therapists and clients react to it in an insidious way. If you're not in recovery, it's not an issue, but many people in recovery have an expectation or want to control a program, meeting, or another person's response, i.e., they are addicted to control.

As therapists, we are only able to guide and help our clients to understand the causes and core issues causing the dysfunction in their lives. In the N/CR process, therapists cannot sidestep their own issues, because they will surface along with the client's issues. In fact, therapists usually clear many of their own issues in N/CR sessions. You will recognize them and simply release them, because you are participating with the client in the release process.

We also need to have other practitioners to work with during our recovery. We cannot read our own book well if we are attached, blocking, or suppressing the causes. In my experience, even if we are committed to growth, we will block and refuse to recognize our attachments. Your body will always tell the truth, if you can get past the mind's blocks.

The final evaluation will only come in the results our clients manifest, as they traverse the path in their journey to transformation. With N/CR, we can go directly to the root cause and the core issues stored in the mind and locate these programs and patterns. We use Kinesiology and the acupuncture points in the body as gates, switches or entry points to release the information. In a short time, N/CR can release and heal any dysfunctional behavior pattern, illness, disease, or pain. We uncover and release the blocks to attaining self-worth, -esteem, -confidence, -validation, -approval and unconditional love.

Lack of love is the cause of illness. The major problem confronting most people today is that they cannot receive love or love themselves. If love does not exist in our reality, how can we recover self-esteem and self-worth, let alone heal ourselves? When we separate from our Source, we shut off the presence of God within. Those who need validation from the outside will interpret any concentrated form of attention as love. In the so-called Münchausen Syndrome, people hurt themselves in accidents or cause illness and disease to get love, and even more staggering, in the Münchausen-by-Proxy Syndrome, parents will harm their children in order to get attention. We will suffer abuse, both physical and emotional, to get the attention we mistake as love.

We have experienced amazing miracles with hundreds of people, such as spontaneous release of disease, emotional dysfunction and genetic defects. Oddly, however, other people either did not respond at all, or the dysfunction would return. This led to the realization that *I* was not doing the healing, that we were not "healers" or even "therapists."

Our only job seemed to be teaching people how to love themselves and receive love. We can help clients to preprogram the situation and rewrite new scripts accepting the past and loving and forgiving themselves and others. We as facilitators cannot install the programs; the client must take responsibility and shift in consciousness. We can help by developing the software and using affirmations to install it; then permanent healing invariably follows.

As a therapist, I cannot change the holographic image that clients hold about themselves; I can only help them make the spiritual shift, thereby causing the healing. If that shift is not made, the healing process will give clients a temporary release. N/CR will work in spite of itself, because we are not working with the Conscious Mind. As a result, we are able to duplicate the process with different people in about 95 percent of cases, but there will always be that 5 percent who will refuse to take responsibility or reject the modality altogether.

When you take control of your life, your Subconscious Mind will cooperate with you, but many times, the Instinctual Mind will try to keep you in survival mode as it was originally programmed to. In an N/CR session, we must ask it to abide by our will by talking to it with an affirmation.

Middle Self is another matter altogether. If Middle Self interferes, we use a different approach to make friends with it so that it won't sabotage you. N/CR accesses the Middle Self's programming and gets it to recognize you as the computer programmer.

I have found that it is not the modality that causes healing to happen, since many allopathic and alternative therapies have claimed provable visible healing. However, they cannot explain why remission happens or how to reliably duplicate the process.

Psychiatrists, doctors, psychologists and practitioners have long recognized the need to release negative emotions. N/CR is a controlled process that gets to the core issue. Double blind treatments with different practitioners working with N/CR have shown that each practitioner has virtually the same experiences.

As practitioners, our effectiveness depends on our ability to get in touch with our clients' "feeling selves." We must build trust, so that our clients feel that we care about and love them. This trust is what allows healing to occur. One thing, and one thing only, governs healing: LOVE, and it works every time.

In Level One training, we focus on effective use of Behavioral Kinesiology and listening techniques for the body/mind. We communicate with Kinesiology and intuitive listening. Verbal communication is done through affirmations. When we locate the causes and core issues of the dysfunction, we communicate with specific affirmations, which are tailored to reprogram the Subconscious Mind. We have developed a body-map over the last ten years, which indicates the locations of most emotions (see figures below).

As the figures show, fear is stored on the left side of the body; anger on the right, with rejection along the spine. In fact, we have uncovered sixty individual locations for specific other emotional, dysfunctional programs.

As if the universe is trying to give us the answer, many doctors and medical researchers are discovering the answers to the puzzle of healing. In a *Discovery* magazine article called "A Bug in the System," scientists reported on the causes of disease syndrome. But they have no cure, prognosis or correction; they have labeled it "a genetic defect." Cellular breakdown is caused by the cell's mitochondria losing the ability to process and absorb nutrients. The doctors attribute this cellular breakdown and malfunction simply to genetic defects. However, regardless of why the cell loses its original blueprint, N/CR erases the cellular memory of rejection and lack of love, and helps the cell recover its original blueprint, so it replicates healthy new cells.

With counseling, physical therapy and almost all alternative therapies, we can remove the energy causing the pain or discomfort but, if we do not treat the root cause, we are just releasing a symptom. We have just masked the problem until the same catalyst or stimulus recurs and causes the energy to build up again, reactivating the disease or dysfunctional emotional program. With N/CR, we locate the core issue, uncovering the belief and/or the Subconscious Mind's program.

When the Subconscious Mind files an experience, it creates a record and program, with energy that makes small chemical changes in the body.

Many scientific studies in the field of Psychneuroimmunolgy have validated this. Two chemicals that activate neurotransmitters cause these changes—neuropeptides, the special chemical mediators and communicators that link the brain/mind and the immune system together. Our thoughts, feelings, and emotions affect our autonomic nervous system. Our mental states activate these specific thought, emotion, and feeling messenger neuropeptides. Because they are bi-directional in their action, they can function in reverse, affecting our behavior and mental state when we try to block or deny negative feelings and emotions.

Cytokinins are the second chemical in the equation. These are also bi-directional and negatively or positively influence both the immune system and the endocrine system. Working on the cell surface recep-

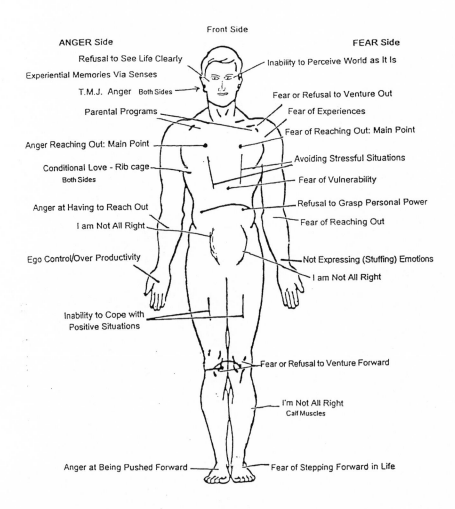

tors, cytokinins either stimulate or inhibit the immune and endocrine systems. Negative attitudes, feelings, thoughts, and actions depress these systems to produce an inhibitory effect, causing illness, disease and/or depression. Over-stimulation of cytokinins from feeling depressed can cause endocrine and immune system burn out. This has the same effect that diabetes has on the pancreas. As a result, the NK cells will suppress the production of T-cells that interact with and destroy disease, virus, bacteria, cancer cells and pollutants.

On the opposite side, normal stimulation from happy, joyous and harmonious feelings and attitudes will promote health and wellness.

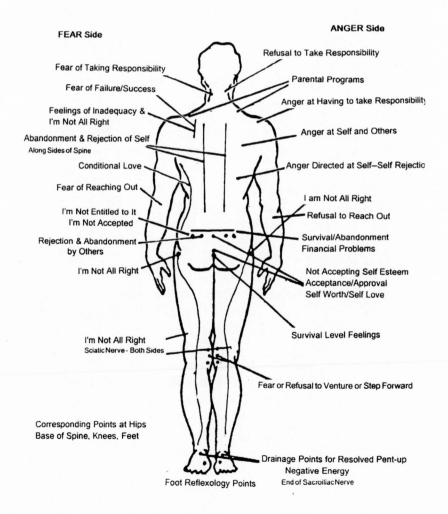

The cytokinins will cause an increase in the production of NK cells and support balancing the immune and endocrine systems, strengthening them to ward of illness, disease and depression.

Each program remembers how we reacted or responded to the incident the first time it occurred. Each time we encounter this situation in the future, we access past patterns to guide our reaction, which reinforces the pattern that determines how we will handle future situations. Eventually these accumulated chemical changes will cause a physical breakdown somewhere in the body.

To release the dysfunctional emotion and program, we must understand the cause, and the reason why you originally reacted the way you did. When we understand the dialogue between your Subconscious Mind and your body, we can "unhook" that dialogue and release it. Then we erase the program's operating instructions, destroy the patterns, and file the record, pattern and program in the Subconscious Mind's archives. At this point, the energy is released and the behavior program is no longer accessible to you.

At the physical level, the cellular memory is released, which allows the muscle or organ to return to its original form. In the case of muscle pain, emotional trauma short-circuited a meridian, which caused the muscle to go into contraction. At the same time, the neuro-pathways were created from the experience. When the trauma is removed, all the effects are released and erased. The original program for the muscles takes over again, and the pain ceases.

In the case of a life-threatening, dysfunctional program, the same process happens. The original endocrine system programs are restored, so the immune system can rebuild the T-cells and leukocytes to destroy the dysfunctional invading cells.

All the physical programs are controlled by the Conscious Mind's computer, i.e., the Subconscious Mind. But because the body is a hologram, all levels must be addressed at the same time. We must work with physical, mental, emotional, and spiritual levels simultaneously, otherwise the treatment will be symptomatic and temporary.

N/CR will access the root cause, because it requires practitioners to get in contact with the client's "feeling self." By doing so, we can listen to information in the Subconscious Mind, which it deposited in muscles, organs, and acupuncture points. We use acupuncture points as switches to "turn on the video and audio," and allow the Subconscious Mind to bring the pictures and experience up to conscious awareness. This, however, is where the similarity with other therapy processes stops because with N/CR, we listen to body/mind and go directly to base cause. Then we get a clear understanding of the cause of the dysfunction. By describing the situation that caused the dysfunction, and then by getting the client to repeat an affirmation, the blockage is released.

My experience with Science of Mind helped me understand and harness the power of affirmation as the key to releasing and filing the record, program and pattern.

The focus of most therapy today, regardless of technique, is to release or suppress the symptoms; unfortunately that does not heal the body. Most practitioners expect some form of remission, cure or healing but, if they don't access the root cause, any improvement will be temporary and symptomatic.

Many people recognize the need to release emotional memories stored in their cells, but few achieve results. Cathartic release does not always indicate that the base cause or core issue has been revealed. Disease and dysfunctional emotional behavior patterns are directly caused by the lack of ability to accept oneself as all right and the refusal to give and receive love! Love can heal anything. To reverse the disease process, we must understand unconditional love and accept it.

Fear, anger, and rejection are the base causes yet, as victims, we try to blame some outside incident, person, or virus. The mind can create any disease it chooses but the only process that heals is love.

N/CR provides clients with a safe space to learn how to love themselves and release the blockages in the body. Then the self can receive the basic needs of all people: love, acceptance, approval and all rightness that foster self-esteem and self-worth.

There is hope. Recovery is possible in every case. The only catch is that clients must desire to take control and discipline themselves to do what it takes. I am a walking example. My book *Your Body Is Talking, Are You Listening?* documents many case histories of people who literally shifted their belief and were healed in minutes. For some, it took days, while others gradually improved over time, depending their willingness to let go of attachment to the core issue that was causing dysfunction, be it *anger, fear or rejection*, which results in lack of love. When the client reconnects to Source, love can begin to heal the body/mind.

When we understand that our mental state controls our heath and wellness, we begin to become disease-resistant. We are no longer contagious nor do we contract illness and disease. Every aspect of our life and well-being is controlled by our feelings, attitudes, thoughts, and actions. Thus we have total control over how our brain/mind instructs our body to react or respond to any given stimulus. A positive response causes the neuropeptides and cytokinins to produce health-supporting activity in our cellular structure. The research done in the field of Psychneuroimmunolgy has proven without a doubt that our mental state is responsible for either a positive response or negative reaction.

For more information on the subject of Psychoneuro-immunolgy, see my forthcoming book *Psychoneuroimunology: The Mind/Body Medicine Connection Book 2*.

Appendix B: What Comprises
an N/CR Session?

We will be working with N/CR, Behavioral Kinesiology, and bio-feedback, if necessary. We demonstrate methods to understand the dialogue, misperceptions, and interpretations that the Subconscious Mind has stored in its memory. The acupuncture points on the body are switches or gates. Putting pressure on these entry points turns on the mind's "VCR" and opens the dialogue with the Subconscious Mind's files.

We must resolve certain basic issues before we can begin the process:

1. The client must be anchored in the body. Many people are out of their body and are unaware they are not functioning in their body, especially if they are confronting a traumatic issue. However, once they know how it feels, they can recognize when this has happened.
2. Electrical polarity must be correct in order for Kinesiology to work properly. If the polarity is reversed, "yes" will appear as "no" and "no" as "yes." We cannot obtain an accurate answer until polarity is balanced properly.
3. Therapists must allow themselves to be loved and love themselves. Separation from Source will cause a lack of love, along with self-rejection. We must accept our entitlement to love.
4. We must find out if the three lower minds are going to work with us. If not, then we must rewrite and reprogram the tapes. We must get Middle Self to recognize that we are not going to destroy it, and to convince it to be our friend.

At this point, we are now ready to ask questions with Kinesiology, or go directly into program releases. We can go directly to the root causes and the core issues stored in the Subconscious Mind's files. This will reveal the programs that have become habit patterns that are causing dysfunctional behavior, illness, diseases or pain in any form. We can release and heal any dysfunctional program in a very short time with use of Neuro/Cellular Therapy.

I recommend taping all sessions for the protection of both therapist and client. Also, the session can be reviewed and transcribed. There will be many parts of the session the client will not be able to recall because the mind may block it out. Many people have found that repeating the affirmations will lock in the new programming.

Q. Why is this particular process so effective?

Unlike other therapy processes, the client is required to participate in the session. The client is not *worked on.* In most treatments, such as Rolfing, Trager, massage, acupuncture, and other body-related processes, you do not participate. In psychology, you will be asked what your problem is, but few clients know what the base cause is, so how can we work with a belief, concept, or a program when we are not sure of the cause? The body will always reveal the base causes and the core issues if we listen to it.

We have to get Middle Self to cooperate with us, as it is one of the main players in the game. The Middle Self knows exactly what is happening in our life, so we need its support. All levels are brought in to play, physical, emotional, mental, spiritual and etheric, all at the same time. The body being a hologram, we access all levels of the mind and body with Kineseology and with clairvoyance to access the records that we need in releasing the programs. We go one further by accessing the ability of the Higher Self.

Q. What should you expect during a treatment?

To understand what a treatment is like, you must first understand what it is not like. No special preparations or clothing are required. You will not experience any deep tissue work that is painful, nor will you be required to accept altered states of consciousness. We do not use hypnosis or guided imagery. You will not expected to dredge up painful, emotional experiences from the past or "lead the discussion" as in analytical psychology. In fact, you do not need to tell us anything. Your body will reveal all we need to know, although we may ask some questions to establish some basic criteria.

Emotions may come up and you may experience flash-backs during the process but they are all momentary and release quickly.

We use affirmations as the means to reprogram and rewrite scripts in the mind. The therapist creates the affirmation, then the client repeats the affirmation. The only person that can reprogram your mind is you; there is no such person as a healer of others. You can only heal yourself. As such, we are only facilitators to direct the process.

Q. What goes on during a treatment?

When we locate the cause or core issue with kineseology, we must determine if it is a belief or reality. If it's only a belief, it may be controlled by a sub-personality. In either case, we can release it with an affirmation that will reprogram the software. If it is body-based, then we have to locate the acupuncture point that holds the incident we are releasing; a momentary pain will occur at that point. As we bring up details of the incident and forgive the cause, it will disappear immediately.

We do not experience the mind's action during the process; it instantly communicates to the body through neuropeptides and signals the muscles to let go of the tension. At the same time, it is rewriting the programs in the computer. Through affirmations, we communicate what we want to happen. It is important to understand that you are giving permission and removing the programs yourself. As the therapist leads you through the affirmation, you are healing your own body. The therapist is actually just a facilitator who has agreed to let you release the negative energy through him/her, providing an opportunity to experience love and forgiveness to release the incident.

Q. How long does this take and how much?

The number of treatments depends on your willingness to let go. Taking responsibility to see life differently without judgment, justification, rejection or fear/anger helps. A typical average is three to ten sessions. Some clients have had over 100 sessions, while others have cleared most of their issues in four to ten. There have been miracles in one session, but they are rare.

A session typically lasts about 80 minutes, charged at $75/hour. Call (800) 655-3846 for an appointment. If you are interested in spreading the word of this work, please call us. We would be happy to work with you.

Q. How can I become a sponsor?

We teach the Neuro/Cellular Repatterning process as a series of five workshops. If you would like to help us present lectures or introductory workshops, please call the number above. We provide a free session if you set up a lecture for us (a minimum of ten people). If you are interested in setting up appointments for me at your home or other location, I will provide you with a free session for each day I work at your location. (There is a minimum number of sessions each day to qualify.)

Appendix C: The Body/Mind Harmonizer: A New Concept for the New Millennium

The Harmonizer Concept

The physical body matches itself to the frequencies in its environment, whether stressful or not. The Harmonizer counteracts the stress in its immediate vicinity, allowing the body to come into earth resonance, which is the most effective frequency for the endocrine system to balance and regenerate itself. The coil-antennae produces a scalar wave field pulsing on and off to create the effect. Technology for the Harmonizer was developed in the early 1900s by Nikola Tesla, who did considerable research into electromagnetic fields and their generation by special coils. He discovered the so-called *scalar field*, a longitudinal wave field that functions outside the space/time of our third-dimensional world. Since it operates beyond space/time, it is unencumbered by the limitations of conventional physics, and is the most effective way to protect the body from disruptive stress of disharmonic fields or vibrations.

We have also found that earthbound spirits, alien entities and extraterrestrials cannot handle the frequencies, and cannot attach to a person in the Harmonizer's field. The scalar wave radiation also blocks abduction and protects from psychic attack. People who have been harassed by earth-bound spirit beings have reported that they have been free of them as long as they keep the unit on them 24 hours a day. This was primarily why we developed this unit. Now we find that it does much more than we expected.

The Harmonizer causes accelerated healing up to ten times the norm, apparently by activating cellular restructuring in the body. Generating a high-frequency bio-electrical field using Tesla technology, the unit reportedly accelerates healing at the cellular level, balances the endocrine system, supports the immune system, rebuilds bone structure, and heals skins cuts and lesions about ten times faster than normal. It also seems to balance the electrical function in the body, which in turn can balance all electrical aspects of the body including blood pressure and neurological function.

The Harmonizer Theory

When it is in perfect health, every living being resonates at its own characteristic frequency. Each component of that being's body also resonates at a particular frequency, and if subject to higher frequencies from its environment, it tried to match those frequencies, which causes stress, and that particular cell, organ or gland is weakened, making it more prone to disease or illness.

A tuning fork in the field of another matched fork that is struck will vibrate at the same frequency. Your body does the same thing. When you are subject to negative vibrations such as stress, fear, or anger in your environment, you begin to identify with this environment and your body begins to resonate with that vibration.

If you go into flight or fight, your adrenals kick in, causing a strain on the immune and endocrine systems. A strong dose of adrenaline helps you handle the perceived danger. Under normal circumstances, when the danger is over, your body should release a shot of nor-adrenaline as an antidote so you can return to normal energy and frequency level of $12 - 18$ Hz. But, if you live in perpetual stress, survival fear or confrontational conditions, your body frequency will rise to $250 - 550$ Hz, over *thirty* times higher than it should be. As your body frequency rises, you begin to function on adrenaline alone.

Electronic devices that emit strong fields also interact with the physical body's electric and electromagnetic fields. The body/mind will identify with the frequency that has the strongest effect on it. The Harmonizer creates a 15-foot diameter field of energy around the body that blocks out other frequencies that are stressful to the body. It emits a low frequency—the Earth resonance signal—and a high frequency that is the ideal frequency for the body's functioning.

The brain's chemicals, such as interlukens, seratonin, interferon, etc. operate at the Earth resonance 12 – 15 Hertz. The immune system and the endocrine system work more effectively when there is no load on the adrenal glands. Negative sensory input or negative thoughts and emotions cause the neuropeptides to slow down, compromising the immune and endocrine systems.

The body's natural electrical field (chi, ki or prana) must be strong to ward off disease factors, but as its frequency rises, the electrical and auric fields weaken, and offer less protection. The Harmonizer causes the mind to focus its energy and operate at optimum health. However, the device is only an adjunct to such measures as proper nutrition. You cannot abuse or mistreat your body and expect the Harmonizer to over-come this. (To learn more about the emotional cause for dysfunction too, as described in my book *Your Body Is Talking; Are You Listening?*)

The following is a greatly simplified explanation of the theory behind the Harmonizer. The information that regulates the various parts of the body is carried by the body's neurological network system. The brain serves as a "switching center" that directs the electrical impulse information and neuropeptides through the meridian system network to the appropriate parts of the body.

Each cell is a mini "computer" in this network, and receives its orders from the mind through the neurological system, carried by elec-trolytes and the neuropeptides. When operating properly, the cells maintain a delicate balance of chemicals. When they go out of balance or get run down, the electromagnetic fields break down or blow out. The cell loses its ability to protect itself properly. The brain/mind's ability to communicate with the cellular computers breaks down and the body becomes subject to attack by diseases, illness and outside forces, and *accelerated aging*—the most damaging effect of increased stress and high frequency.

The results are illness, depression, chronic fatigue, emotional instability and life-threatening disease. Metabolism is affected due to breakdown of the function of the endocrine glands, and the body's absorption of nutrition is impaired.

As the body's internal frequency rises past 50 Hz, the good "happy" brain chemicals shut down and the adrenals kick in larger doses of adrenaline to keep you functioning. The adrenals become overworked, which leads to adrenal insufficiency. When production drops below 30 percent, normal fatigue sets in, similar to low blood sugar tiredness caused by hypoglycemia.

Continued high frequency interference causes breakdown in all systems of the body, resulting in Chronic Fatigue and Epstein-Bar Syndromes, which lead to clinical depression. Many doctor prescribe Prozac, Zolov, Valium or other mind-altering anti-depressants, which can be addictive because they suppress the symptoms and fool the brain into believing that the total body malfunction is a false message. (For a more detailed explanation of how the mind operates, how diseases and illnesses affect the body, and what their causes are, see *Your Body Is Talking; Are you Listening?*)

Low Frequency Operation

The Harmonizer balances electrical, metabolic and electromagnetic system dysfunction by shutting out the disharmonious stress that causes the body to elevate its frequency. It emits a fifth-dimensional etheric scalar field that strengthens all the systems of the body by bringing down the frequency to the optimum level for perfect health.

To be in balance, most devices, plants and animals have clockwise and counterclockwise positive and negative energies. A few plants such as garlic, onion, and some herbs radiate a double-positive field, hence their antibiotic healing qualities. The Harmonizer also radiates a double-positive field, which explains the response it creates.

For more than 200 years of recorded history, the Earth's resonant frequency or Schumann Resonant Factor was 7.83 Hz but, recently, it has risen to 12 – 14 Hz. Our original Harmonizers were built to emit 7.83 Hz, and later models have kept pace with the Schumann frequency. The current 12.5 Hz field helps the adrenals to heal and resume their normal operating level. At this ideal frequency, all organs and endocrine glands function at their most effective level and your body begins to heal because when the body is in the Harmonizer's 15-foot diameter field for a period of time, it will match the Harmonizer's frequency. This may take up to three days depending on your body, but you will notice your body begin to slow down and relax.

High Frequency Operation

The unit also emits a high frequency of 9.216 MHz. When we began our search for the high frequency that would accomplish our purposes, we checked through hundreds of frequencies. Little did we know that the frequency we finally choose was only 0.02 MHz off the actual frequency of the Ark of the Covenant. Apparently, this is a universal frequency that will activate the body's healing modalities and repel anything or anybody who emits a negative energy.

Initially, we were able to get 9.216 MHz chips because Motorola had over-ordered but we have since found other readily available sources. For the latest model, we redesigned the entire circuitry and coil, and used a slightly larger case to accommodate the rechargeable battery pack. As a result, the unit now has a much lower power requirement and is more effective.

When we discovered that we were getting a scalar wave without the circuitry to produce it, we asked some experts about it. All they could say was, "You're dealing with hyper-dimensional physics and it's over our heads and we can't explain it. This is Tesla and Einstein's realm, and we don't understand what's happening."

We are apparently producing an output that no one understands. Nor has any history of this effect been recorded. Two new research consultants joined our team—a radio frequency engineer and a physicist— and they said, "As far as we can tell, it appears that we're on the threshold of a new discovery in quantum physics. We can't measure the scalar field output because it's outside conventional physics, but the radio frequency seems to be a carrier wave for the scalar field."

Harmonizer History

Our first prototype had a weak field, yet it worked so well that we knew we were on to something so we continued our research. The second generation unit had a 100 millivolt output, and the current production unit puts out 800 millivolts. The first unit of the current (tenth) generation had a metal core coil that was absorbing two thirds of the output, so our engineer suggested using a non-reactive plastic core. When we went to a nylon core, we discovered that power output tripled. The next challenge is to build an even more powerful unit that will not interfere with short wave or TV reception, or we would run into trouble with the FCC.

The device uses a triple-wound bifilar toroidal coil/antenna driven by complex electronics that were not available in Tesla's time. Today's computer chip technology has allowed us to reduce the size of the original prototype by over 90 percent. The first generation prototype had a range 18 inches and a battery life of 80 hours. The second generation had a range of 3 feet and a battery life of 260 hours. Early units used expensive 9-volt batteries, and we switched to AA Nicad rechargeable battery packs that lasted about a year. Today's tenth generation has a range of 15 feet and a nickel hydride battery pack that lasts up to four years.

> Warning: Charge the unit for one hour a month, or four hours if it is fully discharged. This is very important, as we have had people return the unit, complaining that battery would not charge. They had over-charged the battery for many hours.

When you first begin to use the Harmonizer, you may find that it needs to be recharged more often than once a month. If your body energy is low and you have been under considerable stress, this will drain the batteries more quickly as the unit interfaces and responds to your body energy level. We have had reports that people have had to initially charge the battery as often as once a week.

Testimonials

Disclaimer: Due to FDA regulations, we make no claims as to what the Harmonizer can accomplish. However, we can report what users have relayed to us. Many claims have been made by users of the Harmonizer but we can not recommend it for anything as we are not psychiatrists or doctors. We are not allowed by law to diagnose or prescribe.

Here, we relay the experiences of those who have used the Harmonizer. For example, many people have reported that it pulled them out of depression in 5 – 14 days without any drugs, and many have ceased taking prescription antidepressants. Two psychiatrists validated this information from their experience.

In my case, I injured my foot with a chain saw, and the wound was not healing well but, as soon as I began using the new Harmonizer, my foot began to heal at an unprecedented rate. I could actually see it heal from one day to the next. The deep gash closed up and healed over in less than two weeks, and today has left only a faint red mark.

1. "It seems to bring programs to the surface that I had no awareness of. It's the best therapeutic tool I have come in contact with." *B.E., California*
2. "I strapped the Harmonizer over a broken leg on the cast where the break was and the break healed four times faster than normal. The doctor was amazed that we could take the cast off in less than four weeks." *J.S., California*
3. "Chronic Fatigue I'd suffered for years disappeared in less than a week." *J.C., Arizona*
4. "I am feeling general well being and able to handle stress more effectively. I'm not getting angry as quickly as in the past. One day, I left the Harmonizer at home and I noticed my stress level began to rise at work." *C.D., California*
5. "Psychiatrists who have purchased the Harmonizer report that it works with depression very well since it reactivates the brain chemicals and supports the rebuilding of normal production of all the essential brain chemicals, allowing the adrenals to slow down and heal. As a result people seem to pull out of depression." *R.N., Virginia*

6. "I put the Harmonizer on a plant that was dying, and it revived in just one day." *T.K., California*
7. "A burn totally disappeared in three days. This was apparently caused by the activation of the cellular restructuring." *J.T., California*
8. "It apparently has caused my immune system to rebuild because I am recovering from a long term illness. It is feels great to get my stamina back." *W.B., New Mexico*
9. "It activates programs in the mind that have been covered up for years. Apparently denial programs are forced to the surface." *H.M., California*
10. "I am finding I have more energy and I sleep less now that the stress is relieved." *G.B., Colorado*
11. "I have been taking drugs for depression, and low thyroid and adrenal function. I continued to take the drugs until they ran out. I noticed that I was getting the same effect from the Harmonizer so I did not renew my prescriptions. That was three years ago and I have not had any depression since. And the new Harmonizer is even better. Thank you so much." *A.P., California*
12. "I handed the unit to friend of mine and he dropped it immediately, saying he couldn't hold onto it. Once I cleared him of attached entities, he had no problem holding it." *J.O.E., California*
13. "I had been to the doctor for my high blood pressure and he pre-scribed medication to control my blood pressure because it was 190 over 120. I checked it again a month later and it was still the same. I bought the Harmonizer and started carrying it with me all the time. Less than a month later, I was down to 120 over 70. The doctor could not understand how my blood pressure would come down to normal. 'That just does not happen to someone your age.' I cannot attribute it to anything other than the Harmonizer." *C.S., Arizona*
14. "It is amazing. I felt burned out and the doctor said my adrenals were very low and wanted me to take drugs to build them back up. I told him I did not take drugs of any kind and would find another way. I started using the Harmonizer, and my adrenals recovered in three days. I do not feel as stressed out anymore. This is truly electronic medicine." *K.S., Oregon*
15. "I have had a umbilical hernia for 25 years, and have consistently refused surgery to repair it, instead doing exercises to strengthen the abdominal muscles so it would repair itself. It had been slow-ing getting smaller, but very slowly. I had the earlier version of

the Harmonizer for four years and while it helped in many ways, it had no effect on the hernia. But with the new high frequency unit, in just three months the hernia has reduced to about one quarter of what it was last year." *A.M., California*

16. "My husband had flu twice this winter and I usually get it from him and end up down for a week. This year, no flu or anything. I can only assume the Harmonizer protected me and kept my immune system up to par so I was not affected." *C.H., California*

17. "For me, the Harmonizer is a miracle because I seem to go out of my body quite often and driving is very dangerous when this happens. I have been solidly in my body since I have been using the Harmonizer." *J.S., California*

18. "I have had serious immune system problems for years. It seems that I catch everything that comes along. The Harmonizer has upgraded my immune system to the point that I am now very seldom sick." *C.K., California*

19. "When I called to find out about the unit, I was willing to try anything as my blood pressure was 210 over 120 and I had lung congestion. My legs hurt so much I could not even walk around the grocery store. In five weeks my blood pressure dropped to 130 over 90 and still continues to fall. I have no lung congestion and I can drive trucks again. I have gone back to work full-time."

20. "As a healer, I touch many clients in my work and would frequently have entities attaching to me from my clients. Today, I would not be without my 'boogie buster' because it protects me so well." *J.N., California*

21. "I have had low adrenal function almost all my life. Stress really takes me down to the point where I can't function. With the Harmonizer, I have recovered totally. I have not experienced any depression or lack of energy since I began using it." *C.K., Colorado*

22. "Accelerated healing of burns has been amazing. I spilled boiling water on my face when I dropped a teakettle. The burn marks began clearing up in two weeks. In a month, they were almost gone except for redness on the skin. Today, there is no scarring and all the marks are gone." *M.K., Arizona*

23. "One of the most amazing results I have found from using the Harmonizer is that old burn scars and keeled scars are disappearing, some of which have been on my body for forty years. It is truly amazing." *H.M., California*

24. "After a motorcycle race, I suffered a serious third degree burn on my leg from an exposed exhaust pipe. The burn healed in less than one month, and in six weeks was just a dark spot. In the past, burns like this have taken six months to heal."

Others have reported a much clearer mind and more vivid memory. People have experienced more clear and active meditations. We have found that the Harmonizer causes an accelerated healing of cuts and wounds on the skin. It apparently is activating some cellular response as skin cuts seem to heal in a one quarter or less time than normal. The only negative aspect that we have found is that it pulls up emotional programs that have repressed in the past, and the person has to deal with them.

We hesitate to list many of the other results people have received so as not to create expectations, and we stress that the Harmonizer is only an *adjunct* to your body. You must work with it, and not expect it to do things for you. Please do not put unrealistic expectations on it as it's only a catalyst for your own healing miracles. You still have do your part in releasing the emotional trauma responsible for the health condition.

New Products and upgrades

The price of the new 800 millivolt 9.216 MHz Body/Mind Harmonizer unit is $295.00 plus shipping. (If you have an old original 12.5 Hz or lower unit, we will exchange it for the 9.126 MHz unit and give you a trade-in value of $50.00.)

A new therapeutic unit is being developed that will have an adjustable power output, from 800-millivolts to 5-volts, *five times* more powerful than the current unit. Projected price is $395.00 or less depending on final cost.

A new "ghost buster" unit will be available soon for clearing buildings and creating an overall balancing/clearing effect in seminar and workshop facilities. Projected price is $450.00 or less depending on final cost.

We are working on a new unit that will operate on 120 volt AC house electricity. It will combine both units plus a programming mode to hook up with a tape recorder or a CD player for use with music and voice tapes for reprogramming the mind. One unit will have a tape recorder built into it. It will use piezo-electric discs similar to ear-phones to input information through the eighth cranial nerve. In this manner, it bypasses the Middle Self, which cannot then tamper or sabo-tage the input (all dysfunction of the body is mind controlled). In our tests, deaf people reported being able to hear the input, also. People have reported that they were able to learn a foreign language in as little as two weeks. A teacher reported that learning-disabled students were able to master lessons that they had not been able to in the past. Pro-jected price on this unit is about $795.00 depending on final costs, and will include some programming software.

To order the Body/Mind Harmonizer, or books and tapes, call or write:

The Wellness Institute
8300 Rock Springs Rd.
Penryn, CA 95663
(800) 655-3846 (Orders only—all major credit cards accepted)
Fax: (916) 663-0134
E-mail: artmartin@mindspring.com
Websites: www.medicalelectronics.org
        www.mindbodymedicineconnection.com
        www.personaltransformationpress.com

Appendix D: Tapes and Books

The first two books are available in most bookstores in the U.S. and in some countries around the world. The other five are available in spiral bound pre-publication format from publisher, Personal Transformation Press.

2011: The New Millennium Begins
$13.95, ISBN 1-891962-02-7
What can we expect the future to bring? How do we handle the coming changes and what do we look for? Prophesy for future earth changes and new planet Earth as it makes the quantum jump from the third to the fifth dimension.

Your Body Is Talking, Are You Listening?
$14.85, ISBN 1-891962-01-9
How the mind works and how to create software for the mind and reprogram it. The cause of illness, disease and dysfunctional behavior defined. Healing miracles and how they are available to everyone. Understanding the body/mind connection in relation to the practice of psychoneuroimmunology with 66 case histories.

Opening Communication with GOD Source
$14.95, ISBN 1-891962-04-1
The author's search for God uncovers a shocking truth—that it's actually a group of wise and ancient beings who have been involved with Earth since the beginning. And following the author's guidelines, you can move beyond the blocks that most of us have and contact them and access your personal page in the Akashic Record. The book culminates in a fascinating dialogue between the author and the Source that resolves many profound mysteries of life.

Journey Into The Light
$9.95, ISBN 1-891962-05-01
The process of ascension and the steps that govern the journey to a light being. Looking for the missing link in evolution. Stepping out of the cycle of reincarnation.

Recovering Your Lost Self
$14.95, ISBN 1-891962-08-6
The author's journey from victim to cause in his life. How you can find your true self and have abundance in your life. Accepting unconditional love in your life through forgiveness and acceptance. Coming to the point where peace, happiness, harmony and joy are reality, not an illusion.

Pychoneuroimmunology: The Body/Mind Medicine Connection
ISBN 1-891962-07-8
What is psychoneuroimmunolgy and the mind/body medicine connection? An overview of the modalities and processes. Integrating the concepts. Research on the modalities. The mind as network computer. Affirmations, software for the mind. Neuro-Kinesiology. Using muscle testing for clearing beliefs and concepts, programs, patterns and records that are causing allergies, emotional behavior patterns, disease, illness and physical breakdown in the body. Neuro/Cellular Repatterning, a method to access the mind's programs, beliefs and interpretations and release them to heal any disease, illness or dysfunction in the mind/body. Miracle healings on demand with love and forgiveness. Supporting the body with nutritional and herbal products.

Tapes

Tapes are available on the guided imagery to train yourself to access the records and on the process for contacting your teacher and accessing the Hall of Records.

1. The Seven Chakra Guided Imagery:
   Train yourself to step out of the body to enter the Temple and the Hall of Records.

2. Accessing your Akashic Records:
   On the process and the various forms and methods of finding the answers to all your questions.

3. Psycho/Physical Self Regulation:
   Originally a tape for runner and walkers to regulate, flush the body of toxins and burn fat for energy. Can be used to train yourself to eat properly and reduce weight.

Resources

Paul Solomon and the Fellowship of the Inner Light,
620 14th Avenue, Virginia Beach, VA 23451
Membership $25.00; books and tapes available; send for catalog.

Keirsey, David and Bates, Marilyn. *Please Understand Me; Dancing to Different Drummers*.
Explains the Keirsey Temperament Sorter test. Available in bookstores or from the Wellness Institute.

Dyer, Wayne, *You'll See It When You Believe It*, and *Real Magic*
A must-read assignment.

Price, John Randolph, *Superbeings*
Available in bookstores or the Wellness Institute.

Whitworth, Eugene *Nine Faces of Christ*
Available from the Wellness Institute.

Neuro/Cellular Repatterning

If you are interested in spreading the word of this work please call us. We would be happy to work with you. We provide a free session if you set up a lecture for us (a minimum of ten people).

We teach the Neuro/Cellular Repatterning process in a 5-workshop series. If you would like to help us present lectures or introductory workshops, please call the Wellness Institute.

If you are interested in setting up appointments for me at a designated location, I will provide you with a free session for each day I work at your location (there is a minimum number of sessions each day to qualify).

Appendix E: Glossary

This book uses terminology that is not in common usage today. This glossary will help in understanding them.

A Course In Miracles: a set of three books that describes how we can change our view of forgiveness and love, and achieve peace and happiness through understanding who we are in relation to the Holy Spirit. The teacher's manual tells us that we are all students and teachers at all times in our life. The lesson manual shows us how to change our concept of who we are each day.

Addiction: compulsion or obsession about a situation or a substance that will cover up, meet a need or avoid a situation. The paradox: getting too much of what you do not need to satisfy an emotional imbalance in life.

Ascension: an evolutionary process of becoming a light being through releasing all the emotions and control sub-personalities that drive our life. Being able to reclaim our personal power and become a "no limit" person. The final result is getting off the cycle of return (reincarnation).

Back-up files: each day, the mind backs up all its files just as you would with a computer to save and protect your files.

Clairvoyant, Clairaudient: using our sixth senses to see and hear beyond normal restrictions of sight and hearing.

Collective Mind: a collection of information from all areas of the universe. Could be also described as the Akashia.

Conscious Rational Mind: the mind that we use to input information and data to the Subconscious Mind's files.

Cosmic phone line: a connection into the higher forces with no discernible source.

Dark Forces: beings from the astral plane, commonly described as demons, devil, satanic or Luciferian beings.

Denial: the first level of locking up programs so you do not have to deal with them. They can be located in any of the four minds.

Denial-of-denial: when an incident is too traumatic to deal with, we lock it up in denial-of-denial so that we cannot access it at all. However, it can affect our mental state even though we are unaware of it.

Divination: gaining answers using any form of an instrument, such as dowsing, pendulums, or oracles.

Ego or File Manager: the aspect of our mind that files the records in and retrieves information from the Subconscious Mind's data files. (I prefer the term *Middle Self.*)

Grace: that which is accorded to us to clear karma. When we acknowledge we have learned the lesson from a karmic experience, contract, or agreement, we can claim Grace and the Lords of Karma will delete the lesson from our Akashic Record.

GOD: (uppercase) the GOD Source or Presence of GOD.

God: (lowercase) the Christian or religious reference to God.

Holographic Mind: the soul level of mind that is in direct contact with Higher Self. It has access to all the records in the mind and Akashic. Will provide help when you request it. The all-knowing mind.

Karma: contracts that are created by dishonest, unethical or out-of-integrity behavior. If you kill someone even if in the line of duty, a karmic agreement is created. If you harm someone in anyway, you create a karmic contract.

Kinesiology: a form of divination that uses the various muscles of the body to answer questions. When accessing the mind through muscle testing for answers, the neuromotor responses are indicated through either strong or weak muscular response depending on how you assign Yes or No.

Lords of Karma: beings from the spiritual plane that reside with the GOD Source and help us file our flight for each life. They maintain the Akashic Record.

Love: a manifestation of actions and feelings that support growth, happiness, joy, peace of mind and acceptance.

Middle Self: the middle mind made up of the Conscious Mind, Instinctual Mind and Inner Middle Self. All the sub-personalities are installed in the Middle Self files. Quite often, it is misidentified as Ego because it exhibits the qualities that people generally ascribe to Ego.

Mystery School: an exoteric school that has existed for thousands of years. Many teachers who have been given the information by GOD Source have carried the tradition on. The teachers are chosen by the White Brotherhood and GOD Source. Many self-proclaimed teachers have set up mystery schools, calling for discernment as to who are the true teachers.

Psychoneuroimmunolgy: a new concept developed by Robert Adler, a faculty member of the Rochester Medical School, where he is now Director of the Department of Psychoneuroimmunology Research. The basic concept is that mental states control the distribution and production of chemicals that communicate with the various systems within the mind/body. They control the immune and endocrine functions, which in turn control heath and wellness.

Quickening: the increase in planetary vibration caused by the shift in energy on the planet.

Spiritual Practice: a discipline one follows in an effort to develop spirituality.

Spiritual Journey: the path to transformation that entails learning many lessons in letting go of limitations, emotions, and karma.

Spirituality: the result of learning the lessons on the path; the process of becoming a person who functions with honesty, ethics and integrity.

Universal Laws: the laws that govern the universe. The specific laws are set up to control interactions and apply to all planetary systems and star groups. (On this planet, we do not seem to acknowledge this simple form of law.)

About the Author

When I met Art Martin, he was beginning to recognize his abilities and was looking for himself. We all want to find ourselves and put considerable effort into doing it. With Art, it became almost an obsession. He sold his restaurant and went on the path full power ahead. It often seemed as if he would blow himself out of the water because he took on so many projects and studies, but it's all come to fruition in the present time. Starting from a dysfunctional childhood, he has overcome the obstacles.

We meet pivotal teachers in our life who direct us to the true path if we can let go of the fear of control. I met Art at one of those seminars fifteen years ago. Paul Solomon and Ronald Beasley proved to be two of those teachers for us.

Twenty years ago, information about ascension was minimal but we both were interested in the process of ending the cycle of return in this lifetime. Art has nailed down the process into viable, understandable terms. He was not satisfied with how people were putting all the responsibility on the spiritual world to do it for us, and felt there were earth plane lessons to learn first. I feel he has detailed the process that shows the transition and how it is done in his books.

The reason he has not taken full credit for the material is that he feels much of the information is drawn from many sources and teachings he has studied. There is little new material coming out today. Almost all of it has been written or taught at some time in the past, even if it was destroyed or not written down. Any thought that entered anyone's mind at any time in history was recorded in the Akashic Records. In that way, those who can access the collective source of records can have anything they desire. Art's ability to access these records has given him the information he needed to finish this work.

Art's ability to listen and evaluate really impresses me. If it works, he uses it. If it doesn't, he discards it. Watching the transition from a judgmental, manipulative, controlling, authoritarian person to a person who can observe a situation and evaluate it without trying to be "better than" amazed me. He was quick to discredit process therapies in the beginning. As I observe him now, I can see he has let go of the need to be right and know it all. Art's work is a representation of this ability to be open and accepting.

One of his greatest strengths is the ability to be vulnerable and let his feelings out. His self-validation has allowed him to let the vulnerable side show without being rejected. In the beginning, he was so concerned over what people thought of him that he'd go out of the way to win their approval. Now he just gets acceptance without even trying now. After much hard work over the years, he has finally achieved his goal.

His family is a good example of his work. He went through many trying times in his early years. Putting off having children till his mid-thirties proved to be a good decision. His children were fortunate that they did not come into his life until he had his life on track. They were fortunate to grow up with his new perceptions of life.

Art's interest in helping people change the world is heartwarming. He feels that everyone can have a life full of peace, harmony, joy and love. I feel he is doing that in his work.

Gwyn Bishop, a friend, client, and coworker.